Politics of Representative Bureaucracy

Politics of Representative Bureaucracy

Power, Legitimacy and Performance

Edited by

B. Guy Peters

Maurice Falk Professor, University of Pittsburgh, USA

Patrick von Maravić

Professor Emeritus, University of Alberta, Canada

Eckhard Schröter

Professor, Zeppelin University, Germany

Edward Elgar PUBLISHING

Cheltenham, UK • Northampton, MA, USA

Published by
Edward Elgar Publishing Limited
The Lypiatts
15 Lansdown Road
Cheltenham
Glos GL50 2JA
UK

Edward Elgar Publishing, Inc.
William Pratt House
9 Dewey Court
Northampton
Massachusetts 01060
USA

A catalogue record for this book
is available from the British Library

Library of Congress Control Number: 2014950728

This book is available electronically in the **Elgar**online
Social and Political Science subject collection
DOI 10.4337/9780857936011

MIX
Paper from
responsible sources
FSC® C013056

ISBN 978 0 85793 600 4 (cased)
ISBN 978 0 85793 601 1 (eBook)

Typeset by Columns Design XML Ltd, Reading
Printed and bound in Great Britain by T.J. International Ltd, Padstow

Contents

Contributors

Robin Hambleton is Professor of City Leadership at the University of the West of England, Bristol, Director of Urban Answers, and was Dean of the College of Urban Planning and Public Affairs at the University of Illinois at Chicago from 2002–07.

Tassilo Herrschel is a Reader in Urban and Regional Development and Governance at the University of Westminster.

Kenneth J. Meier is the Charles H. Gregory Chair in Liberal Arts at Texas A&M University and holds a joint appointment as a professor of public management at the Cardiff University School of Business (Wales).

Tabitha S.M. Morton received her PhD from Texas A&M University in 2013 and is an instructor in the Department of Political Science at Texas A&M University.

B. Guy Peters is Maurice Falk Professor of American Government at Pittsburgh University, USA, and Professor for Comparative Governance at Zeppelin University, Germany.

Eckhard Schröter is Professor of Comparative Public Administration in the Department of Public Management and Governance at Zeppelin University, Germany.

Bas van Gool is a Lecturer in Governance Studies at Vrije Universiteit Amsterdam.

Patrick von Maravić is DAAD Visiting Associate Professor in the Department of Political Science at the University of Alberta, Canada, and at the Department of Public Management and Governance at Zeppelin University, Germany.

1. Delivering public services in multi-ethnic societies: the challenge of representativeness

B. Guy Peters, Eckhard Schröter and Patrick von Maravić

POLITICS, REPRESENTATION, AND BUREAUCRACY: HOW TO CONNECT THE DOTS

The politics of representative bureaucracy highlight the procedural, political, and conflictual nature of representation in public organizations. In very general terms "representative bureaucracy" can be described as the "body of thought and research examining the potential for government agencies to act as representative political institutions if their personnel are drawn from all sectors of society" (Dolan and Rosenbloom, 2003, xi; see the chapter by Bas van Gool on the intellectual history of representative bureaucracy). Understanding the politics of representation prompts us to take a closer look at the conditions under which public organizations act as representative institutions and when they do not. Questions of representation, whether seen under the label of diversity management or representative bureaucracy, are per se political. Representation as seen through political lenses means viewing it in the light of manifest or latent social conflicts (Lipset and Rokkan, 1967: 5). Political considerations determine who is represented and who is not, who is included and who is excluded, and to what extent individuals or groups acquire and exercise power, status, or authority in order to act or stand for an idea or group in the public service. These issues are important in any society but are especially relevant in societies that are deeply divided along religious, ethnic or class lines.

The clearly discernible trend towards greater cultural variety in what used to be more rigidly defined "nation states" emphasizes the need to understand the politics of representative bureaucracy (von Maravić et al.,

2013; Joppke, 1998). With the fast and widespread growth of geographical mobility in almost all OECD-countries and a globalized economy that has resulted in more and more people migrating for work, but also on humanitarian grounds or to find political safe havens, attention has increasingly shifted towards the role of large public service systems in increasingly heterogeneous societies (Hooghe et al., 2008; Castles and Miller, 2009). This pressure is most strongly felt in large urban conurbations that serve as centers of gravity for both migrating low-skill and high-skill workers (see the chapter by Robin Hambleton in this book). The global flows of migration – coupled with intensified European integration and amplified by prospects of an ageing and shrinking European population (Tassilo Herrschel in this book) – is likely to catapult the question of opening up public sector workforces to more ethnic and cultural diversity to the top of the political and administrative reform agenda. And with emerging political and normative considerations, which follow the discourse of the "politics of identity" or "politics of recognition" debate (Taylor and Gutman, 1994; Benhabib, 2002; Parekh, 2006; Kymlicka, 2010; Vertovec and Wessendorf, 2010), focusing on bureaucracies as representative institutions, the inclusion of any kind of minority is no longer contingent on functional necessities or politically opportunistic behavior but rather has turned into a manifestation of minority rights per se. From this flows a politically powerful symbolic meaning attached to pressures to open public sector organizations because working for "government" can be interpreted as a strong signal of a successful integration of minority groups into the State and into normal social roles.

This volume (in conjunction with its sister publication *Representative Bureaucracy in Action*), as with it its assembled authors, sheds light on a core theme of the study of public administration. By seeking a more profound understanding of the causes, facets, and consequences of the politics of representation in the public sector, the authors not only underscore the necessity of a pluralistic and interdisciplinary perspective, which ties in insights from history, sociology, urban politics, political, and organizational theory, as well as public administration/management, but highlight this by reaching out to different theoretical perspectives and empirical insights in order to understand a phenomenon that transcends not only our distinct academic disciplines but also our traditional focus on public organizations. By seeking answers to questions about the origin and evolution of the concept of representative bureaucracy (Bas van Gool), the comparative study of representative bureaucracy (the editors), the role of politics, identity, and structure in cross-nationally studying representation (Kenneth J. Meier and Tabitha S. M. Morton), the relationship between representativeness, the merit principle, and patronage (B. Guy Peters), the link between urban politics and migrants (Tassilo Herrschel), the potential myths of the performance claim in the field of diversity management and representative bureaucracy (Eckhard Schröter and Patrick von Maravić), and the role of leadership in managing multi-cultural cities (Robin Hambleton), this volume delivers new perspectives on these challenging questions and defines gateways for further research.

This introduction aims at stressing three distinct arguments that can be read as intending to move the debate about representativeness in the public sector forward. First, we argue that the study of representative bureaucracy will eventually profit by breaking it loose from its traditional anchoring in the dichotomy between passive and active representation and opening it up for perspectives that allow us to capture additional and other "channels for the expression" (Lipset and Rokkan, 1967: 5) of interests. In particular, we wish to broaden our perspective so as to include aspects of both political and bureaucratic representation. Second, and related to the first claim, we hope to throw light on the institutionalization and freezing of different types of representation and draw attention to factors that may help us to explain this variation among administrative systems in the future. And thirdly, we elaborate on the lessons for theorizing public organizations, arguing that public sector bureaucracy plays multiple and potentially competing roles. On the one hand, public organizations are political simply by virtue of implementing public programs, and they therefore face pressures to be representative and to foster public participation. On the other hand these organizations are responsible for managing and implementing policy and therefore must have some concerns with efficiency and effectiveness. All public organizations have some of these contradictory pressures, but they may be exacerbated in societies with fundamental social cleavages.

CONCEPTS OF REPRESENTATION IN MODERN DEMOCRACIES: POLITICAL AND BUREAUCRATIC

Approaches to Political Representation

The concept of representation is one of the cornerstones of the architecture of modern democratic theory, just as much as the empirical–analytical body of research on political representation constitutes a defining component as political science as a discipline – past and present. From this productive line of thought, however, the study of representative bureaucracy appears to be oddly disconnected. Within the academic "public administration" and "public management" communities too, issues of "representativeness" in the civil service as well as questions about the representative role of public agencies are all too often considered to be a sideline to the major flow of research on public sector organizations, and is typically associated with a narrowly defined set of normative assumptions and research questions (see also below). This apparent, though hardly uncommon, lack of communication between neighboring and yet separated research communities produces – as we see it – significant losses for all parties and academic (sub-)disciplines involved: students of representative bureaucracy, comparativists in public administration and management studies, or political scientists and sociologists analysing the theory and practice of political representation in modern democracies. A brief look into their respective research discourses and debates – showing the existing degree of overlap, but also their specific limitations and omissions – might help to illustrate the potential benefit in approaching issues of representation more comprehensively, thus acknowledging the capacity of public bureaucracies to act as representative institutions.

Put at its simplest, representation is the act "of make present again" (Pitkin, 1967). The author's penchant for the study of the use and origins of words also reminds us of the fact that "representation" is something *indirect* (hence its recurrent clashes with advocates of *direct* democracy), something that involves delegation or trusteeship, and is closely associated with more differentiated societies and complex institutional rules and structures – in short, arrangements in which mediators or representatives are needed "to present *again*" what escapes our immediate observation or experience. Most of our conceptual tools that we currently refer to in our discussion of representativeness in politics and administration were introduced about half a century ago (borrowing, of course, from philosophers of the classical era and the age of enlightenment, see Dahl, 1989, for an overview of the genealogy of the concept) and with Hannah Pitkin's work (1967) being one of the most influential contribution to this debate. Her discussion of four analytical dimensions help to meaningfully define the relationship between representatives and those represented: formalistically (pertaining to the formal status of representatives and the way how they are chosen, e.g. in elections), descriptively (with an eye to the extent to which representatives are like those represented), symbolically (asking about the degree of acceptance that representatives enjoy in their constituencies), and substantively (focusing on the activities of representatives and the extent to which they serve the interests of those represented). Interestingly, students of political representation and representative bureaucracy were at this point conceptually rather well-aligned as they both addressed similar dimensions: descriptive and substantive representation or – in Frederik Mosher's terms – passive and active representation. Conventionally, however, the mainstream of political science research would portray the process of political representation first and foremost as a legislative affair, based on formal authorization of representatives by way of elections (e.g. in single-member constituencies) and conceptualized as a retrospective principal–agent relationship. In the face of new political challenges and empirical research findings, it has been increasingly difficult, however, to capture the full scope and depth of representative processes using that classical model. One of the first critical questions raised was prompted – not much different from the debate about government bureaucracies (Kingsley, 1944) – by the concern about the class bias of legislative institutions (Schattschneider, 1960) and later refined in order to acknowledge the diversity within constituencies (Mansbridge, 1999): how can the effective representation of disaffected citizens and of marginalized constituency members be improved? Another problem arises if public policies are more and more shaped and determined by international actors, institutions and decision-making processes that transcend the reach of national legislatures, let alone the boundaries of parliamentary or congressional districts. On top of that, elected representatives enjoy no monopoly to the claim of aggregating and articulating collective interests, and in fact a flourishing associational life (e.g. social movements, self-help groups, and civic associations) as well as powerful organized interests are strong rivaling factors. In response to these critical observations and comments, theorists of political representation have suggested interesting deviations from or refinements of earlier concepts: In the context of deliberative democracy, the idea of "discursive representation" has been introduced (Dryzek and Niemeyer, 2008) to capture the increasingly elusive nature of global governance where a well-defined *demos* is missing. From this perspective, in transnational public policy making it is not so much people, institutions or networks thereof that represent interests but discourses, defined as a set of categories and concepts with common assumptions and judgments. Other authors have addressed the capacity of citizens to represent themselves in voluntary associations and have ventilated the corresponding term of "citizen representatives" (Warren, 2009). In still other contributions to this complex debate, redefined and complementary roles and attributes of representatives have been floated so as to move away from traditional formalistic and retrospective relationships. From those vantage points, for example, political representation is also conceptualized as *advocacy* (Urbinati, 2002) or "*surrogacy*" (Mansbridge, 2003) in order to cater to underprivileged interests or constituents outside their districts. While a great many of new concerns and recent political changes have been sought to incorporate into contemporary notions of representation, one major transformation of modern political systems appears to be conspicuously missing from this discourse: the extent to which public bureaucracies – in varying degrees as regulators, owners of government property, or purchasers, if not providers of public goods and services – have come to affect the day-to-day life in modern societies. As a matter of fact, public agencies, as Chris Ansell (2012) has put it, find themselves in a difficult position: on the front end of problem solving, but "on the tail end of the chain of representation" (p. 2).

Public Bureaucracies as Representative Institutions?

Consequently, rather little attention has been paid to the potential capacity of public bureaucracies to act as representative institutions. It is only at the fringes of a rich and productive stream of theoretical and empirical scholarship on political representation that – under the rubric of non-democratic forms of representation – members of the bureaucracies have been recognized as potential representatives of the citizens they serve. As if the mainstream of "political representation" research had adopted a predominantly instrumental and passive view of public bureaucracies, the role of the administrative machinery of government in this context is primarily reduced to executing the will of political leaders (as authorized by the legislature) without being involved in the political struggle over power. To be sure, this image of public bureaucracy, of course, conforms best with the formal orthodoxy of the constitutional chain of democratic legitimacy – starting at the ballot box and – funneled through legislative and executive institutions of government – eventually leading to street-level bureaucrats. And yet, the widespread neglect for public agencies and their members in the discussion of representation seems all the more surprising as a broad movement in public administration and policy research has demonstrated how actively public administrators are involved in all phases of the public policy-making process and the extent to which a seemingly passive function such as policy implementation is politically charged and constitutes an integral part of a political process.

What is more, students of public administration (and later: public management) have not rushed in significant numbers to fill that gap in the representation literature. Owing to the bureaucratic paradigm – modeled upon Max Weber's ideal-typical depiction of the administrative staff organization under legal–rational authority – the supposedly rule-bound, impersonal behavior of officials moved to the center of attention and left little room for an image in which personal attributes of officials – other than their exam qualifications, perhaps – would play a larger role in assessing the quality of administrative performance. In a similar vein, the normative concern with the fight against corruption, nepotism and cronyism, the effort to stem the tide of "agency capture" and, last but not least, the necessities of dealing effectively and efficiently with complex and knowledge-based policy problems has highlighted – for good reason, to be sure – the benefits of having a professional, impartial and merit-based career civil service based on expertise and loyalty to the government of the day. In turn, alternative ways of selecting, recruiting and promoting administrative staff, including party-politicization or patronage, tend to be seen as deviations from the norm and have been given a bad name (for an in-depth discussion, see Peters in this volume). Without explicitly referring to issues of political representation, however, a number of major research themes in comparative public administration can easily be linked to our discussion. Picking-up on the question of party-political considerations in filling civil service positions, much of the literature suggests that the representation of party members in public bureaucracies is not only a widespread phenomenon, but may also serve a legitimate concern on the part of political leaders and societal interests. By the same token, neo-corporatist arrangements between organized interests and government institutions can also be interpreted in terms of the representation of specific occupational groups, social strata, and political interests in and by the bureaucratic apparatus. Also, couched in terms of decentralization, de-concentration or regionalism and localism, the territorial base of administrative structures reminds us of the fact that the very meaning of this principle of organization is to represent local and/or regional interests and – given the fact that oftentimes local and regional identities are also defined by linguistic, religious and other socio-cultural characteristics – that it can conveniently serve as a vehicle for representativeness in national administrative systems. Finally, findings from comparative research into role understandings and job-related attitudes of senior civil servants strongly support the view that administrators in significant numbers adopt role perceptions of advocates of both diffuse and organized interests and see themselves in their official capacities as interest mediators.

REPRESENTATIVE BUREAUCRACY: CORE CONCEPTS, VALUES, AND CONSEQUENCES

Core Concepts: Passive and Active Representation

The term "representative bureaucracy" has traditionally been used when referring to the relationship between the demographic makeup of the public sector workforce (particularly with regard to class, gender, race, ethnicity, as well as cultural traits such as language and religion) and the society it is supposed to serve (Kingsley, 1944; Meier, 1975; van der Meer and Roborgh, 1996). Conventionally, the theorems of representative bureaucracy are couched in terms of a search of control over administrative power. Sparked by the concern to keep public bureaucrats responsive to the public at large (Subramaniam, 1967) and further fuelled by the deeply ingrained belief that existing external constraints of bureaucratic power are inherently inadequate, the design of representative bureaucracy was meant to serve as an effective internal measure of controlling government officials' behavior. In contrast to the logic of external control mechanisms, protagonists of representative bureaucracy tend to see achieving attitudinal congruence between administrative officeholders and the general public as key to their approach. In this tradition, the concept of representative bureaucracy directs the attention to the relationship of the socio-demographic, -linguistic, and -ethnic compositions of societies and the workforce of the public sector and raises questions about the extent to which public sector workforces mirror the composition of the societies – *passive representation* – they are supposed to serve. It also examines the consequences of representativeness for the quality of service delivery, the management of large organizations, the legitimacy of the state as such, as well as questions of sharing power among societal groups (Peters, 2013). One central empirical question in this field of research is not only whether the bureaucracy looks like a given segment of the population in terms of its ethnic, racial, social, gender or occupational characteristics (Meier, 1975; Selden and Selden, 2001; Sowa and Selden, 2003), but also whether these groups – *active representation* – *actively* promote the interest of their groups (Mosher, 1968). And a prior question, centrally addressed in this volume, concerns the extent to which public sector organizations or entire civil service systems embark on representation strategies, why they do it or not, and through which means representation actually occurs (compare Meier and Morton, Schröter and von Maravić in this volume). The puzzle is essentially about making sense of the variety of forms and mechanisms of representation, which we encounter when comparing representation across countries and time.

The argument for researching representative bureaucracy comes often from a normative position assuming that the question of having or not having an ethnically representative public bureaucracy has implications for fair and effective policy-making and implementation, and the associated aim of integrating minorities into society by giving them the opportunity to become part of government, or even to control a bureaucracy that is dominated by a (ethnic) majority group and which does not care for the problems of minorities (Dolan and Rosenbloom, 2003; Subramaniam, 1967; van Gool, 2008). This notion that groups can hold regimes accountable by becoming part of them (Subramaniam, 1967; Mosher, 1968) has long been present in the literature. But access to the civil service is not always automatically given but depends, as Guy Peters argues in his chapters, on a number of factors, for example group belongings, access to education or just think of the different traditions of citizenship (Brubaker, 1992; Joppke, 1998), which do not automatically favor newly arrived migrants and their entry to the public service. This situation gives rise to fundamental questions about the universal appropriateness of merit-based recruitment (see Peters in this volume).

Value Base and Competing Paradigms

Arguably, the prevailing notion of human nature, as argued in greater length in the chapter by Eckhard Schröter and Patrick von Maravić in this book, employed by the advocates of representative bureaucracy serves as a good starting point of our overview of their value and belief systems. Clearly, the anthropological picture of (wo)man that guides most of the normative debates and empirical studies on workforce diversity is that of a social animal or *zoon politicon*, defined by a strong sense of group identity and driven by a strong impetus for communication and interaction with other members of their community. It flows from this identity politics that a strong collectivist undercurrent can be discerned in the representative bureaucracy approach – not unlike the dominant strand of the participatory democracy literature. Starting from this value base, we can contrast the notion of representative bureaucracy with competing ideal-typical models of organizing public sector agencies, starting with classical Weberians' views and moving on to highly individualist and market-driven principles of organization.

The classic Weberian ideal of the career public servant recruited on merit and capable of acting *sine ira et studio* with both superiors and clients pervades discussions of public bureaucracies (Gerth and Wright

Mills, 1948; Weber, 2002). This model is assumed to produce the most capable public servants and also to provide for the greatest possible equality in the recruitment, promotion, and retention of public servants. Further, the equality implied in the merit system can be justified in democratic terms, with all citizens having equal opportunity for public employment. While the model of political neutrality and merit recruitment has a powerful normative standing, we should not assume that it is necessarily the best means of attaining all the goals of personnel management in the public sector. In particular, we should not assume that merit-based recruitment will necessarily produce the most representative public bureaucracy. Legal mechanisms, such as affirmative action regulations in the United States or gender quotas in other countries, can help to break open traditional forms of recruitment and open up the access for traditionally non-represented groups but also nepotism and patronage, as Guy Peters argues in this volume, can be mechanisms, despite the well-known ethical and democratic problems, to overcome the under-representation of minority groups.

In stark contrast to what representatives of the bureaucratic school of thought have to offer on that account, advocates of public organizations representative of the society they serve hold organizational values that are diametrical opposed to the concept of impersonality as manifested in ideal-typical Weberian bureaucracies or, in other words, organizations that are structurally and culturally geared to let real people and their feelings, identities and non-work related qualifications vanish behind the veil of abstract rules and neatly delineated office structures (Dolan and Rosenbloom, 2003). In a similar vein, protagonists of market-driven social coordination (cf. Lindblom, 2002; Self, 1993, 2000) – based on assumptions of man as a rational actor – tend to be just as far away from the core values of the "representative school of thought". It is not the uniformly defined model of man or woman with externally pre-set utility functions and cost–benefit calculations to guide their behavior that appeals to advocates of diversity strategies in public, or for that matter, private sector organizations. Rather, their belief system rests on the assumption that organization members are defined by their ethnic, linguistic, or religious backgrounds – to name just a few sources of identity – and that they rely on social interaction with other individuals to develop their own preference structures as well as for the purpose of self-actualization.

Consequences of Representative Bureaucracies: Intended Benefits and Improvements

As noted above, the lion's share of the "representative bureaucracy" literature is propelled forward by a strong normative impetus. The mainstream of this strand of research shares the general assumption that it is in essence good to be provided and will eventually lead to better decisions, more effectively implemented policies, and higher levels of service quality as well as customer satisfaction. More "representative" and "diverse" staff is also believed to be a boost to employees' morale and motivation and thought to unleash innovative and creative potential. Clearly, the question of staffing public organizations according to social, ethnic, racial or linguistic characteristics – to name but a few – of a given segment of the population seems to carry important implications for the delivery of public services as well as the sharing of power in society. What is often obscured by a general claim to the improvement of administrative performance (see also Schröter and von Maravić in this volume) deserves a more differentiated and detailed treatment to which we turn below.

The majority of scholarship on diversity and representativeness in public (and private, for that matter) organizations focuses on the improved quality of organizational output. Seen from this perspective, good administration – particularly in multi-cultural environments – depends on the diversity of judgment, information and social skills that bureaucrats bring to the administrative apparatus – not unlike Kingsley (2003: 18) who called for the "pooling of diverse streams of experience" or Mosher (1968: 16) who advocated bringing together "different perspectives, knowledge, values, and abilities". The key message of this argument is echoed by advocates of increased diversity in the management of for-profit organizations who show in their work how workforce diversity is positively associated with higher creativity, better problem solving, and a more flexible adaptation to organizational change. In a similar vein, empirical research in public service delivery has demonstrated that the output quality significantly increases if the socio-demographic and -cultural traits of service providers match those of their target groups.

The intended consequences of representativeness, however, are not limited to the output dimension. While representativeness may make it easier for service providers to accomplish their service mission, it is also said to have a positive impact on organizational behavior more generally. In particular, the working climate – so it is argued – will considerably benefit from a more diverse workforce, with all the positive ramifications for human resource management in its wake. In particular, this "inward-looking" perspective on representativeness and diversity highlights research findings that report increased employer attractiveness, workers' loyalty and job satisfaction, but less personnel fluctuation and absenteeism. While representation is still a major factor in all of this, attention seems to shift in this segment of the discussion towards "diversity" as a goal in its own right. To be sure, it is likely that employers (public or private) will try and capitalize – as a way of employer branding – on the suggested positive corollaries of having a diverse workforce as it radiates a sense of open-mindedness, tolerance of minorities, equity and fairness, multi-culturalism, and modernity.

A third dimension of improving administrative performance through strategies of representativeness zooms in on external relations with specifically defined stakeholders and constituencies. In addition to questions about the quality of service output, it adds an interesting twist to the discussion as it acknowledges the value of having close and deeply rooted relations with customers or clientele groups as a quality of public organizations in its own right. This perspective also recognizes the profound political nature of external relations. Not only can representative bureaucracies contribute to higher levels of trust and legitimacy, they can also opportunistically use their well-established ties with supportive citizen groups as a resource for political bargaining and bureaucratic politics to strengthen their own cause. In essence, this category of functional justifications of representativeness falls into two subcategories: one being primarily concerned about customer relations as defined by the private-sector service management literature, another being more interested in questions of democratic accountability and responsiveness as discussed in political science circles. As for the former, diversity is presented as a quality that allows for more tailor-made products, opens up new markets, gives better access to specific clientele groups and helps focusing on customer demands. If seen from the latter perspective, a bureaucracy that mirrors the composition of society it serves tends to be more responsive to public interests.

What runs across most of these arguments discussed above is an implicit claim that representative bureaucracy would not only improve performance, as spelled out before, but enhance the legitimacy of public sector organizations overall. Though overlapping with expectations about improved external relations and better quality of services rendered and decisions made, the concern here does not lie with specific outputs or clientele groups. Rather, a more diffuse and systemic level of support seems to be at stake that exists independent of individual experiences of administrative performance. A passively representative bureaucracy, so the argument goes, carries "independent and symbolic values" (Mosher, 1968: 17) that are prerequisites for democratic societies: it signals a "commitment to equal access to power" (Selden and Selden, 2001: 309), serves potentially as a vehicle for upward social mobility, thus integrating minorities or marginalized groups into the mainstream of society, and manifests the "consensual and equalitarian ethos of the community" (Subramaniam, 1967: 1014).

Consequences of Representative Bureaucracies: Unintended Drawbacks and Potential Pitfalls

While advocates of representative bureaucracy as a major principle for organizing public agencies tend to present the effects of this reform strategy in the most favorable light, any more comprehensive perspective cannot overlook a series of potentially significant drawbacks and ramifications.

Most fundamentally, any effort of making public organizations look more socially representative in terms of "passive representation" is almost bound to pit – in principle – *group* rights of minorities or marginalized collectives against *individual* rights of other contenders for civil service jobs. In this context, decision-makers are likely to face at one point the ethical question of whether (and if so, how?) to discriminate against a member of an already well-represented group in order to advance the cause of an underrepresented societal group. Concomitantly, this problem is often accompanied by the potential conflict between meritocratic standards of selecting, recruiting, and promoting public officials. If the top priority of organization principles is accorded to maintaining formally equal access to civil service positions, and to preserving the predominance of formal qualifications, expertise, and professional standards, the quest for representativeness will probably be perceived as an attempt to open the gates for political patronage, cronyism, and to put the expertism at risk. If highest emphasis, however, is placed on the economy and efficiency of public organizations, the concern with representative bureaucracy is more likely to lie with the extra costs associated with this approach. In fact, personnel numbers may be driven up – well beyond the limit of the required minimum – in an effort to accommodate additional requests for representation. Also, expenses for running human resource management systems might go up as the composition of the workforce is becoming more complex and services have to be offered to different groups with different needs (language or otherwise).

Assuming, however, most if not all of these problems can be avoided, we still face another category of potential problems – problems that appear to be the flipside of what representative bureaucracy is meant to achieve. As personnel departments aim at recreating the socio-cultural complexity of modern societies, they also invite additional degrees of fragmentation into their own organizations, including the extra challenges for intra-organizational coordination that come with them. Seen from a wider angle, this possible side-effect reminds us of the in-built tension between the general welfare that public bureaucracies are supposed to serve and those particular group interests that representative bureaucracy is all about. In fact, the pursuit of effectively including hitherto non- or underrepresented groups might even backfire. The recognition of "minority status" or "preferential treatment" in public organizations can be interpreted as a way of creating its own constituencies, so that social cleavages may be cemented and perpetuated. Rather than "*re-presenting*", i.e. making present again existing social cleavages, strategies towards representativeness might actually create new divisions (or reinforce and revive older ones) in society as the move towards representativeness can be opportunistically used to set new incentive structures for organized interests. And, finally, those additional divisions are perhaps even more forcefully felt *inside* public organizations as "intra-minority" competition seems to be one of the more frequently observed (unintended) consequences of representative bureaucracy.

Again, let us assume that these repercussions are adequately addressed and dealt with – as they, within limits, can be with an extra effort to the management of human resources and institutional change. A more fundamental category of open questions – related to basic assumptions of the "representative bureaucracy" concept and its relations with "political representation" – has still to be discussed. Theoretical reasoning as well as empirical research findings suggest that public policy making processes may inch closer and closer to the state of "*ungovernability*" if more and more actors, including non-elected officials in public bureaucracies, lay claim to legitimately represent specific constituencies. (This problem brings back to memory the role perception of policy-driven and highly politicized senior bureaucrats – or "pure hybrids" – who are likely to compete for the same turf as politicians.) On top of that it creates conceptual problems for the notion of accountability, if we deal – lacking any recall mechanisms or re-election requirements – with administrators and their relations with external stakeholders and constituencies.

So far we have worked on the assumption that bureaucratic "representatives" actually intend to perform their roles as prescribed by the mainstream of the "representative bureaucracy" literature. A new picture, however, opens up, if we take issue with the proposition that "active representation" is primarily or exclusively sought after to promote the standing of marginalized groups. Rather, measures to improve "active representation" can just as well be used as a way of tokenism – a way to comply formally with popular expectations or legal requirements without addressing the question of substantive representation seriously. In other cases, to bring this discussion to full circle, it may be a vehicle for rewarding old – or buying new – political friends and supporters. Besides, the hypothesized link between "passive" and "active" representation is not as strongly established as much of the "representative bureaucracy" literature seems to suggest. Research on professional or elite socialization has shown how earlier socio-cultural attachments to minority groups may over time give way to new social identities, attitudinal patterns, and role understandings so as to conform more closely with their professional or organizational peers. As a matter of fact, minority members have been known for occasionally over-identifying with values and behavioral patterns of majority groups in order to blend in more easily. Even if members of marginalized groups in administrative positions still identify strongly with their socio-cultural inheritance, their propensity to act on their behalf as trustees, delegates, or stewards of their collective cause in their official capacity may be very low or non-existing.

THE CONTINGENCY OF REPRESENTATION OR, WHAT IS TO BE REPRESENTED?

What representativeness actually means appears to be highly contingent on the prevailing societal conflicts and cleavages, the specific function of the civil service within society, as well as its traditions and mechanisms of recruitment. The country studies in the volume *Representative Bureaucracy in Action* (von Maravić et al., 2013) illustrate not only why and how the issue of "representativeness" and "diversity" matters in public sector employment, but also highlight the driving forces that either keep the debate from moving forward or propel the institutionalization of some form of representation. Not only do traditional migration countries such as the United States of America, Canada or Australia cope with questions of the ethnic-cultural compositions of their societies but so also do European countries with a growingly diversified ethnic–cultural composition, often enough concomitantly to the existing linguistic–ethnic cleavages as for example in Switzerland or Belgium.

However, how issues of representativeness actually play out institutionally, what representativeness actually means, and to which groups it refers may vary among countries (see chapter by Peters, Schröter and von Maravić in this volume). Is it a question of geographic representation as in the case of Southern Italy, castes as in the case of India, an issue of indigenous groups in Mexico, people of African or European decent in South Africa, religious groups in the Netherlands and also formerly in Switzerland, entire regions as with Wallonia and Flanders in Belgium, or upper-middle class as in the case of Great Britain at the time when Kingsley wrote his account of the underrepresentation of the rest of society in the civil service? Thus, although government may attempt to produce more or less representative personnel systems, their efforts may be shaped in part by the nature of the surrounding society, (labor) market, and institutional setting. It is therefore not sufficient to focus the study of representative bureaucracy on ethnic diversity and migration alone but we must consider the societal conditions that establish the prerequisites for the nature of representation in a society's administrative system. The question then is not just whether bureaucracies act as representative institutions but whom do they represent, how, and why (see also Wimmer, 1997).

What representation actually then means in an administrative system and to what extent public organizations are (see the chapter by Kenneth M. Meier and Tabitha S.M. Morton in this book) turned into representative bodies raises questions about the influence of a variety of institutional as well as socio-cultural factors that range from currently as well as historically existent cleavages, the traditional role the state encompasses in a society (liberal vs. organic) to the institutionalized forms of interest group articulation and mediation.

Social Conflicts

Considering the variation among countries of how representation essentially plays out, we propose that historical and salient social cleavages offer one explanatory factor for further investigation (Lipset and Rokkan, 1967: 1-64). Lipset and Rokkan understood "social cleavages" as arising "out of a great variety of relationships in the social structure [...]" (1967: 6) but were also clear in seeing that "only a few of these tend to polarize the politics of any given political system" (1967: 6). In other words, we think that there are good reasons to believe that the extent to which a countries' administrative system acts as a representative institution depends on the nature of prevailing social cleavages in a society. The type of cleavage, e.g. ethnic, language, or class polarization, appears to be a necessary though not yet sufficient indicator for the type of representation we find in a given administrative system. And yet we lack systematic analysis across administrative systems that would allow us to move beyond hypothesizing causal relationships but determine to what extent a distinct form of representation can be understood as an expression of manifest or latent social conflicts (cf. Lipset and Rokkan, 1967: 5). The extent to which a country's administrative system is a function of salient social cleavages depends furthermore on the ability of groups to articulate and advocate those conflicts over a significant period of time in the political arena. It is therefore plausible to assume that salient social cleavages play then a role in shaping the representative nature of a country's administrative system, when specific issues, e.g. ethnic conflict, dominate the political agenda. Though social cleavages shape the nature of representation, there is no reason to believe in a deterministic relationship as other factors mediate this relationship.

Channels of Representation

One of these mediating factors can be seen in the different ways interests are being articulated and political preferences are being transmitted into a political system. The ability to organize the interests of a group and translate those concerns into the political arena by actively advocating a group's concerns, seems to be a factor that shapes the way bureaucracies respond to the specific demands of a group. The related, though yet still open question, however, concerns the influence of more general features, such as the type of electoral or interest group system, of a nation's system of political interest articulation. While majority electoral systems often lead to a two-party system, for example in Westminster democracies, the "winner takes it all" logic makes it difficult for minority groups to articulate their political will in the political arena (Lijphart, 1999). This could account for why the absence of proportional representation in the legislature is being (often) balanced by a tendency towards proportional representation in public sector organizations. This, at least, suggests the case of the United States as well as the case of the Canadian political system, though it is contradicted by the United Kingdom (Andrews, 2013; Turgeon and Gagnon, 2013; Peters, in this volume). Political systems, which determine the composition of the legislature by using proportional representation, tend to give more room for smaller parties to be represented with their ideas and agendas and therefore offer a channel for articulating societal conflicts. Does this automatically make representation in public organizations superfluous?

We may assume that this is not necessarily the case but it could make us think of alternative mechanisms of representation vis-à-vis the bureaucracy.

The two different logics of determining representation within parliament are not only related to the number of parties in parliament and the tendency to form coalition governments but also to interest group systems. While consensus democracies, to use Arend Lijphart's (1999) term, do not follow the more antagonistic pluralist logic of interest group articulation of Westminster systems but instead incorporate a few selected interest groups into the policy-making process, which tends to lead to the exclusion of other interest groups, this corporatist style of policy-making (cf. Schmitter, 1974) is necessarily more dependent on finding a consensus among different groups. However, as indicated before, this more institutionalized way of interested articulation does not necessarily lead to a greater openness for less well-organized groups (Lehmbruch, 1977; Katzenstein, 1987b, 1985). Nevertheless, the ability of groups to articulate their interests in the political arena, the one way or the other, seems to be having an effect on either stabilizing existing institutional solutions or pushing them towards change. However, this form of "corporatist" representation may provide an alternative form of indirect representation of interests to the bureaucracy and could be more relevant in countries such as Germany or Austria. This specific type may provide a functional equivalent to the recruitment of "representatives" in the civil service as we see it in Canada or the United States. At least, the case of the German civil service suggests that the influence of relevant organized interest groups happens directly at the edge of relevant government departments, allowing them to institutionalize the partisan shaping of decision-making processes without being necessarily part of the civil service (Derlien and Mayntz, 1989; Katzenstein, 1987a). But this could matter for other countries as well. Lipset and Rokkan (1967) argue that the interest group system constituted a second pillar of democracy in Norway and other Scandinavian countries that enabled segments of society who were not well represented by the dominant Labor Party to influence policy. This representation was important for legitimation of the existing political order. As time and society have moved on, a third pillar of representation, within the public bureaucracy, may become increasingly important. Pluralist systems of interest group mediation may offer similar mechanisms, though they are often less institutionalized.

Administrative Traditions and Forms of Recruitment

A third factor that seems to be worth further exploring concerns the influence of national *state or administrative traditions*. By "pooling diverse streams of experience" as Kingsley (Kingsley, 2003: 18) put it, or Mosher's idea of bringing together "different perspectives, knowledge, values, and abilities" (Mosher, 1968: 16) citizens, they both argued, are better served as it improves the quality of governance. In principle, advocates of representative bureaucracy share the idea that a bureaucracy that mirrors the composition of the society it serves is more responsive to public interests and will therefore, as Selden and Selden point out, "better serve democratic principles" (Selden and Selden, 2001: 308). This very general argument, which seems to prevail in the representative bureaucracy as well as diversity management literature, provokes the question whether this might not only be true under very specific institutional, historical, and cultural conditions and is therefore difficult to generalize for all administrative systems. Our assumption would be that, when considering the variety of administrative traditions and cultures (Painter and Peters, 2010), the extent to which bureaucracies function actively as representative institutions is not only highly contingent upon different administrative traditions but also on the different roles the public service plays within societies. This idea is being nourished by the distinction between a liberal and an organic state tradition. The former, also labeled as a *public interest state* (Pollitt and Bouckaert, 2004: 53) is generally associated with Westminster political systems, whereas the *latter Rechtsstaat model* is more representative of the political systems of France, Germany, Switzerland, and Austria. This distinction, especially with regard to administrative system, rests on different beliefs of the role of state in society, the existence of administrative law, and the education and recruitment of public servants.

In the German and French administrative tradition, the state is a transcendent entity, its citizens members of an organic society. As bureaucrats personify the power and overarching capacity of the state, they take an essential role in shaping or even bringing about society. Their devotion, loyalty, and accountability is essentially a consequence of their specific training as professionals in the practice of law and administration of power. In this context it seems relevant to remind us of the different career systems that are embedded in the different administrative traditions. In the continental tradition, especially Germany and France, university graduates enter a career at an early age of their life and then proceed through the ranks often within the same organization. Attending specific training programs as in the case of the ENA in France is often a prerequisite for entering a civil service career. Obviously, this does not only form a specific expertise but is also the basis for a shared set of values among elite member of the administrative class. Being member of a state elite, especially in France (cf. Birnbaum, 1977; Suleiman, 1984), carries the connotation of being able to take the right decisions for society and all its members. The idea of representation is officially non-existent in these systems, although the idea of "égalité" has prevailed ever since the French Revolution in 1789, also, at least as a principle, in the French civil service. Nevertheless, the idea of representation can be seen to exist in a different, rather indirect form as civil servants perceive themselves, due to their expertise and training, to be able to consider all necessary interests and take justified decisions as a consequence of their competencies and social status. Representation is therefore not so much a binary-coded issue of absence or presence but rather concerns the institutionalized mechanisms, by which a civil service system legitimizes and institutionalizes distinct forms of dealing with it. Related to this, is, of course, the more general acceptance of hierarchy and subordinance that legitimizes (to a certain extent) elite circle decisions. This is quite the opposite to the notion of state and bureaucracy in Anglo-Saxon countries, though one should be quick to point out that these are here very broad generalizations, which cannot do justice to each country. Still, one must not go as far as Margaret Thatcher's observation, "there is no such thing as society" (in an interview, 1987), but it underlines the importance of the individual in society and its relationship to government. "Stateless society" (Stillman, 1991) expresses the attitude that the state, especially within the United States, arises from a contract among members of society and is being held accountable by its members. The boundaries between state and society are more distinct in the liberal tradition than in the *Rechtsstaat* tradition. In addition, as the legal foundation of the state is less important compared to the *Rechtsstaat* tradition the training of public servants rests less on law. Representation is important in this administrative tradition as it defines a distinct form of holding government accountable, as being a "mirror" of society, means actually to be able to reflect all existing values and interest in society.

Social cleavages, forms of interest mediation as well as administrative traditions are in our view relevant, though not necessarily sufficient to understand why we observe variants of representation in administrative systems. In some instances the social groups who may have something to gain politically and in terms of employment simply do not mobilize, or do not mobilize effectively. This may be from lack of understanding of politics in democratic systems, or because the groups feel threatened in some way. For whatever reason, simply existing may be insufficient for a group to gain representation in representative bureaucracy. There is no "dearth", as Lipset and Rokkan (1967: 6) pointed out, of well-founded hypotheses but making sense of them systematically and empirically will be a major task for the future, which will hopefully lead us to a more comprehensive understanding of the dynamics, facets, and contradictions of the politics of representation in the public sector.

IN CONCLUSION: LESSONS FOR A THEORY OF PUBLIC ORGANIZATIONS AND PATHWAYS FOR FURTHER RESEARCH

Public bureaucracies are creatures of society and politics. The study of representative bureaucracy vividly reminds us of the fundamentally important and bidirectional relationship that exists between the dynamics of societal developments – be it class divisions, gender inequalities or other socio-cultural cleavages – and the most basic questions of how to staff public organizations. At the same time, the essentially political nature of the functions public agencies perform is highlighted. While public organizations – trusted with the task of the delivering public goods and services – will have to answer to questions about their effective and efficient performance, they are also inherently involved in those crucial processes of political interest mediation and representation, as well as generating system-wide public support and legitimacy. In order to fully appreciate these societal and political dimensions of public sector employment, however, our analytical lenses need to be adjusted accordingly. If we only employ ideal-typical bureaucratic models of organization or focus exclusively on purely efficiency driven managerialist prescriptions, our analysis of civil service systems will fail to see and recognize important societal and political implications.

While "representative bureaucracy" certainly qualifies as a contested concept in the field of public administration, it is also a highly relevant approach to advance our understanding of how public organizations work. One of the most significant lessons that can be drawn from what has been outlined above is that it does matter who is recruited into public sector jobs. Again, it is crucial to point out that the representativeness of public organizations affects both their internal and external affairs and has an impact on efficiency and effectiveness just as it does on legitimacy. As a consequence, it matters that those employees are capable of influencing policy and administration in ways that may advantage the social groups from which they are recruited. While this form of legitimation may not always please members of the dominant groups in society, it is crucial for managing the politics of contemporary political systems, whether democratic or non-democratic.

Thinking about the importance of representative bureaucracy naturally leads on to thinking about the importance of lower levels of the public bureaucracy, and the face-to-face contacts between citizens and their public servants. The familiar literature on street level bureaucracy has pointed out that these interactions not only determine who gets what in a material sense, they also affect the image of government and public bureaucracy with the public. Most citizens have limited interactions with their elected officials but they have frequent interactions with public servants, ranging from police to school teachers to tax collectors and beyond. This insight can just be added to the list of reasons why the capacity of public bureaucracies to act as representative institutions should be taken seriously.

Representative bureaucracy is not important only for political reasons, however, and it has substantial relevance for the management of public organizations (cf. Ely, 2004; Pitts, 2009; Pitts and Wise, 2010). The logic of representative bureaucracy is to some extent the antithesis of the logic of New Public Management that has dominated thinking about public organizations for the past two decades. Representative bureaucracy assumes that participation and involvement are more important for a well-functioning organization than is the drive toward market efficiency (see Pollitt and Bouckaert, 2004). While the market model of governing assumes that citizens will be better off if services are provided efficiently and at the lowest possible cost, more participatory conceptions of management assume that citizens and employees will be better off if more people can be involved in decision-making. With regard to the broad and increasingly influential field of performance management in particular, the lessons from the study of representative bureaucracy can be condensed in a single message that appears simple and yet difficult to digest: organizational performance is a multi-dimensional concept, ranging from the quality of output and the effects on internal management to the consequences for the building-up of political support and public trust.

The above having been said, however, having multiple social groups within public organizations may also generate some management issues. As has long been apparent for both public and private organizations informal organizational structures exist alongside the formal structures and provide alternative forms of control. If these informal structures are defined by ethnic or gender characteristics then cooperation within the organization may be impeded if the various informal structures and groups are in conflict with one another. It flows from this that representative bureaucracy as a reform strategy may indeed be the source of new challenges for public personnel management that have to be addressed by comprehensive measures of "diversity management".

Representative bureaucracy may also raise important questions about the accountability of public organizations. Positive representativeness has been lauded as a mechanism for providing some differential consideration to minority group members and women. If indeed that is a consequence of increased representativeness then decisions being made within the bureaucracy may not apply the law equally to all citizens. While we can make a case that the more disadvantaged members of society should receive special consideration if that is indeed done then the average taxpayer and citizen may believe that his or her interests are not being served adequately. Thus, there is a need for some balancing of principles of equality and compensation when attempting to determine just how much representativeness should be linked to policy choices.

Despite a long-standing intellectual tradition and a rich body of literature that refers to representative bureaucracy as a field of scholarly work, our knowledge of the conditions under which public organizations are more or less likely and able to act as representative institutions and what the consequences for administrative performance are going to be is still underdeveloped. How exactly reform approaches towards "representative bureaucracy" play out in different institutional contexts, cultural settings and for various types of public agencies is still an agenda item for further research in comparative public administration. To what extent citizens and their voices, opinions and interests can be represented by members of public bureaucracies and how this channel of interest representation relates to other forms of political representation can in turn be best answered if we wed the still rather separated research traditions of political and bureaucratic representation together. Why does passive representation in public bureaucracies translate into active representation in certain cases but not in others? What role perceptions and attitudinal dispositions towards their clientele groups do public administrators hold? These questions apparently require further research into the sociology of public sector organizations and their members. As illustrated by this shortlist of research questions and approaches, we supposed that much can be gained in this field of inquiry if we pursue a distinctly comparative and interdisciplinary research agenda that frees itself from narrow normative limitations and recognizes the inherently political nature of public bureaucracies. It is to this research agenda that this publication as well as its sister volume seeks to make a contribution.

2. The comparative study of representative bureaucracy: an analytical framework

B. Guy Peters, Eckhard Schröter and Patrick von Maravić

INTRODUCTION

This chapter will place the numerous empirical papers on representative bureaucracy in a broader context. Rather than describe in detail the different findings across countries (see von Maravić, Schröter and Peters, 2013), this chapter will instead attempt to understand the factors that may have generated those differences. The fundamental argument for the chapter is that representative bureaucracies do not arise just out of normative commitments or as a mere reflection of existing social conditions, although those factors will be significant. Rather, individual public bureaucracies are embedded in complex social, political, and administrative systems that place pressures on organizations to become more representative, but – at the same time – also place restrictions and limitations on the willingness and capacity to change in that direction. In sum, in the following we set out to discuss a frame of reference for the comparative analysis of representative bureaucracy across national borders.

We will look at several factors that can explain the relevance of issues of representation, as well as those factors that might also explain the success or failure of representativeness. These factors typically are aspects of the social and political systems, rather than public administration per se, but administration itself will also influence the extent to which representativeness, and especially more active versions of representativeness, is likely to be effective. In all these explanations for representative bureaucracy, however, there should still be room for agency so that some individual administrators may be crucial in facilitating, or impeding, representative bureaucracy being implemented.

Since Donald Kingsley (1944) advanced the notion of representative bureaucracy (see also van Gool in this volume for an in-depth discussion of the perception and intellectual genealogy of the term), the term has become commonly used to describe and to understand questions of class, ethnicity, and gender – among other socio-structural and -cultural divisions – within the public bureaucracy. There has been a good deal of development of theory concerning representative bureaucracy per se, but there has been somewhat less theoretical and analytic development concerning representative bureaucracy in comparative perspective. Although there is evidence collected about this concept in a number of different administrative systems (see von Maravić, Schröter and Peters, 2013) representative bureaucracy has not been considered from a directly comparative perspective (see chapter in this volume by Meier and Morton). Such a comparative perspective would locate representative bureaucracy in the context of other dimensions of the political and administrative systems, as well as in the context of the social system within which administration is embedded, and help to build a more theoretical understanding of this concept.

Ours can only be a modest contribution to this end. We proceed by investigating three broadly defined sets of contextual factors that can be effective in shaping the trajectory of representative bureaucracy in any given country: (1) social context, including socio-demographics, cultural dispositions, and socio-economic aspects; (2) political environment, including constitutional settings, modes of interest mediation, and particular policies pertaining to representativeness; (3) characteristics of the public sector, including civil service systems, administrative structures, and the specific mix of providers of public services. Each set of those variables will be briefly introduced at a conceptual level, before we, in a more cursory treatment, shed more light on selected aspects to illuminate and exemplify their relationship with representative bureaucracy. This suggested remit of our discussion alone forbids – for the purpose of this chapter – a full-blown comprehensive and in-depth analysis. Rather, we aim at navigating the debate of representative bureaucracy in comparative perspective by highlighting important, though often unduly neglected, determinants of national trajectories of representative bureaucracy, thus pointing in possible directions of future research.

SOCIAL ROOTS OF REPRESENTATIVE BUREAUCRACY

Dimensions of Social Context: Socio-demographics, Cultural Dispositions, and Socio-economics

Public bureaucracies are creatures of societies. As such, their forms and functions – including the size and composition of their workforces – will tend to reflect characteristic traits of their social habitats. For the sake of clarity of our argument, we may group those characteristics into three different – though to some extent overlapping and interrelated – categories: socio-demographic, socio-cultural, and socio-economic factors. Clearly, socio-demographics play a potentially major role in explaining cross-country differences in the relevance, institutional form, and outcomes of representative bureaucracies. Traditionally, well-established concepts such as social class (Kingsley 1944), including questions of upward social mobility, have received wide currency in this context. In addition, the core concern of the "representativeness" debate has been with ethnic, linguistic, and religious divisions that may run through societies. Regional identities, often deeply rooted in cultural and political history and couched in terms of strained "center-periphery" relations, are also frequently referred to as major justifications for the need of representative bureaucracies. Additional factors, such as age or gender, receive today more attention than two decades ago. Some of these societal features, however, have given way to socio-structural factors that have been with us as long as any form of society or community exists but are now redefined in their relationship to representativeness: gender issues have moved to center stage, new social and political communities have been formed based, for example, on the sexual orientation of their members, and demographic changes in many societies worldwide have sharpened age-based inter-generational cleavages. Still other rifts running through society are easily conceivable and likely to dominate future discussions about representative bureaucracies, such as the emerging divide between "digital natives" and "digital nomads". What we gain from this overview of societal characteristics is the insight that social cleavages may serve as necessary, though not as sufficient conditions for representative bureaucracy to take root. The sheer existence of socio-demographic dividing lines tells us very little about how much political saliency is accorded to this divide, and how this saliency may be translated into any particular form of representation. It is rather the category of socio-cultural dispositions that may provide further guidance for our comparative study of representative bureaucracy. The prevailing value patterns in any given society can be expected to amplify or to mute specific calls for representation of social groups. If public bureaucracies are primarily, or even exclusively, perceived as sources of (technical, legal, or other professional) expertise (rather than as part and parcel of the political machinery), social support for Weberian-type merit-based recruitment policies is likely to be high and moves to make public bureaucracies more socially representative will be less pronounced. Even if the question of social representation in public bureaucracies is an issue of social debates, some calls for representation will be perceived as more legitimate than others. Again, the dominant pattern of social and political values and attitudes at any given time and place – as exemplified by the secular trend towards post-materialism – serves as an effective filter or amplifier of demands for more socially diverse and representative bureaucracies. Third – and finally – social pressure for or against the notion and practice of representation in public sector organizations is also deeply rooted in socio-economic considerations. Selection and self-selection of minority members for employment in the public sector, in other words, is often a direct or indirect function of the job market. From the public employers' perspective, the intake of members of certain social groups may serve a functional need. As seen from the opposite perspective, socially and/or economically marginalized and underprivileged groups may turn to the public sector for the lack of employment opportunities elsewhere.

We should be quick to remind ourselves, however, that the above consistently treats social factors as the independent variable with representative bureaucracy being the dependent variable. Of course, this relationship can cut both ways. Representative bureaucracy as a policy program may be able to create its own constituencies by defining certain social groups that need to be represented. It may also provide incentives for intra-minority competition over preferential treatment or for new groups or communities (if only "imagined communities") to get official recognition as a "minority" or "marginalized" group. By the same token, the proactive selection, recruitment, and hiring of minority members by public bureaucracies can effectively change public perceptions of those minorities and re-allocate economic opportunities in society. In a nutshell, the dynamics of representative bureaucracy as an administrative reform policy are not to be underestimated. With that caveat in mind, we can now turn to a more detailed and empirical discussion of the social roots of representative bureaucracy.

Social Cleavages and their Political Context

If societies were perfectly homogenous then representative bureaucracy would be a meaningless concept. But all societies are heterogeneous, albeit to different degrees, and hence the concept is meaningful and is important in terms of how societies manage their social cleavages (cf. Lipset and Rokkan, 1967; Henjak, 2010) and develop their public bureaucracies. The presence of social differences within societies has become even more relevant as gender has become politicized, so that even countries that may be otherwise largely homogenous must consider equal, or even compensatory, treatment of women within public sector employment.

As we consider the role of social cleavages and how they relate to the development of representative bureaucracies we need to remember that these cleavages may be subtle, and also continue to change. Societies that to the outsider may appear very homogenous may be divided internally in ways that are politically relevant (Stubager, 2010) and very important to the members of the society. Further, although Kingsley was primarily concerned about the effects of social class on administration that cleavage has lessened in intensity in many developed countries[1] to be replaced by more "post-material" values (including gender), as well as by immigration, as the foundations of difference in societies. Further, the continuing relevance of ethno-nationalism in countries such as Spain (e.g. Basque Country, Catalonia) and the UK (Scotland) emphasizes the relevance of representativeness.

The above points to the importance of politicization of social cleavages in defining the relevance of representative bureaucracy. If social differences are not considered politically relevant, or indeed are considered to undermine other fundamental values within the society or policy domain then representativeness may not be a significant factor in recruitment. For example, the French political and administrative systems have tended not to recognize differences because of the importance of the concepts of equality and fraternity within the political myths governing the system.[2] At the other extreme the social cleavages may be so intensely politicized, that the issue of representativeness of the bureaucracy is both difficult to calculate and perhaps too sensitive to address directly. For example, Belgium – a country with a long history of "representative" language policies in the public sector – now tends to avoid when possible a national census that might identify *changes* in the ratio of the linguistic groups within the country (see van de Walle et al., 2013).

As well as the existence and politicization of social cleavages, the legitimacy of the social group within the political system may also be relevant (see also Chapter 1). In some cases, the minority segments of society who would likely benefit from representative bureaucracy – both as employees and as clients – are long established within the society. Other groups who are more recent additions to the society may not be considered to have the same legitimate claims. For example, within the United States, African Americans appear to be considered by some as having more legitimate claims than do people of Hispanic origin, largely because the Hispanics are often thought to be illegal migrants even if they are actually citizens. In many European countries, large influxes of immigrants have tended to stretch the sense of belonging within the societies and hence may make claims for representativeness less viable politically (see Goodman, 2012).

Despite the number and intensity of social cleavages, the political relevance of representativeness and the viability of political pressures to push administrative systems in that direction may be a function of the pattern of coping with difference. The obvious difference is between societies that have stressed assimilation versus those that have stressed multi-culturalism (see Turgeon and Gagnon 2013). In the former case, the attempt has been not to emphasize social differences, but rather to encourage all members of the society become integrated into the larger society. On the other hand, societies that emphasize multi-cultural responses to difference may also emphasize the need to make all institutions of society, including the public bureaucracy, more representative of those differences.

Socio-economic Push and Pull Factors

The above discussion has been primarily from the perspective of equality of opportunity for employment, but as already noted representative bureaucracy may also be driven by the nature of the clientele of government. If governments must serve a diverse clientele, especially when language is an important basis of the social cleavage, then it may be more efficient to promote representative bureaucracy. The representativeness may be especially important at the "street level" (Meyer and Nielsen, 2012). Representativeness may also enhance the legitimacy of government to clients who might otherwise feel threatened by employees from the dominant community.[3] This argument for representativeness is more relevant for street level bureaucracy than for the upper echelons of the system, but in comparative perspective it is crucial to consider service delivery to disparate populations. This can be seen in the case of Germany where the state administered police forces as well as tax authorities have been among the most active administrative institutions in recruiting staff with migration background, e.g. Turkish or Serbo-Croatian. Often publicly justified as a mechanism of integration, the functional aspect behind hiring staff with specific language skills, cultural sensitivity, and insider knowledge of these specific communities cannot be overlooked when it comes to fighting crime or tax evasion. These staff members are often regarded to work especially in areas that are related to their ethnic origin, e.g. juvenile delinquency by immigrants, cross-border organized crime. However, this may sometimes create conflicts on both sides as those staff members do not necessarily want to be reduced to this specific trait of their origin (see Dudek, 2009).

Finally, the political relevance of representative bureaucracy may be a function of the economic opportunities available to members of the minority groups who might seek public employment. For example, African Americans were excluded from many white-collar jobs (especially in the South) and therefore employment in federal government jobs was particularly important.[4] These economic factors may in fact make the public sector over represent perceived minority employees. For example, the relative paucity of good jobs in Southern Italy led to a significant over-representation of this group in the civil service (see Capano and Carboni, 2013).[5] And Germany is an example for more functional pressures to seek a job in the public service. Increasing salaries and the growingly unattractive blue-collar jobs in the public sector led to a situation in which municipalities increasingly depended on immigrant employment. At the same time, minorities were highly attracted to the job security and relatively high income. Nor should the symbolic attractiveness of working for "the State" be underestimated.

In summary, numerous characteristics of the social and economic systems within which government functions influence the demand for, and the possibilities for, representative bureaucracy. As is often the case, the very situations in which there is the greatest need for representative bureaucracy, i.e. those in which there is a large and disadvantaged minority community, may be the cases in which actually creating such an administrative system will be the most difficult task for government. When there is a significant minority community the dominant community may wish to hold on to its social and economic advantages so that political and legal actions may be needed to produce the changes.

REPRESENTATIVE BUREAUCRACY EMBEDDED IN POLITICAL SYSTEMS

In addition to the social and economic pressures for representative bureaucracy, the nature of the political system within which the bureaucracy functions also influences the emphasis placed on representativeness in public administration. It may be difficult to separate some aspects of politics from public administration (discussed below), but there are some elements of how the governing arrangements as a whole are constructed, and how they are considered by the population, that influences the representativeness of the public bureaucracy. As with societal forces, we may be able to identify separate classes of determinants (or shaping factors) that can be grouped together to help to streamline our argument. First, we can pick up on our discussion of socio-cultural patterns and employ the concept of political culture as a potentially powerful independent variable. To be sure, political culture is a somewhat vague term, and often is the residual explanation for political behaviors,[6] but ideas do matter in political life (Schmidt, 2010). Most fundamentally, ideas about the rationale of the state and the foundations of citizenship are likely to leave their imprints on national designs of (more or less) representative bureaucracies (see below). Second, the influence of institutional arrangements and the structural layout of governing systems (the "polity") need to be carefully considered, including both the horizontal and vertical dimensions of the diffusion or concentration of political power in any given system. Horizontally, political power can be systematically dispersed between the branches of government or among key actors such as political parties. Vertically, political systems differ in the degree to which they allow for political decentralization. By definition, institutional designs that favor power diffusion – such as in political systems with proportional representation, strong traditions of judicial review, and elaborative arrangements of "checks and balances", and also in federal and politically decentralized countries – tend to be more inclusive of various political forces and provide more access points for the representation of political interests. While this logic applies primarily to the concept of political representation, we seem to be on safe ground to assume that those access points can also be effectively used to promote the representation of societal forces in public bureaucracies. Third, this very process of interest representation is of crucial importance for the development of representative bureaucracies. Arguably, some governments enjoy a greater degree of autonomy from special interests as represented by pressure groups than others. When interest groups tend to dominate the policy-making process and the universe of organized social groups is highly pluralistic (as is typically the case in the United States), it might be conducive to more effective collective representation of groups that represent minority interests. In European neo-corporatist systems of interest representation – though waning since their heydays in the 1970s and early 1980s – governments may find it easier to resist conflicting group demands. Once recognized by states as important collective interests and granted preferential access to policy-making decisions, corporatist actors, however, tend to enjoy influential positions in political systems, particularly when they are organized as "peak organizations" as most of the representatives of the "old social question" – pitting capital against labor – are. In contrast, new social movements or members of newly-formed groups (such as representatives of migrants' interests, newly established faith-based organizations or advocates of group rights based on the concept of identity politics) are likely to face more difficulties in making their voices heard vis-à-vis the executive-bureaucratic apparatus. These questions feedback to our earlier discussion of national political cultures and regime types as more fragmented and divided societies may altogether call for distinct approaches towards interest mediation – approaches that differ from majoritarian, "the-winner-takes-it-all" systems and place a premium on power-sharing and consensus-building. They have been introduced to the comparative study of democracy as the as *politics of accommodation* (Lijphart, 1976) as in the case of the Netherlands or *consociationalism* (Lehmbruch, 1967) for Austria and Switzerland.

Notions of the State and Conceptions of Citizenship

Another factor within the political system affecting the relevance of representative bureaucracy is the conception of citizenship (cf. Brubaker, 1992). In addition to the basic distinction between *jus solis* and *jus sanguinus* is the question about how easily non-citizens can be naturalized, and their position in the political system until they do become citizens. If citizenship is conceptualized in terms of *jus sanguinus*, and if becoming a naturalized citizen is virtually impossible, then the public sector will have fewer groups about which to be concerned in terms of representation. A country such as Switzerland, for example, has a number of dimensions of social cleavage (see Kübler, 2013) but pronounced barriers to naturalization means that immigrant groups would be less politically relevant than in many other countries. The administrative system here has been reasonably successful in integrating members of the various communities within the country but much less so in coping with immigrants.

As well as the influence of conceptions of citizenship, the place of fundamental rights in the political system is important in defining just what role representation will play in public life. A stronger foundation of social and political rights will mean that individuals can make more claims on government – both as potential clients and as potential employees – than in systems which have weaker conceptions of rights. For example, the diffusion of the right for non-citizens to participate in local elections in the countries of the European Union (see Bauböck, 2005) has meant that groups who might have been easily excluded from consideration become an active part of the electorate and hence political leaders must pay greater attention to their demands.

The Politics of Interest Representation

As well as having these conceptions of fundamental rights for minorities and women, the extent to which those ideas can be translated into action through instruments such as affirmative action laws will also influence the capacity to build representative bureaucracies. Some few countries such as India have enshrined this demand for compensatory opportunities for marginalized groups into their constitutions, but most that are interested in providing additional opportunities for the disadvantaged use affirmative action laws or regulations (see van Gool and de Zwart, 2013). Still, there are marked differences in the extent to which governments have acted to attempt to promote the representativeness of their public service.

The capacity of social groups to press for employment and other benefits from the political system is also a function of the structures available for political participation. More fundamental rights may be important for representative bureaucracy, but the right to participate is also important. In particular, if a minority within society is able to place political pressures on the dominant community then they may be able to obtain both employment opportunities and services delivered in ways that best correspond to their preferences, e.g. in their own language. So long as the minority community is politically powerless then pressing demands for representativeness will be difficult.

Conventional forms of representative democracy may perform well for citizens and particularly for the more advantaged groups in society, but tend to be less functional for non-citizens and for minorities. Therefore, alternative forms of participation may facilitate the involvement of the less-advantaged in politics, and that access to political power may help to facilitate their inclusion also into the bureaucracy. Political systems such as those in Scandinavia and the Low Countries that have developed alternate channels of participation that are more open to less conventional participants may empower groups that otherwise would be excluded.[7]

The extreme form of these alternative forms of participation would be clientelistic politics (see Grindle, 2012). Although clientelism is frequently denigrated, and for some good reasons, there can be virtuous consequences.[8] If members of minority groups can gain some political power then they as *patrons* can provide opportunities in government for their clients. Even if the *patrons* are not members of the minority they may still need to build a political following among the minorities. Even in less extreme cases, the "personal vote" (Golden, 2003) that can go to a political leader based on patronage and pork-barrel spending may also be conducive for recruitment of minority group members into public positions.

Policies and Policy Diffusion

In addition to the "polity" (e.g. fundamental rights) and "politics" (e.g. interest mediation) dimensions of political systems, the content of public policies also significantly affect the extent to which representative bureaucracy as an administrative and political concept is being perceived and implemented. The broad church of "Welfare State programs" provides ample room for our discussion of this "policy dimension". For example, the extent of Welfare State services provided by government will be relevant for the ability to develop representative bureaucracies, especially for the inclusion of women into the public services. The availability of parental leave programs and subsidized child care through the public sector will be important for the participation of women in the labor force (Gornick et al., 1997), including the public bureaucracy. Further, the traditional role of women as care givers is becoming more relevant at the other end of the life cycle with parents living longer. If the public sector provides inadequate provisions for care of the elderly, then women may be less likely to remain active participants in the labor force for a full career (Viitanen, 2005). Education, to turn to another example, is also an integral part of the extended Welfare State and is a key factor in explaining upward social mobility (see "social roots of representative bureaucracy"). Particularly in public administration, which tends to rely heavily on merit criteria for recruiting its employees (see also the section on administrative systems), the root cause of the underrepresentation of minorities and women in qualified positions can often be traced back to socially selective educational systems. Therefore the nature of the national education system influences the capacity to build representative bureaucracy, especially at the upper echelons of the public service. Consequently, comparative studies of education policies point their critical fingers to school systems that may have the effect (rather than uplifting people) to petrify existing social relations (see for a critical discussion of Germany's multi-layered educational system Liebig and

Widmaier, 2009). Thus, a prior question for the development of representative public bureaucracies may be how to develop greater equality of opportunity for all affected groups in the first place.[9] In this context, anti-discrimination policies gain in importance for the discussion of comparative developments in representative bureaucracy. In many instances, however, these policies are no longer the sole prerogative of the nation state. Rather, they are increasingly exposed to pressures from international organizations and supra-national institutions that champion equal opportunities and anti-discrimination legislation. It flows from this that norm diffusion across country borders – and sometimes cascading down from inter- and supranational organizations and courts – can also be an effective driver in reform measures that bring administrative systems closer to social and cultural representativeness.

THE RATIONALE AND FABRIC OF THE PUBLIC SECTOR

The final and most proximate influence on the creation and success of representative bureaucracy will be the nature of the administrative system itself. Although obviously influenced by the nature of the political system within which it functions, the administrative system itself affects the development of representative bureaucracy. To some degree these administrative systems will take their lead from the values and legal provisions of government, but they may also have their own internal dynamics that influence outcomes. First, the dichotomy between law and management as the defining characteristic of administrative practice is one important dimension of administrative systems that can influence the capacity of those systems to become more responsive. Highly legalistic systems, e.g. Weberian systems, tend to permit less latitude for development of affirmative action and other instruments for enhancing representativeness. The influence of the managerial conception of administration tends to be subtle, but it does allow more latitude in recruitment and in the management of personnel once hired. On top of that, the established system of selecting, recruiting, training, and hiring public sector personnel is most significant as a precursor to the development of representative bureaucracies. While some civil service systems (e.g. in continental Europe) make a point of separating public sector employment from other walks of life – by way of a special social and/or legal status, narrowly defined entry requirements, state-run training programs, rigid rules governing employment conditions or life-long career orientation without much lateral mobility between sectors – in other countries (such as

Anglo-Saxon democracies) the boundaries between job markets in the public, non-profit and for-profit sectors are much more permeable. The extent to which civil service systems tend to be relatively "open" or "closed" can be expected to have important ramifications for the capacity of public bureaucracies to serve as socially representative institutions. As a rule, "open" public personnel systems with more flexible recruitment channels, a higher frequency of lateral movement into and out of the public sector, and a preference for position-based (as opposed to career-based) job placement stand a greater chance to respond more quickly to calls for the inclusion of underrepresented social groups.

Moving beyond human resource management, we also need to consider the structural layout of the administrative apparatus more carefully. A major clue in our search for explanatory variables emerged from our discussion of political decentralization. In a similar vein, the shift of administrative responsibilities to lower levels of government moves public services and their providers closer to the communities they are supposed to serve.[10] Being directly exposed to local or regional political and social pressures, public authorities are more likely to reflect demand-driven needs for social representation. As cases in point, school teachers or police officers – if in the employ of locally based authorities (as in the United States) – may more clearly mirror the social composition of their local clientele, if compared to educators and police forces who are on the payroll of central (as in France) or state governments (as in Germany).

Finally, our frame of reference for the comparative analysis of representative bureaucracy needs to take account of the increasingly blurred lines of the public sector. The delivery of public services is no longer monopolized by public administration proper – nor has it ever been. More recently, however, the "provider mix" in public service delivery has been a staple of "new public management"-inspired reform trends in many countries worldwide. Consequently, the universe of service providers is increasingly populated by hived-off agencies, not-for-profit organizations, corporatized entities, and commercial enterprises. In the context of "representativeness" and "diversity", the role of non-profit membership organizations, self-help groups, or clientele-based "welfare associations" in the provision of public services is of particular interest. By their very nature, they are meant to represent their clientele groups and mobilize their members to serve their own communities, thus offering broad and direct avenues for social representation. While some administrative systems (as in the United States or Germany) have traditionally worked closely with "third-sector" organization in public service delivery, others are (re-)discovering this mode of co-producing public services in the wake of the "new public management" or more participatory and community-based reform approaches.

The Role of Merit Recruitment versus Patronage

Public administration tends to rely heavily on merit criteria for recruiting its employees, though meritocracy is per se not the only legitimate rationale for making hiring decisions. Before we turn to mechanisms of patronage as the most fervently discussed rival of meritocracy as a recruitment and selection principle in the public sector, let us briefly reflect upon the various and somehow conflicting ways in which the importance of the merit principle in the civil service may play out. Merit systems are designed to provide equality of opportunity, but may not produce equality of outcomes, especially when the criteria for recruitment involve formal educational criteria and minority group members and women may not have equal opportunity for, or equal interest in, attending institutions of higher education. Therefore, merit systems may become an effective barrier to achieving equality of recruitment rather than the means of achieving that equality. We should also not lose sight of the fact that "elite recruitment" based on merit criteria can also be opportunistically used to obscure motives of social selection. Most notably in those country cases that modeled their national training institutions upon the French Ecole National d'Administration (ENA) or tend to recruit high-ranking officials from elite universities such as Oxford and Cambridge in the UK, training in and recruitment from those institutions also tends to promote social cohesion among future members of the administrative elite.

Following from the above discussion of merit recruitment, the use of patronage appointments – though often burdened with negative connotations – may offer particular advantages for achieving more representative bureaucracies. Given the constraints on merit systems, and the linkage to the educational system, patronage appointments provide an opportunity for political or even administrative leaders committed to greater equality to appoint more women and members of minority groups to position in government (see for a more detailed discussion Peters in this volume). Of course, the patronage appointments are not necessarily made on the basis of normative commitments by the political leadership to the norms of fairness and equality. Patronage appointments may be made in order to appeal politically to minority constituencies. For example, any Cabinet in the United States must now contain minority group members and women, even for political parties that do not have strong constituencies among minorities or feminists.

And having the freedom to make those appointments may permit politicians to circumvent conventional restraints on recruitment to make bureaucracy more representative while at the same time building their own political base.

The Role of "Implementation Structures"

The nature of the "implementation structures" (Hjern and Porter, 1981) utilized within an administrative system may also have an influence on the capacity to build representative bureaucracy, and perhaps more importantly may reduce the pressures toward representativeness. If the public sector utilizes private organizations – for profit or not – to implement many of its programs then the pressures to employ more minority group members for street-level bureaucratic positions may be reduced. Further, these types of positions are often filled disproportionately by women so the overall representativeness of bureaucracy may be diminished. The use of non-governmental organizations to provide public services has been a standard prescription from New Public Management, but the (presumed) efficiency of that practice may be gained at some social cost. However, countries vary significantly as to the degree to which labor market administrations employ minority organizations to implement their programs. Labor market politics are usually seen to have a fundamental impact on immigrant groups that face unemployment or underemployment (see Hellström, 2010). The Canadian labor market administration relies, despite a high degree of organizational fragmentation, on community and immigrant groups as service providers, whereas in Sweden, which is often considered to be an egalitarian country that stresses social inclusion, immigrant organizations play a minor role in the labor market. Questions, as to what extent the type of implementation structure influences the outcome in this specific field, may offer a field for further empirical exploration.

CONCLUDING THOUGHTS

We are arguing that the representativeness of bureaucracy, and indeed of all political structures, is important for understanding the manner in which these organizations function. As well as their internal functioning, however, representative bureaucracy provides insights into the relationships of public administration to the remainder of the political system, and to the society as a whole. The analysis of representative bureaucracy addresses not only the manner in which the public sector recruits its members from the society, but also its capacity to provide services effectively to that society.

We must also remember that not only has representativeness an important functional dimension for public bureaucracies, it has also an important political dimension (for a more detailed discussion of functional and political considerations see Schröter and von Maravić in this volume). While representativeness of the bureaucracy may influence the service provision it can also speak to the manner in which various segments of society, especially those typically disadvantaged politically, may become involved in governing. Indeed, for some groups who may be excluded from other aspects of political life involvement in the bureaucracy provides some foundation for future political influence. Thus, this is not just a study of the nature of the public bureaucracy, as important as that may be, it is also a study of political representation and political influence considered more broadly. Seen from this angle, representativeness also provides a comparative insight into the ways in which various countries manage the relationships among the often-contentious segments of their societies.

Having said this, the comparative study of representative bureaucracy can only benefit from the systematic inclusion of societal, political and administrative variables that define the environment in which public sector organizations operate. While the issue of "representativeness" is at stake, so we believe, in practically every contemporary administrative system, the perception and definition of the problem, the nature of public debates as well as the policy measures to deal with questions of "representativeness" differ significantly from country to country (and also within countries, for example by levels of government or types of public sector organizations, see Schröter and von Maravić in this volume). There is no unidirectional or even uniform trajectory towards representative bureaucracy. Rather, "representativeness" comes in very different shapes and sizes. In order to bring some order to this variety, we set out to systematically explore the landscape of contextual variables that are likely to define the contours of national profiles of "representativeness" in public sector organizations. What we ended up with is less of a comprehensively compiled list of research results, but more of a roughly sketched agenda for future research.

NOTES

1. The economic crisis beginning in 2008 may have reactivated that cleavage, although more in terms of a "consumption cleavage" based on having employment or not rather than the more traditional conceptions of social class.
2. We do not use "myths" in a pejorative sense here, but only to note that all political systems have useful half-truths that bind citizens together and create the justifications for some aspects of the political arrangements within the system.
3. This potential for fear is perhaps especially important when serving immigrant populations. Even if in the host country legally they may have concerns about being expelled or perhaps losing their benefits simply because of their immigrant status.
4. In addition, training for various jobs (blue and white collar) was available through the military that might not have been available in the civilian world.
5. Historically, the patronage politics of the Christian Democrats also played a significant role in this pattern of employment (Warner, 2001).
6. That is, if all other explanations fail, then an observed outcome must be a function of political culture (Elkins and Simeon, 1979).
7. One interesting discussion of this as the "European Polity Model" can be found in Heisler (1974), although the examples here are dated the basic pattern of inclusive participation remains in place in many European countries. On the importance of inclusion see Acemoglu and Robinson (2012).
8. See the chapter by B. Guy Peters in this volume for a more extensive treatment of this argument.
9. In an increasing number of educational systems women are becoming the majority, and in the United States at least there have been some calls for making the educational system more friendly to males. Likewise, some minority groups – notably Asian Americans – tend to outperform members of the dominant community.
10. This idea finds a more refined treatment in the chapter by Eckhard Schröter and Patrick von Maravić in this volume.

3. The "performance claim" of representative bureaucracy: does organization matter?

Eckhard Schröter and Patrick von Maravić

INTRODUCTION

Representative bureaucracy both as a field of scholarly work and administrative reform has already a long history of occupying an important place in the theory and practice of public administration and seems to be even further on the rise as public sector organizations operate in increasingly multicultural societies (Kingsley, 1944; Mosher, 1968; Meier, 1975; Selden and Selden, 2001). It seems to be fair to suggest that much of the debate has been propelled forward by what we wish to label as the "performance claim" of representative bureaucracy. Regardless of their specific research focus, the general assumption of most studies in this area of interest appears to be that representative bureaucracy is a good to be provided and will eventually lead to more qualified decision-making in the public sector, more effectively implemented policies, better-served and more-satisfied clientele groups, not to speak of better motivated and more innovative staff. As a matter of fact, a rich body of empirical studies points at a positive association between workforce diversity and overall organizational performance (Riccucci, 2002; Bradbury and Kellough, 2008; Pitts, 2006, 2009). It flows from this already well-established strand of organizational research that many students of public administration have come take this performance claim for granted. This situation, however, may also give rise to the question whether a bias in case selection could be at work, so that most of the empirical and normative literature on this subject unduly focuses on a very specific segment of the universe of public sector organizations.

Thus, we set out to take issue with an under-complex version of the performance claim as it seems to underestimate the high degree of variety of public sector organizations. Admittedly, the suggested link between workforce diversity and enhanced performance has many facets and calls for further clarification as to what is actually meant by improved organizational performance in this context. For example, some authors argue that in more diverse organizations the quality of decision-making increases, whereas others have observed improved employer–employee relations and still another strand of research has found a positive correlation with representative and customer/clientele relations. While dissecting the overall performance claim into these more specific components we also seek to unearth their theoretical and normative underpinnings.

Our concern with the generalizability of this claim, however, takes center stage of our analysis. One is tempted to ask whether one coat fits all types of public sector organizations. When researching diversity in public sector workforces, we argue that the diverse nature of public sector organizations needs to be taken into account. To this end, this chapter seeks to conceptualize and discuss against the backdrop of the performance-enhancing claim four stereotypical public sector organizations in order to capture the variety of organization tasks as well as the varying degrees of discretion, clientele orientation, and professionalism. Consequently, we will go well beyond the current focus of empirical research that lies predominantly with local service providers as the most popular point of reference of the performance claimants. In doing so, we identify a wide array of under-researched organizations, where the promise of the "performance claim" does not hold so easily.

The argument of this chapter is unfolded in three steps. While the first section offers a cursory overview of the theoretical and normative underpinnings of the discourse on "representative bureaucracy", the second part of discussion takes a closer look at four clusters of arguments of organizations that are said to benefit from more diverse workforces. In our third section, we invite readers to embark with us on an analytical project that is best understood as a thought experiment and is designed to bring institutional variety back into diversity research, thus generating a hypothesis about the inherent limits of the four dimensions of the "performance claim".

THEORETICAL AND NORMATIVE UNDERPINNINGS

As difficult a task it is to bring all or at least the mainstream of an established line of theoretical and empirical research under one umbrella without doing injustice to individual works and their authors, it may just as well be necessary and helpful for our future discussion to shed some light on the shared normative foundations and belief systems of the "representative bureaucracy community". To be sure, membership of this community tends to be in flux and is difficult to neatly define as boundaries are fuzzy and tend to overlap with neighboring epistemic communities. Moreover, their common intellectual project is nourished by various theoretical sources and normative convictions. Having said this we still suggest to see the mainstream of the representative government literature as a line of thinking in organization studies and public administration that exposes a common set of core beliefs and values.

The term "representative bureaucracy" is used by students of public administration when referring to the relationship between the demographic makeup of the public sector workforce (particularly with regard to race, ethnicity, cultural traits such as language, religion, and gender) and the society it is supposed to serve (van der Meer and Roborgh, 1996). In very general terms representative bureaucracy can be described as the "body of thought and research examining the potential for government agencies to act as representative political institutions if their personnel are drawn from all sectors of society" (Dolan and Rosenbloom, 2003: xi). One central question in this field of research is whether the bureaucracy looks like a given segment of the population in terms of its ethnic, racial, social, gender, or occupational characteristics, or if the bureaucracy advocates interests of a specific segment of the population (Mosher, 1968). The argument for researching the issue of representative bureaucracy comes often from a normative position assuming that the question of having or not having an ethnically representative public bureaucracy has implications for fair and effective policy-making and implementation, the aim of integrating minorities into society by giving them the chance to be part of government, or even to control a bureaucracy that is dominated by a (ethnic) majority group and which does not care for the problems of minorities (Subramaniam, 1967; Dolan and Rosenbloom, 2003; van Gool, 2008). It is not surprising that this has institutional consequences for administrative regimes such as the accessibility, recruitment, self-understanding, and management of the civil service, which go in hand with the *opening* of the civil service for personnel with a migration background. The issue of representation and staffing carries important implications for the delivery of public services, the sharing of power in a society as well as it symbolizes equal opportunities and equity (Groeneveld and Walle, 2010; cf. Wimmer, 1997).

Conventionally, the theorems of representative bureaucracy are couched in terms of a search of control over administrative power. Sparked by the concern to keep public bureaucrats responsive to the public at large (Subramaniam, 1967) and further fueled by the deeply ingrained belief that existing external constraints of bureaucratic power are inherently inadequate, the design of representative bureaucracy was meant to serve as an effective internal measure of controlling government officials' behavior. In contrast to the logic of external control mechanisms, protagonists of representative bureaucracy tend to see achieving attitudinal congruence between administrative officeholders and the general public as key to their approach. In addition to this well-established account of representative bureaucracy's conceptual foundation, however, a more fundamental value base can be identified on which most of the modern architecture of diversity strategies in the public and, for that matter, private sectors has been built. For this purpose, we take a number of hints and pointers from cultural theory as a navigating tool to chart the terrain and locate the representative bureaucracy community.

Arguably, the prevailing notion of human nature employed by the advocates of representative bureaucracy serves as a good starting point of our cursory overview of their value and belief systems. Clearly, the anthropological picture of (wo)man that guides most of the normative debates and empirical studies on workforce diversity is that of a social animal or *zoon politicon*, defined by a strong sense of group identity and driven by a strong impetus for communication and interaction with other members of their community. It flows from this that a strong collectivist undercurrent can be discerned in the representative bureaucracy approach – not unlike the dominant strand of the participatory democracy literature. In stark contrast to what representatives of the bureaucratic school of thought have to offer on that account, advocates of public organizations representative of the society they serve hold organizational values that are diametrically opposed to the concept of impersonality as manifested in ideal-typical bureaucracies or, in other words, organizations that are structurally and culturally geared to let real people and their feelings, identities and non-work related qualifications vanish behind the veil of abstract rules and neatly delineated office structures (Dolan and Rosenbloom, 2003). In a similar vein, protagonists of market-driven social coordination (cf. Lindblom, 2002; Self, 1993, 2000) – based on assumptions of man as a rational actor – tend to be just as far away from the core values of the representative school of thought. It is not the uniformly defined model of man or woman with externally pre-set utility functions and cost–benefit calculations to guide their behavior that appeals to advocates of diversity strategies in public, or for that matter, private sector organizations. Rather, their belief system rests on the assumption that organization members are defined by their ethnic, linguistic, or religious backgrounds – to name just a few sources of identity – and that they rely on social interaction with other individuals to develop their own preference structures as well as for the purpose of self-actualization.

The high value accorded to groups and particularly to group rights is another defining feature of the diversity cluster in the recent public administration and management literature (Groeneveld and Walle, 2010). This collectivist undercurrent in the representative bureaucracy mainstream, however, is intimately coupled with a deeply rooted commitment to a pluralist representation of group interests and an inherently inclusive approach to group interest mediation (Taylor and Gutman, 1994). This peculiar cross of "high-groupness" and the (quasi-multicultural) endorsement of plurality in group representation sets the pro-diversity approach apart from normative foundations of public management that only accept the methodological individualism as a legitimate yardstick to evaluate human behavior (as preached by adherents to the creeds of the "new institutional economics" and the "new public management"). By the same token, it alienates followers of the "diversity band wagon" from the tenets of more "grid" and "single group"-oriented supporters who, as for the former, primarily believe in the legitimacy of formal structures (if they do public management the hierarchist way to paraphrase Christopher Hood, 2000) or, as for the latter, consider the shared norms and values of a given single group as their first and foremost point of reference (as do outright "egalitarians" to use Hood's terminology again).

It flows from this more inclusive group-oriented stance of members of the representativeness camp that models of interest representation and political decision-making that operate under the "winner-takes-it-all" rule do not resonate well with them. Consequently, a distinctly more consociational, consensus-oriented, and power-sharing style seems to be in order. Necessarily, any elitist assumptions of strong leadership, quick, uniform, and efficient – in a nutshell: non-participatory – decision-making procedures, or "experts-know-best" attitudes are sources of potential clashes with the worldviews of diversity advocates. In this regard, the representativeness community shows a greater proximity to exponents of egalitarianism, but a similarly large distance to the camps of hierarchists and individualists.

On the ground level of organization practice, this fairly abstract pattern of assumptions about the human nature and societal values translates best into principles of organization that empower employees, gives them greater participation in administrative decision-making and subjects them less to superiors and procedural controls. Empowerment is seen as conducive to foster the connection between passive and active representation as employees enjoy greater discretion and flexibility in dealing with clientele groups and the public at large. Clearly, advocates of representative bureaucracy would find it difficult to see organizations as a "nexus of contracts" as suggested by neo-institutional economics or to subscribe to the Weberian notion of an "iron cage". Their preferred mode of social control does not (primarily) rely on "intelligently designed" incentive structures or formal procedures. Rather, organizational cultures and sub-cultures seem to play a decisive role in the way organizations are governed.

Given this set of underlying values and normative expectations, advocates of representative bureaucracy seem to be predisposed to expect diversity strategies to translate into a broad range of consequences positively associated with organizational performance.

DISAGGREGATING THE "PERFORMANCE CLAIM": FOUR DIMENSIONS OF PERFORMANCE

While the linkage between workforce diversity and improved administrative performance has been a common concern of generations of authors in this field, the indiscriminate reference to a uniform and seeming monolithic "performance claim" only obscures a high degree of internal complexity and differentiation that characterizes the debate. In fact, the suggested virtues of representative bureaucracy that have been extolled by a growing body of scholarly literature over the past decades seem to fall into different, though partially overlapping, categories. By disaggregating the cluster of performance claims into more specific components, we are also able to develop a better understanding of the multi-faceted nature of the meaning of performance. From the following brief review of literature on workforce diversity in private as well as public organizations, four different dimensions of performance can be distinguished, which refer to the quality of organizational *output*, e.g. improved products or policies; the *throughput* within an organization, e.g. job satisfaction, less absenteeism; *clientele relations*, e.g. higher customer satisfaction; as well as, what one might term, *diffuse system support*, e.g. the more general legitimacy of government activity. Though all these categories are present in the discourse, they do not attract equal attention and differ to quite some extent by the quantity of published work.

The Output Claim: Improved Quality and Mission Accomplishment

The majority of scholarship on diversity in public as well as private organizations centers on what can be labeled as *Quality-of-Organizational-Output claim.* This position views the "human potentialities" (Krislov, 1974: 4) in their whole variety as a prerequisite for a well performing administration and ultimately rests on the assumption that workforce diversity prevents an organization from the dark side of groupthink and increases the chance for more effective and creative solutions (Pitts, 2006). Good administrative performance in multi-ethnic environments therefore seems to depend – if judged from this perspective – to a great extent on the quality of judgment, information and social skills that bureaucrats bring into the administration – just as Kingsley was convinced that "superior insight and wisdom" is the result of the "pooling of diverse streams of experience" (Kingsley, 2003: 18). No contemporary advocate of diversity management, as we will illustrate in the remainder, would today reject this claim.

Private as well as public management scholars alike have focused in their work on this output claim. The generic management literature seems to be quite unanimous in their support of the link between workforce diversity (in terms of professional skills, age, gender, cultural, or ethnic backgrounds) and increased performance, learning, creativity, flexibility, or the ability to adjust to environmental changes (Thomas and Ely, 1996). Cox and Blake (1991: 54), for example, showed in their investigation of workforce diversity that it has a positive competitive advantage as it leads to higher creativity, better problem solving, and a more flexible adaptation to organizational change. Hamilton et al. (2004) find that ethnically heterogeneous teams are more productive than homogeneous ones. Ancona and Caldwell (1992) offer positive findings of functional diversity on team performance and innovation. They argue that bringing together different "thought worlds" leads to higher chances of improving a product as the different perspectives help to rule out errors (cf. Simons et al., 1999). Leung et al. (2008) published an article with the title "Multicultural experience enhances creativity [...]" in which they argue that the confrontation with multiple cultures can enhance team creativity. Cox et al. (Cox, 1991; McLeod et al., 1996), in an experiment involving students, found that racially heterogeneous groups produced higher quality ideas in a brainstorming exercise than homogeneous groups.

Reviewing the public sector literature in this field, a similarly positive picture arises as much scholarly work has been aimed at analysing how public organizations can fulfill their task missions more adequately thanks to increased representativeness. For example, research that probed the relationship between racial, ethnic, and gender representation on one hand, and the capacity of local police forces (i.e. in the context of suburban riots in Paris in 2005, 2006, and 2007; (Meier and Hawes, 2009) or school districts to reach their policy goals on the other, is best suited to serve as cases in point (Keiser et al., 2002). In particular, Meier and Stewart (1992) and Meier (1993) found that the presence of minority public school teachers was positively associated with constructive educational performance of minority students. Wilkins and Keiser (2004) present evidence of the passive–active link in child support enforcement for women. Similarly, Meier and Nicholson-Crotty (2006) found that the percentage of women in local law enforcement is positively linked to the number of reports and arrests for sexual assault. Brudney and colleagues (2000) confirm the view that race and gender can affect public attitudes and Hindera (1993) investigates the policy impact of three ethnic and racial groups of federal civil servants (black, white, and Hispanic) as they implement federal equal employment opportunity policy. Pitts (2005), using data from Texas public school districts, also points towards the complex relationship between ethnic diversity and organizational outcomes in public education. He shows that diversity among teachers is positively associated with performance outcomes. In addition, Pitts (2009) shows in a more recent study on US federal employees that diversity management is strongly linked to work group performance and job satisfaction. This benefit of increased job satisfaction is more seen by people of color than by white employees, Pitts argues.

The Throughput Claim: Improved Employee Satisfaction and Employer Branding

Part of the studies identified for this review focus on what can be called the *throughput claim,* referring to the assumed positive impact of diversity on human resource management and internal management generally. From this point of view, organizations in both the public and private sectors are expected to gain from diverse workforces irrespective of their specific mission statements and the goods and services they are supposed to render. The main focus seems to be on the relationship between the employer and the employee especially with regard to questions of increased employer attractiveness, workers' loyalty and job satisfaction, less personnel fluctuation and absenteeism (Thomas and Ely, 1996; Acquavita et al., 2009; Choi, 2009). In much of the private sector management literature, the concern lies less with questions of representativeness, but with diversity as a goal in its own right. Ely (2004: 232) shows in her study that an organization's demographic composition affects the individual's workplace experience favorably. In a similar vein, Pitts (2009) finds also positive evidence of the link between diversity management and job satisfaction. Taking a more neutral position, Green et al. (2005) in their analysis of data on human resource (HR) professionals employed by large US manufacturers that neither age differential nor gender differential has a negative impact on job satisfaction or the organizational commitment of HR professionals.

This does not mean, however, that students of diversity management are blinded by the promising light of performance enhancement. Rather, authors also point at potential conflicts that arise when diversity increases (Pelled et al., 1999; Hamilton et al., 2004). Pelled et al. (1999), for example, show that diversity shapes conflicts to such an extent that functional background diversity would shape task conflicts but ethnic background is positively associated with emotional conflict. Romzek and Hendricks (1982) have pointed out in an early study that organizations need to be aware that employees who represent outside group interests may not develop desirable levels of organizational involvement, which can eventually even threaten the goal attainment of an organization (cf. von Bergen et al., 2002). Correspondingly, Choi (2009) shows that employees in US federal agencies that effectively manage diversity are more satisfied with their jobs than those working in agencies without effectively managing diversity. This suggests that possible downsides of raising workforce can and need to be addressed by accompanying measures of diversity management.

Employers may also use diversity as a resource to create an image of their organizations that sends powerful messages to both insiders and outsiders of the corporation as it radiates a sense of open-mindedness, equity and fairness, modernity, and multi-culturalism. As for "employer branding", publicized diversity strategies and related success stories may help to appeal to newly targeted recruitment pools and to attract sought-after talents who tend to be attracted by organizational values typically associated with diversity programs such as tolerance of minorities, multi-ethnic and -linguistic working environments.

The Clientele Claim: Improved External Relations

The third dimension of the performance claim focuses on the relationship between an organization and its clientele or customers. Although the nature of external relations overlaps in part with the output- and system-related categories, it also taps a different dimension as it acknowledges the value of having close and deeply-rooted relations with more specifically defined target groups as a quality of public organizations in its own right. Moreover, it adds a distinct demand-side to the approach of representative bureaucracy: how do people at the receiving end of public service delivery value the fact that they interact with representative bureaucracies and, more specifically, with representatives of their own community? On top of that this dimension recognizes also the profound political nature of external relations. Not only can representative bureaucracies contribute to governmental legitimacy, they can also opportunistically use their well-established ties with supportive citizens as a resource for political bargaining and bureaucratic politics.

As a closer look reveals, this dimension is, in turn, divided into two major categories: One stream of arguments is primarily driven by concerns about customer relations, whereas the other strand of thought is nourished by considerations about democratic accountability. As perceived in much of the private management literature, diversity allows for tailor-made products, new markets, better access to specific clientele, and a focus on customer demand (Thomas and Ely, 1996), whereas in the public (pre-New Public Management) literature the focus lies more on questions of responsiveness and accountability of government (cf. Subramaniam, 1967) and has to be read against the historical circumstances of 1940s and 1960s (Groeneveld and Walle, 2010: 241, 245). The claim that citizens are better served in a representative bureaucracy is present in Kingsley's and Mosher's work as already came across in the output-oriented section (cf. the "pooling diverse streams of experience" as Kingsley (2003: 18) put it, or Mosher's idea of bringing together "different perspectives, knowledge, values, and abilities" (Mosher, 1968: 16) improves the quality of governance. In principle, advocates of representative bureaucracy share the idea that a bureaucracy that mirrors the composition of the society it serves is more responsive to public interests and will therefore, as Selden and Selden point out, "better serve democratic principles" (Selden and Selden, 2001: 308).

It does not come as a surprise that this focus seems to shift in the backwater of New Public Management reforms more to questions of customer satisfaction of public services. In keeping with the customer-oriented "performance claim", Bradbury and Kellough (2008) found that African American citizens respond particularly favorably to governmental behaviors that specifically target the interests of the African American community and that African American citizens and administrators hold markedly different attitudes from white administrators. In any event, catering to diverse communities seems to present an extra challenge to public service providers. So, Andrews et al. (2005: 501) observe lower levels of consumer satisfaction with public services in more ethnically diverse neighborhoods.

The "Diffuse System Support" Claim

Last but not least, we suggest conceptualizing a "diffuse system support" category, a term borrowed from Easton's classic work (1965, c.f. 1975: 440–450), to denote a cluster of benefits that society at large can derive from fostering public bureaucracies that mirror the demographic makeup of the communities they serve. When Easton talks about the "diffuse support" of a system, he means the more general evaluation of what an object *is* and not what it *does* and refers to a "reservoir of favorable attitudes of good will" (Easton, 1975: 444) that helps members of a society to accept decisions although they might be opposed to them or might even have negative consequences for them. This means that in the short run the level of support is independent of specific outputs or performance.

Though the smallest portion of work has been done on this dimension of the performance claim, it seems to be implicitly present in many studies mentioned before. So, Krislov's statement comes to mind that representative bureaucracy is also about gaining societal "support for policies" by drawing a "wide segment society into government to convey and merchandise a policy" (Krislov, 1974: 4–5). The diffuse system support claim becomes especially visible when authors argue that a representative bureaucracy could be of advantage when it comes to implementing controversial policy programs, unpopular policy decisions, e.g. redistributive measures or budget cuts, and therefore help the organization in critical times, for example in times of economic recession or, more generally, in times of environmental uncertainty (Pitts et al., 2010: 882).

The central claim is that a representative bureaucracy would not only improve performance, as spelled out before, but enhance its legitimacy overall (Groeneveld and Walle, 2010: 240), which in Easton's terms understanding of the concept of legitimacy would mean that passive representativeness could support a person's conviction "that is right and proper […]" and that it "reflects the fact that in some vague or explicit way [a person] sees these objects as conforming to his own moral principles, his own sense of what is right and proper in the political sphere" (Easton, 1975: 451). On the other hand, it does not come as a surprise that "separatist ethnic and linguistic groups" (Easton, 1975: 451) do not consider a political authority legitimate that turns them into second-class citizens and deprives them of their rights. In accord with this view, Mosher was convinced that a passively representative bureaucracy would carry some "independent and symbolic values" (Mosher, 1968: 17) that are the prerequisite for a democratic society as it underlines such things as equal opportunities and an open civil service. And also Selden and Selden express the opinion that advocates of representative bureaucracy stress the importance of "a symbolic commitment to equal access to power" (2001: 309) that goes in hand with passive representativeness. An open civil service to which everyone has access was in Mosher's eyes the fulfillment of Lincoln's dream of a government "by the people" and this not only for symbolic reasons but Frederick Mosher was convinced that public employment is an important vehicle of social mobility, which is an important element of a free society (Mosher, 1968: 17–21). Groeneveld and van de Walle even use words such as "harmonious society" (2010: 241) to which a representative bureaucracy could contribute, and the authors continue to maintain that representing "those who count" (Groeneveld and Walle, 2010: 241) is a means to balance and share the power among different groups and resembles the picture of a "consensual and equalitarian ethos of the community" (Subramaniam, 1967: 1014). What also shines through these statements, however, is the possibility to use instruments of "passive group representation" opportunistically as symbolic politics as already Frederick Mosher observed (1968: 17).

BRINGING ORGANIZATIONAL DIVERSITY BACK IN

Public sector organizations come in all shapes and sizes and are trusted with a mind-boggling variety of missions. As a consequence of increased societal complexity and further propelled by reform doctrines such as the "new public management" the degree of institutional differentiation of providers of public goods and services with increasingly blurred boundaries between the public, not-for-profit, and for-profit sectors has reached unprecedented levels (cf. Pollitt and Bouckaert, 2004). While this universe of organizations has become more and more diverse, we wonder whether this increased differentiation is aptly reflected in the mainstream of research of "representative bureaucracies". Also, we are interested in exploring how different performance claims – as defined above – are likely to play in different organizational settings as one can safely assume that the nature of services rendered and the technologies and steering modes employed to deliver them, structural lay-outs and prevailing cultural patterns, as well as environmental factors will have important ramifications for the role "diversity strategies" and "representativeness" can play in shaping organizational performance.

For the sake of clarity – and at the expense of a more refined argument – we selected four stereotypical cases of public sector organizations that represent distinct categories and differ on a number of important variables. As indicated above, we contend that *task-related differences* between organizations matter: Are administrative units charged with service delivery, planning or "law-and-order" functions? Is their task-profile primarily distributive, redistributive or regulatory in nature? On top of that, our case selection is guided by considerations about differences in organizational structures and cultures. This category of *institutional factors* contains questions such as: Where is the organization located on the central–local continuum? Does the agency in question enjoy a smaller or greater degree of autonomy from centralized supervision? How close is the administrative unit to their clientele group – geographically and functionally? Is there a designated constituency, or does the organization serve a more diffuse group and/or the public at large? Do organizations foster more strongly or weakly developed organizational identities? Do organizational cultures tend to be of an individualist or collectivist nature? Finally, a host of important *staff-related properties* come to mind: Is the relevant staff group part of the "rank and file" members or do they belong to administrative elite circles? How much discretion do administrators have in decision-making and how direct is the link between individual decision-making and the results produced? How do officials perceive of their organizational role? Do they accept for themselves a traditional bureaucratic role description or are they more attached to professional loyalties?

What follows are narratives that circle around stereotypically constructed cases, which are meant to capture the essence of distinct and highly relevant public sector organizations. As the bewildering multitude of all possible combinations of task-specific, institutional and staff-related characteristics defies a clear-cut taxonomy, these case reports were chosen as an alternative approach to illuminate the plurality of administrative units. Rather than presenting or scrutinizing empirical findings, this exercise aims at generating hypotheses and fleshing out new agenda items for further research.

CASE A: THE PROFESSIONAL SERVICE ORGANIZATION

Case Characteristics

This stereotypical case has been a centerpiece of scholarly debates on representative bureaucracies. As a matter of fact, the universe of public and non-profit organizations is widely populated by agencies with service-oriented task profiles that go hand-in-hand with a pronounced clientele orientation. In most cases, they are engaged in the implementation of public policy programs that qualify – primarily, though not exclusively – as "distributive" policies. As for examples, agencies rendering educational and personal social services, but also health providers and – blurring the boundaries between order and safety vs. service functions – services such as community policing spring to mind.

This type of organization could also be aptly termed a "street-level bureaucracy", only that most employees are unlikely to conceive of their jobs in a more traditional bureaucratic sense. Rather than embracing bureaucratic role perceptions, many individuals in these organizations enjoy a certain degree of professional autonomy as teachers, social and community workers or health experts. Less constrained by formal rules and procedures, they are better able – more often than not supported by organizational cultures that encourage individual initiative – to use their leverage in the provision of services as they see fit. While typically located at the receiving end of the policy-making cycle, "professional service organizations" and their staff, be it as field offices of government departments, locally based non-profits or as part of city governments, are – in terms of geographical distance, but also as a consequence of functional requirements – particularly close to the community and client groups they cater to.

Discussion of Performance Claims

In this case, most, if not all, parameters seem to have set so as to accommodate the requirement for successful diversity strategies to take root. Not surprisingly, references to relevant research findings are available in abundance and, more importantly, the wealth of empirical evidence produced is predominantly unidirectional in its support of the overall performance claim (e.g. Meier and Bohte, 2001; Pitts, 2005; Meier and Hawes, 2009).

Understandably, much of the scholarly attention has been centered on the output dimension. Of crucial importance to creating an organizational habitat in which the logic of representative bureaucracy can fully unfold its performance-enhancing potential is the degree of professional autonomy and individual discretion granted to service providers. Empowered employees at street-level can also use their leverage to form long-term links between their clients – relations that work both ways as public service providers benefit just as much from better access to their client groups as the other way around.

Much of the supportive arguments seem also to hold true if applied in the context of a more system-wide perspective. Arguably, the "face-to-face" delivery of personal social, health or educational services has a decisive impact on individual socialization processes. In particular, the way services are rendered can be a critical factor in shaping attitudes of minority groups towards government and society at large. It flows from this that the impact of "professional service providers" as classified by this case category not only transcends the narrow boundaries of local neighborhoods or school districts, but may also have legitimizing or de-legitimizing – as the case may be – consequences for the public sector as a whole.

If taken to their logical extremes, of course, the output- and group-related advantages of minority representatives may develop negative side-effects, if not outright self-destructive consequences (such as preferential treatment or access for certain client groups at the expense of others, debilitating levels of inter-minority group competition, further fragmentation of service delivery or the division of the organization into minority-based sub-cultures). Nonetheless, the chance of improving overall performance seems to outweigh risks that can also be kept at bay by corresponding measures of "diversity management".

In a nutshell, representative bureaucracy – if seen from this organizational angle – appears as a low-risk and high-gain strategy for organizational leaders to adopt with potential benefits to be expected from all dimensions of the performance claim.

CASE B: THE TOP-LEVEL POLICY-MAKING ORGANIZATION

Case Characteristics

Somewhat aloof from the hands-on management of individual casework, the archetypical policy-making organization marks the other polar end of the spectrum. Positioned at or close to the pinnacle of administrative and political hierarchies, the contours of their task and competence profiles resemble closely that of ministerial bureaucracies. Given the well-established reform trend of "agencification" in many central or federal governments and shifts towards a "regulatory state" in many OECD-countries, we can also identify a sub-category of policy-making organizations: powerful executive agencies and independent regulatory agencies.

The higher echelons of administrative officials give advice to political executives, are involved in long-term policy planning, prepare new pieces of legislation and tend to be busy gathering political (though not necessarily partisan) support for policy initiatives emanating from their departments. In doing so, they also cultivate professional relations with other actors in their policy arenas (including legislators, representatives of special interests and leaders of political parties), and help coordinating policy proposals in the face of departmental egoisms and professional silos. In a nutshell, senior civil servants in policy-making positions perform inherently political functions (Aberbach et al., 1981; Peters and Pierre, 2004).

In view of their politicized job profiles, the term "senior bureaucrat" captures, if at all, only partially the essence of most leading staff members' role perceptions in policy-making organizations. As evidence from comparative studies suggests (Derlien and Mayntz, 1989; Peters and Pierre, 2004), the prevailing pattern of work-related attitudes and role understandings among top administrators in most central (or federal) government departments seems to conform rather with the role model of a "political bureaucrat" than with the Weberian-type of a "classical bureaucrat". By definition, top administrators are also separated from "rank-and-file" bureaucrats by their elite status. As a rule, they have reached unrepresentatively high levels of formal post-secondary education and to a large extent their careers are the product of prestigious educational institutions. In addition to extended educational biographies, most top-level bureaucrats can also look back on a long tenure in their organizations. Even as members of the administrative elite, higher civil servants still face a more or less rigidly defined organizational grid (as expressed in inter- and intra-departmental lines of jurisdictions or positional differences), but just as many if not more constraints are likely to emanate from informal, unwritten rules and conventions that effectively govern the behavioral patterns of elite administrators.

Discussion of Performance Claims

Given the high degree of individual discretion and the close proximity to positions of political authority that higher civil servants enjoy as administrative leaders, it is understandable that expectations about the potential role of "minority representatives" in the higher echelons of government departments run high. Disappointingly, however, the level of our empirical knowledge of the relationship between workforce diversity and organizational performance in top-level "policy units" is still relatively low.

The very factors that may lead us to have hopes about "trustees of minority interests" in ministerial bureaucracies – such as high-ranking positions and hybrid functions in the grey area between the realms of politics and administration – can, however, also be used to build a case against effective minority representation. For one, long organizational tenure and high-levels of educational attainment can also be interpreted as powerful forces to weaken the initially strong ties that tend to bind members of any community to their social origins (Daley 1984; Selden et al., 1998; but also Meier and Nigro, 1976, for different results). Consequently, elite administrators – remote as they are from their parental background and primary processes of socialization – have been found to be less influenced in their job-related attitudes and role understandings by social class or ethnic origin than by their much later adopted organizational and professional role models (Mosher, 1968). Second, the high degree of (party) politicization of top officials' work environment has to be taken into account. So, party political complexions of high officials could – unless national party systems are organized along ethnic cleavages – more effectively shape role and policy perceptions than social and ethnic origins.

Even if members of racial and ethnic minorities in policy-making positions should adhere to a strong sense of loyalty to their minority communities as part of their role understandings as public administrators (see Romzek and Hendricks, 1982), the effect on organizational performance is still less than clear. As far as political accountability and the policy-making capacity of government are concerned, the notions of "neutral competence" and loyalty to the "government of the day" are effective and legitimate rivals to the normative assumptions of "representative bureaucracy". Also, the risk of a more fragmented and incapacitated government with agencies being increasingly captured by particular group interests (as captured by LaPalombara's, 1964, "*parantela* relations") and turf battles between minority groups cannot be ignored in the context of calls for "representativeness" in policy-making organizations.

From an internal managerial point of view, explicit diversity strategies can be seen as diametrically opposed to principles of organizing the higher civil service that accord more weight to the importance of social and professional cohesion among top administrators. While national administrative systems differ significantly in the extent to which they promote these organizational values – probably best illustrated by reference to the almost antagonistic models of (former) Whitehall's "village life" on one end of the spectrum and the image of US "government by strangers" (Heclo, 1977) on the other end – a common concern for an effective coordinative capacity in the higher civil service seems to be widely recognized (see also Peters, 1987). Though not without its own shortcomings (such as a tendency to provide a hotbed for group-think and in-breeding), a more homogenous organizational culture shared by top administrators can serve as a functional equivalent to achieve this goal.

Despite these possible downsides, the value of having an elite group of "political bureaucrats" that mirrors the racial, ethnic, or linguistic composition of society at large can be immense from the perspective of organizational and political leaders. In extreme cases (as in ethnofederalist regimes), where the divides between ethnic groups run particularly deep and are likely sources of (militant) tensions, power-sharing in the higher ranks of the bureaucracy may appear as an adequate response to pacify societal conflict and provide an extra dose of legitimacy to state authorities (Wimmer, 1997). In milder cases too, measures of passive representation may help to smooth relations with stakeholders and to raise levels of government legitimacy. And yet, this approach can be likened to a tightrope walk as one easily slips into mechanisms of political patronage and inter-minority group competition at highly politicized levels.

To sum this brief discussion up, an aggressively pursued "diversity strategy" appears against the backdrop of this case to be an ambivalent and potentially risky policy option with at best tenuous links to the improvement of organizational performance as earlier defined as the "output" or "throughput" dimensions. Gains from highly visible and potentially policy-relevant representativeness strategies, however, can be primarily reaped from actions of political symbolism.

CASE C: THE HIGH-RELIABILITY AND HIGH-RISK ORGANIZATION

Case Characteristics

Returning to the ground level of direct and concrete delivery of administrative tasks, our third case report portrays organizations with largely safety-related and "law-and-order" functions. Emergency services are typical representatives of this case category as they respond under high time-pressure to non-routine events, often of catastrophic magnitude, that present major threats to order and safety at local, regional or (inter-) national levels. Stereotypically, though frequently locally based this category of first responders does not cater to specifically designated clientele groups, but attend non-discriminatorily to victims of natural or anthropogenic disasters. In addition to fire fighters, special police forces or medical emergency teams, we also suggest conceptualizing an important sub-category of experts who are supposed to be in control of highly complex technical systems such as nuclear power plants, air traffic control centers or the infrastructure of public utilities (for the discussion on high-reliability organization see also Perrow, 1984; LaPorte et al., 1989; LaPorte and Consolini, 1998; Bigley and Roberts, 2001; Roe and Schulman, 2008).

Mostly, these functions can be classified as "high-risk" as there seems to be a drastically shortened learning curve in case things go wrong. The chances of learning from experience is limited and – given the essential nature of services provided to the community – failure to perform the mandated functions successfully jeopardizes the established order and safety, if not existence, of the affected community – not to speak of the danger for the individual health and safety of the officials in question.

In most instances, this type of organization features a powerful combination of extremely high scores on the "groupness" scale and on the "grid" dimension. Not only is the importance of formal rules, close supervision, and standard operating procedures well-understood and seen as legitimate. On top of that it is a deeply rooted collectivist organizational culture based on tightly knit and socially cohesive networks that oftentimes effectively supports and complements these formal constraints. This carefully nurtured sense of belonging or camaraderie – plus strong pressures to adopt an agency-sanctioned role perception, of course – has team members even prepared to sacrifice, under certain circumstances, their individual health for the sake of collective goal achievement.

Discussion of Performance Claims

Evidence from empirical studies of how strategies to make bureaucracies more representative of society impact on high-risk and high-reliability organizations tends to be a scarce commodity, but we may also be able to draw on more readily available evidence from a variety of law-enforcement agencies (such as regular police officers on their beat or border control agencies and child protection offices).

Taking first a throughput perspective for our evaluation of performance claims, the prospect of making high-reliability and high-risk organizations significantly more diverse in terms of their staff composition is very likely to be perceived by long-tenured members as nothing less than an outright threat to organizational stability and integrity. While quickly moving targets, a flexible work environment and the occurrence of unforeseen events may generally call for more outside-the-box thinking and innovative approaches to problem-solving (just as much of the literature on innovation management and cognitive diversity suggests), the extremely hazardous and risky nature of their day-to-day business may lead many first responders to believe that reliance on time-tested and well-trusted technologies and behavioral patterns serves as the best survival guide. Since chances of learning from own mistakes are severely limited and the stakes of failure for both the organization and the individual are prohibitively high, experimental approaches to problem-solving are rarely encouraged.

Externally imposed changes to a tightly-woven, trust-based group culture (or "esprit de corps") and a well-established set of response patterns are bound to be met with fierce resistance from the inside, thus posing a major challenge for accompanying measures of diversity management (such as additional training sessions, interactive workshops or special job placement schemes to sensitize staff members to diversity issues and/or to socialize new entrants better into existing structural and cultural settings).

Not only tend these changes to be associated with relatively high organizational costs, they may also result – in addition to the desired consequences – in adverse effects on performance as far as immediate output quality and relations with external groups are concerned. While scholarly work that lends support to the (output-related) performance claim has shown that minority representatives in police forces effectively help to ease tensions in conflict-ridden neighborhoods (such as the Parisian suburbs, see Meier and Hawes, 2009), other research into the police force points into a different direction. As a matter of fact, minority police officers have been on the record to resent the idea of being on duty in their own ethnic quarters out of fear of strained relations with their own kin and a perceived lack of authority (Dudek, 2009). In other cases, minority members are reported to be driven by organizational pressure into overcommitment that runs exactly counter the desired consequences.

One may conclude from this that representative bureaucracy can be depicted in this short portrait as a controversial high-risk strategy that comes with a high potential of intra-organizational conflict.

CASE D: THE BUREAUCRATIC MASS SERVICE PROVIDER

Case Characteristics

Finally, our attention shifts to a routinely neglected case of organizations: classical, seemingly outdated and more or less monolithic machine-type administrative units. Though probably underresearched, this type of organization can still be considered as the backbone of the service industries in the public and private (e.g. in banking and insurance) sectors. As workhorses of the welfare state, for example, agencies of this type administer entitlement programs of all kinds and provide financial transfers (Rose, 1984, 1985).

Lacking most of the typical appeal to researchers that earlier cases had to offer (such as policy relevance in the formation or implementation phases, proximity to political power, high levels of technical and professional expertise, eye-to-eye contact with citizens, or exotic and extreme mission statements), this type of organization – regardless of whether it is located in the public, non-profit or for-profit sector – catches our eyes just because it is easily overlooked. It is extreme only in the sense that of all cases it comes closest to the depiction of the Weberian ideal-type of a bureaucratic administrative staff.

This case evokes the picture of a large-scale executive agency that performs mass functions of a non-technical nature. The sheer volume of the caseload necessitates the widespread use of standard procedures and a neatly defined division of labor both horizontally and vertically. While the organizational grid seems to manifest itself very strongly – alongside with formal job descriptions and role expectations of impartiality and objectivity – the sense of "groupism" tends to be, if at all, only marginally developed, as professional communities, party-political obligations or strong policy-driven commitments are likely to be the exception among most of the clerical staff that populates the organization. The most striking feature of this bureaucratic type of massive service provider, however, is its reliance on conditional programming that effectively limits the amount of discretion on the part of administrators. Combined with the stereotypical anonymity of most clerical staff to their clients and given the fact that most of these organizations are just as remote – in terms of location as well as in the way of steering and accountability – from policy-makers as they are from citizens, this case appears as the epitome of faceless and bloodless administrative machinery geared to operate efficiently and seamlessly in the background.

Discussion of Performance Claims

The relationship between organizations of this category and most of the claims on performance links made earlier can be best described as a case of mutual indifference. Rarely has research on representative bureaucracy looked into the workings of orthodox bureaucratic machineries with an eye on ramifications for organizational performance. Also, there is little indication, if any, that mass service organizations of this kind provide fertile grounds for the performance-related promises of diversity strategies to flourish. What prevents the anticipated positive consequences of minority representation from making significant inroads along the output dimension into mass service providers are the strictly limited room of maneuver available to administrators, the lack of any established relations with designated constituencies they serve and the difficulty of associating individual employees personally with the consequences of their work in a principally anonymous, more or less automated process governed by legal rules or – increasingly more likely in the wake of public managerialism – algorithms of performance management systems.

As for the throughput dimension of organizational performance, employees are primarily subjected to bureaucratic role descriptions and do not typically form strong group- or professionally-based organizational cultures – a scenario of high gridness and low groupness that Hood (2000) describes as "fatalist". Also, most of the technologies employed to process the high volume of caseload in mass service organizations are likely to be comparatively simple and stable. It remains doubtful whether the positively associated consequences of more motivated and innovative staff can come to fruition in this environment. And yet, the large body of rank and file personnel that is typically associated with mass service providers represents a major resource that can be utilized in the logic of the "performance dimensions" identified before. Public sector organizations could use their considerable impact on the labor market to present themselves as model employers with regard to job opportunities and employment conditions for minority groups, thus gaining from access to new recruitment pools, but also capitalizing on symbolic actions that may transcend into diffuse system support.

To summarize our last case report we seem to be on relatively safe ground in suggesting that minority representation in most of these service machineries goes generally unnoticed as far as the anticipated quality of organizational output is concerned. As a result, in this context the "representative bureaucracy" approach appears as a low-risk and low-cost, but also a low-benefit strategy for organization leaders unless the more diffuse gains from system-wide implications are factored in as well.

CONCLUDING THOUGHTS

This chapter adopted a perspective that looked at representative bureaucracy through the eyes of distinct types of organizations. To be sure, there are many compelling reasons to embark on diversity strategies in the public sector with a view of making the socio-demographic composition of its workforce as representative as possible of the society it is supposed to serve. In most of the contemporary debates, however, the normative – and oftentimes empirically substantiated – assumption that "representativeness" in public bureaucracies will eventually, *ceteris paribus*, result in improved performance of administrative organizations has taken center stage. This background gave rise to the question whether the widely shared contention of the performance-enhancing qualities of workforce diversity can adequately serve as a coat that fits public sector organizations of all shapes and sizes equally well.

By introducing two elements of variation – with regard to our understanding of "performance" and the categories of public organizations under scrutiny – earlier sections of this chapter reminded us of both the multi-faceted nature of benefits that can (or cannot) be reaped from "representative bureaucracy" – and, for that matter, from any other organizational reform measure – and of the pluralist and diverse universe of organizations delivering public goods and services. As the discussion has shown, the positive effects of "representativeness" and "workforce diversity" on organizational performance are highly contingent on task-specific features, institutional characteristics and employee-related properties of public organizations.

The energy of testing the "performance link" in empirical studies has been highly unevenly distributed – a finding that might be seen as indicative of a "selection bias" in much of the representative bureaucracy research. Consistent with value patterns that underscore this research tradition, the segment of locally based service organizations that provide personal professional services to a specific clientele, primarily at "street-level" and in "face-to-face" contact, has taken most of the limelight, whereas stereotypical bureaucratic providers of impersonal mass services, policy-making agencies, or work units that respond to emergencies do not feature prominently. It is in these three latter categories of organizations, however, that our thought experiments cast serious doubt on the validity of the proposed link between actively pursued diversity strategies and organizational performance. Consequently, the goal of administrative performance improvements has to be balanced against competing organizational values and benefits need to be discounted against extra costs incurred through the pursuit of representativeness in public bureaucracies.

The literature review has also shown that empirical evidence on the – intended and unintended – consequences of diversity strategies in the public sector is still relatively sparse. As this chapter was first and foremost an exercise in generating hypotheses and reminding readers of currently existing blind spots of the discourse on performance and representativeness, its conclusion is best understood as a suggested research agenda and a call for – in view of the existing variety of public sector organizations and multiple meanings of "performance" – more systematic and – across national and disciplinary boundaries – better orchestrated research activities in this field.

4. Reconsidering political and bureaucratic representation in modern government

Patrick von Maravić and B. Guy Peters

INTRODUCTION

Political systems are distinct in the way they institutionalize the relationship between political and bureaucratic representativeness. Political representation is generally considered to be the hallmark of modern democratic government and its absence a feature of authoritarianism. Yet, the *locus* in which representation is anchored – parliament or administration – varies among countries and across political systems. This chapter therefore sets out to explore the way political systems organize and balance this relationship and what consequences arise from it. It seeks to understand the logic and institutionalization of representation both across different types of political regimes.

Two major institutions characterize the rise of modern democratic government since the nineteenth century: professional bureaucracy and representative government. Concomitantly with the rise of these twin institutions in the nineteenth or early twentieth century, dominant theorizing of modern representative government has implied the doctrine that representation lies in parliament and government and not in bureaucracy. Authors as varied as Max Weber, Carl Schmitt, Hans Kelsen, Reinhard Bendix or Robert Dahl emphasized this point in their writings. Reinhard Bendix (1980: 235), for example, argued "representation is to be distinguished from government", formulating an idea that shaped our thinking about the relationship between political and bureaucratic representation in the twentieth century.

The reification of public administration or *the* bureaucracy as an apolitical and neutral tool of politics (in parliament is representation, in bureaucracy not) has become a master narrative in modern democratic theory, classic administrative theory and modern public management reform parlance. Ever since the slogan "no taxation without representation", which galvanized public opinion in the *British Colonies and Plantations in America* against Britain following the passing of the *British Stamp Act* of 1765 by the British parliament and called for representative democracy, political representation has been first and foremost equated with elected delegates, whereas appointed officials and bureaucratic institutions have been unduly neglected. This ahistorical and simplified view neglects the propensity of rulers – both democratic as well as authoritarian – to use bureaucracy as distinct political tool of representation and as a strategy of rule. This is, however, for different reasons, different ends, and by different means.

For a long time political scholarship has disregarded the potential and empirical propensity of bureaucracy to function as a representative body or even considered political and administrative representativeness to be reconcilable. Bureaucracy has generally been depicted as a non-majoritarian, politically neutral, and merit-based institution that functions as an instrument of the parliamentary will and shall stay outside of the political struggle over power. One may say, that the rich theoretical and empirical scholarship on the representative function of parliament and different types of representation (cf. Pitkin, 1967; Eulau and Wahlke, 1978; Mansbridge, 2011) has left bureaucracy, as one scholar recently put it, on the "tail end chain of representation" (Ansell 2011: 4).

To the same extent, students of representative bureaucracy ever since Kingsley's classical study on the nature of representation in the British civil service have neglected the political dimension of representation in democracy. As much as students of political representation have underestimated the extent to which bureaucracies can and have been functioning as mechanisms of representation, advocates and students of representative bureaucracy have focused mainly on the interrelation between the passive and active dimension of representation in public organizations. In doing so, they have paid insufficient attention to its relationship with political representativeness and ignored normative as well as functional questions in theorizing modern democracies (Mosher 1968: 11–14). Instead, the question whether passive representation leads to functional representation has been at the center of administrative scholarship (Krislov, 1974; Meier 1975: 197)

The conceptual, normative, and empirical flaws of this position have yet not been sufficiently explored in the literature of representative bureaucracy, diversity management, or comparative politics in general. Yet, they also have not been adequately scrutinized by students of politics and practitioners in the developing world. However, students of ethnic conflicts – among them Crawford Young (1976), Donald L. Horowitz

(1993), Andreas Wimmer (1997) – and consociationalism – among them Arend Lijphart (1976), Gerhard Lehmbruch (1967) – have long recognized the role bureaucracies take in the struggle of plural societies over the resources of power. Nuanced questions concerning the balance between the twin goals of political stability and effective governance through power sharing between elites from different social groups, seem to have been replaced today with rather simplistic and vague ideas of performance in diversity management and representative bureaucracy.

Against the background, we would like to understand in more general terms the role of bureaucracy in plural societies (Lijphart, 1977), the conditions under which bureaucracies fulfill representative functions, and why some regimes (including democracies) turn towards bureaucracy as a tool of representation while others do not. Also, this chapter looks into the likely consequences of more or less representativeness in terms of the functionality and legitimacy of institutions or, for example, in view of societal conflicts.

We argue, *first*, bureaucracies, either alone or in context with other political institutions, such as parliament, can take on the role as a representative institution. Bureaucracy can take an important role in giving voice to underrepresented people but can at the same time also serve as a strategy of rulership – in democratic as well as authoritarian systems – securing political stability through distributing administrative posts among rival ethnic, regional, religious or political groups. *Second*, bureaucratic representativeness can contribute to stabilizing regimes but at the same time may inflict high costs in terms of adaptability, the freezing of ethnic cleavages, patronage, and legitimacy. *Third*, the reasons why some regimes embrace representative bureaucracy still lie in the dark. We therefore review potential push and pull factors, which need further elaboration.

All those aspects trigger questions about the match or mismatch of bureaucratic and political representativeness and its consequences for legitimacy, public policy-making, and parliament as the primary place of representativeness. Notwithstanding these concerns, the relationship between political and bureaucratic representativeness merits further conceptual and empirical investigation as it does not only shed light on a neglected relationship but points first towards different ways of how political systems organize and balance this relationship and, second, towards potential tensions and conflicts between these two branches of government.

REPRESENTATION AND NON-REPRESENTATION IN POLITICS AND ADMINISTRATION

The concept of representation is conceived to have both fundamental normative as well as positive value for the study and quality of modern democracies. Representation is the act, Hannah Pitkin suggested, "to make present again" (Pitkin, 1967). The underlying idea is that parliament and government can speak legitimately for all people in society and make their voices present in the policymaking process. Different mechanisms have been discussed throughout history to ensure a fair and effective representation of the people, ranging from lot in the Athenian democracy to elections in our modern democracies (Manin, 1997). This notion of making present again is tightly coupled with ideas of trusteeship and delegation and cannot be understood unless one bears societal differentiation, complexity, and geographical size in mind. It is therefore something indirect and stands in conflict with ideas of direct democracy. The locus of representation, it seems especially in normative democratic theory, lies in parliament, the place in which deliberation and articulation takes place.

This notion of political representation needs to be viewed in the light of the almost concomitant evolution of another powerful institution in the nineteenth century, the bureaucratic form of administration. At the beginning of the twentieth century, Max Weber posited that the process of rationalization would infiltrate and dominate all areas of society. The institution that proved in his eyes this force at work was that of *legal–rational bureaucracy* (Gerth and Mills, 1948). Characteristics such as public office, hierarchy, scientific knowledge, division of labor, written documents, and the recruitment on the basis of merit, were supposed to mark the end of private government, patronage, and hereditary appointments to public office as we know it from feudal times, which lasted in some western countries, such as the United States or Great Britain, into the late 1880s. A neutral and depoliticized bureaucracy was viewed, by scholars such as the later President of the United States, Woodrow Wilson, to be a prerequisite for democratic government (Wilson, 1887). Silberman (1993: 59) describes this in *Cages of Reason* as "administration not only substitutes for politics, it also becomes the representative of the public interest". This doctrine receives an even more ideological basis by the doctrine of "elevating", another term by Bernhard Silberman (1993: 58), public administration into a systematic science.

This view that bureaucracy shall function outside of political turmoil and conflict, has turned into a cornerstone of normative democratic theory. We select a number of authors whose quotations underline this point. However, we need to bear in mind that the selected authors represent different academic traditions. Hans Kelsen and Carl Schmitt may rather stand for a Continental European tradition that views public administration more from a legal perspective standing above societal conflict, whereas Reinhard Bendix and Robert Dahl conceive public administration in the American tradition as a non-partisan actor under the auspices of political control and leadership. Let us quote some examples to underline this point:

> If the democratic principle [...] must essentially be limited to the legislative process and to the selection of the highest executive organs, that is, if it must not penetrate that part of government commonly referred to as the executive sphere (judicial jurisdiction and administration) then this simultaneously demarcates the sphere beyond which the influence of political parties must not reach.
>
> Hans Kelsen (1920: 83)

> And administration carried out in accordance with the principle of democratic identity is practically impossible and, according to democratic principles, not even a theoretical problem, because in administration (in contrast to the government) there is no representation.
>
> Carl Schmitt (1928: 297)

> Representation is to be distinguished from government.
>
> Reinhard Bendix (1980: 235)

> "Meritocracy" then could refer to a bureaucracy based on merit that operates within a democratic regime, under the full control of elected leaders.
>
> Robert Dahl (1991: 57)

Yet, despite this powerful normative notion of a professional and neutral bureaucracy, that operates on the side of partisan political conflict and implements the law, students of public administration have continuously drawn our attention to the problem that it actually matters who works in public administration, who is represented, and who is not. This view unfolded particular leverage when a group of scholars in the England of the 1920s, especially Harold Laski (1921) and his doctoral student Donald Kingsley (1944), began to question this modern master narrative of democratic governance not only on empirical but also normative grounds. Studying the composition of Whitehall staff and its recruitment basis from the upper middle class and from institutions such as Oxford and Cambridge, they coined the term "representative bureaucracy" as a powerful critique against an unrepresentative civil service and its detrimental consequences for those not being represented. This term is today used to refer to the relationship between the demographic makeup of the public sector workforce (particularly with regard to race, ethnicity, cultural traits such as language and religion, and gender) and the society it is supposed to serve (van der Meer and Roborgh, 1996).

The underlying normative connotation of representative bureaucracy is the following: Proponents assume that the question of having or not having an ethnically representative public bureaucracy has implications for fair and effective policy-making and implementation, the aim of integrating minorities into society by giving them the chance to be part of government, or even to control a bureaucracy that is dominated by a (ethnic) majority group and which does not care for the problems of minorities (Subramaniam, 1967; Dolan and Rosenbloom, 2003; van Gool, 2008). The issue of representation and staffing carries important implications for the delivery of public services, the sharing of power in a society as well as it symbolizes equal opportunities and equity (Groeneveld and Walle, 2010).

Conventionally, this theorem of representative bureaucracy is couched in terms of a search of control over administrative power. Sparked by the concern to keep public bureaucrats responsive to the public at large (Subramaniam, 1967) and further fuelled by the deeply ingrained belief that existing external constraints of bureaucratic power are inherently inadequate, the normative plea for a more representative bureaucracy was meant to serve as an effective internal measure of controlling government officials' behavior.

Obviously, though the two concepts differ in terms of *where* they anchor representation, they both have the idea to "make present again" at their core. We therefore think that combining both concepts may offer a distinct conceptual lens, which will allow us to develop a better understanding how and why political systems, both authoritarian and democratic, make use of those instruments.

FOUR TYPES OF REPRESENTATION

In reality, regimes institutionalize political and bureaucratic representation differently. They appear as a duo but as solos too. And though the idea of political representation is firmly tied to our general ideas of modern representative government, we find variation when looking at the actual institutionalization of representation. The postwar period of the 1920s in Germany and Austria and the ongoing societal turmoil and transformation of political systems from powerful monarchies to democratic systems of government, made Hans Kelsen (1920) and Carl Schmitt (1928) reflect about the combination of democratic and authoritarian principles. Concepts such as *mixed government* and *mixed constitution* are at the center of those reflections. By doing so they remind us to differentiate between *political form principles*, such as democracy, aristocracy, and monarchy, and *organizational form principles,* such as lot and elections, federalism, party systems etc. Both authors discussed at length whether the idea of an "autocratically" organized bureaucracy would suit democratic principles of governance or whether the democratization of bureaucracy should be pursued as Austro-Marxists, such as Otto Bauer (1923: 237), and others at this time of post-monarchical struggled requested. Both scholars were convinced of the necessity and prominently supported by Max Weber's view that the concentration of expertise in the bureaucracy and, among other features, strict meritocratic form of recruitment would provide a necessary complement to deliberation and politics in democracy. They firmly believed that there is no such thing as a "pure" democracy or a "pure" autocracy. All political forms mix organizational components. As indicated, the same question was discussed for authoritarian regimes as Hans Kelsen noted in *The Essence and Value of Democracy* (1920: 84):

> Just like democracy, autocracy tends in practice to develop a collegial – and, hence, parliamentary – organ, which is based on the division of labor, for its legislative activities. On the other hand – and again like democracy and in part for the same reasons – it inevitably creates a bureaucracy for its executive functions.

It would lead us astray, to go deeper into this discussion. However, these basic ideas set the conceptual ground for further exploring the relationship between representation in parliament and bureaucracy. We suggest embracing these ideas conceptually by imagining different degrees of political and bureaucratic representativeness and combine those two concepts in a simple table in order to generate additional insights:

Table 4.1 Types of ideal-typical distinction between political and bureaucratic representation

Type	Description	Examples	Ends	Means
TYPE A Low bureaucratic, low political	Hegemonic control of all branches of government: long-term one-party rule, monarchy, sultanism	North Korea under Kim Il Sung, Nazi Germany 1933–1945, Romania under Ceauşescu, Saudi Arabia, often military regimes	Absolute control and compliance	Despotism, arbitrariness, and surveillance
TYPE B Low bureaucratic, high political	Election or lot, professional bureaucracies, merit-based recruitment	Germany, France Normative ideal of democratic theory; Rechtsstaat tradition	Legitimacy, legal and effective government	Elections, lot, merit-based recruitment for civil service positions
TYPE C High bureaucratic, low political	Personal and corporatist rule (monarchs); e.g. authoritarian monarchy Inter- and intraparty representation of different societal, geographic, ethnic cleavages	Yugoslavia under Josip Tito (1943–80) Libya under al-Gaddafi (1969–2011) Austrian Empire in the nineteenth century Corporatist regimes in Latin America	Long-term regime stabilization through creating support of relevant groups Fusion of incorporation and expertise	Patronage, spoils, rents, concessions
TYPE D High bureaucratic, high political	Parliament and bureaucracy as channel of representation	Netherlands since 1917, Lebanon, United States of America, Canada	Accountability, avoiding oligarchy Compensation for injustice; accommodation Welfare-state proxy	Merit recruitment, quotas, affirmative action, chance, patronage

We achieve this aim by an ideal-typical distinction between political and bureaucratic representation that can be either low or high. The combination of these two dimensions of representation in a matrix allows us to distinguish four different types of relationships that go beyond pure democratic political systems but help us to capture the logic of different forms of representation across both authoritarian and democratic regimes (see Table 4.1). It raises a number of questions, among them whether there could be a bureaucratic representativeness without political representativeness, or is political representativeness a necessary but not sufficient condition. The following paragraphs will describe in greater details our findings.

Type A: Low Representative Bureaucracy, Low Political Representation

Type A cases of representation concern those systems of rulership, which deny its citizens basic political rights (see Linz and Stepan, 1996). In those regimes is not only the political representation low but also bureaucracy does not fulfill this function. This *type A* representation is typical for revolutionary regimes that depend on either eliminating or controlling both the legislature as well as bureaucracy but also long-term one-party governments, sultanistic regimes that institutionalize personal rule in all branches of government as well as technocratic systems. It is partisan by all means. Bureaucracy is an agent for social change and often subject to radical "cleaning" processes, in which representatives of the former regime are to be eliminated. Germany during the rule of Adolf Hitler (1933–45) may serve as an example here. Often the boundaries between decision-making and administration – separation of powers in democracies – do not exist, leading to a politicization of the bureaucracy and bureaucratization of politics. If the idea of representation exists at all, then it is the representation of specific groups, who have gained power and try to overthrow a ruling elite. This type has a highly adversarial character and intentionally stresses the need to be unrepresentative though this paradoxically often with the claim to speak for the good of society. This notion is especially present in Karl Marx's theory of the state, where the working class shall take power for a specific period in order to create a just society (Marx, 1968). Selection of political and administrative leaders is rather arbitrary or happens on the basis of belonging to a specific group. The idea of unrepresentativeness becomes a system of this type, despite the fact that revolutions are often justified to occur in the name of the people.

Type A stresses low political and bureaucratic representativeness. Weber's idea of charismatic leadership may be called to illustrate a notion, in which arbitrariness is a strong characteristic of decision-making. The selection of personnel, especially the one closest to the ruling person or group, is determined by cronyism and personal loyalties, which are not subject to appeal by an independent court system.

Type B: Low Representative Bureaucracy, High Political Representation

High political representation and low representation in bureaucracies has a long tradition in modern theory of democracy. Parliament serves as the locus for deliberation, as Jürgen Habermas points out. In discussing the role of non-majoritarian institutions in majoritarian settings, Johan P. Olsen (2010: 188) summarizes the position by Habermas as follows:

> Legislature and courts are the only two branches of government that are formally empowered to deal with normative reasons. Laws ought to be implemented and prepared by a normatively neutral, technically competent, and impartial bureaucracy. Social and economic power should not be converted directly into administrative power.

The role of bureaucracy in terms of representativeness is either not being considered or treated as an "instrument under parliamentary control" (Krislov, 1974: 27). Juan Linz and Alfred Stepan talk of the need for a democracy to create a "usable" bureaucracy that has the "effective capacity to command, regulate, and extract" (1996, 11). In modern administrative systems, that follow a Weberian logic (Gerth and Wright Mills, 1948), however, the merit principle determines the primary principle for selecting of administrative staff. This does not mean that bureaucratic representativeness in *type B* is impossible. It is rather a question of equal opportunities of access to the educational system and the capacity of these systems to create equal chances to compete for public service jobs. As studies have shown, the composition of western civil service systems is by no means socially representative. Instead, they often show a strong middle-class bias and reflect a tendency of recruiting people from rather similar social backgrounds.

As parliament is supposed to represent the will of the people, theorists of democracy, ever since Edmund Burke's famous *Speech to the Electors of Bristol* of 1774, have focused on fair and effective mechanisms of electing political representatives (Lijphart, 1999). *Type B*, therefore, places all emphasis on political representation. Bureaucracies are instruments to carry out the will of parliament but are not considered to be representative institutions. They are thought of as "cages of reason", as Silberman (1993) puts it. Where free and fair elections shall safeguard equal opportunity of access to political representation, merit recruitment serves as the selection mechanism in public administration. Political representativeness is contingent upon voting rules. Voters choose their candidates in free elections, forcing them to vote for a specific group raises questions about the legitimacy of process (Pitkin 1967: 90).

However, Jane Mansbridge has argued that the "institutionalization" (1999: 652) of descriptive representation can make sense under a number of different circumstances, e.g. in situations of distrust by a group or de facto low legitimacy within a group (1999: 650–652), and involves costs in other values, whereas Pitkin sees "no room" for some kind of enforced descriptive representation (Pitkin, 1967: 90).

However, what 'high' political representation means varies across countries and time. Low political representation, as Philippe Schmitter notes, has not kept us from calling any western country democratic (2009: 55). This despite the fact that low political representation has also been a characteristic feature of many western parliamentary democracies in the nineteenth and twentieth centuries. The French Revolution of 1789 marks for many the advent of basic democratic principles, especially liberty and equality. However, the direct result of the French Revolution was a suffrage, which was manifested in the Constitution of the year III. It produced a "large basic electorate but a very small real electorate" (Silberman, 1993: 98). Only those were eligible to vote who paid taxes or who fought in the army. Limited franchise was a character of electoral systems in western nations throughout the nineteenth and large parts of twentieth century. Prussia's three-class system from 1849 to 1918 is another example for limited suffrage. And Lijphart notes that "only the well-to-do had the right to vote" (1976: 107). Catholics were for centuries subject to systematic discrimination in the Netherlands and held only a disproportionately small share of position of power and prestige (Lijphart 1976: 90). Most western democracies introduced women's suffrage after World War I. However, in a number of western democracies it took much longer – France 1944, Belgium 1948, Switzerland 1971 – to move towards universal suffrage and full political representation (Ramirez et al., 1997: 744). And Desmond King (1995) suggests calling the United States democratic only for the period after the *Civil Rights Act* of 1965, which guaranteed equality for all citizens.

We could continue this list but it should suffice to remind us of the composition of the House of Lords in Great Britain, whose selection principles had been a monarchical – *hereditary rule* – one until recently. Schmitter calls all this a "'bizarre survival of the un-elected" (2009: 55). This is not meant to smash established institutions of democratic systems but to call to mind the different mechanisms that are being established to determine the composition of certain political institutions. This, eventually, leads to the normative question, whether a society at a certain point in its history considers a specific mechanism to be legitimate or not.

The principle in *Type B* is straightforward: bureaucracy should act, as parliament commands it to act. This narrative comes closest to our normative understanding of representation as it features a *locus* for deliberation and an instrument for its execution.

Type C: High Representative Bureaucracy, Low Political Representation

In *Type C*, where administrative representativeness is high but political representativeness is limited or does not exist, a free deliberation among freely elected representatives does not take place. Limited political representation, as discussed under Type B, may happen in democracies as well, when certain groups, e.g. women or immigrants, are denied the right to vote. Although authoritarian regimes often deny full-fledged political representativeness, they often call for elections in the form of plebescites to legitimize their system of rulership (Gandhi and Lust-Okar, 2009; Gandhi, 2010). Research has shown that it would be too easy to dismiss elections under authoritarian rule as pure measures of window dressing. Instead, they can be seen as important mechanisms to enforce cooperation and compliance among rivaling groups. However, it is in most cases limited and not based on the principle of equal opportunities and rights as we will discuss in this section.

While authoritarian regimes do allow partial representation of relevant groups in order to incorporate them into their system of rulership, its main logic is to be seen in the need to organize compliance and cooperation. Authoritarian regimes do not function in a social vacuum but depend on creating institutions that organizes predictable compromises (see Gandhi, 2008: xviii). Neutralizing potential opposition takes different forms, ranging from killings, imprisonment or enforced exile to turning them into shareholders of public administration. Public administration and the creation of ghost posts, public companies, and rents is a relatively flexible instrument to turn potential opponents into dependent creatures of the regime.

This use of the bureaucracy is especially the case in resource-poor countries (Wimmer, 1997) or where natural resources are not equally distributed. The state apparatus is then turned into a ‘milk cow’ that nourishes different groups for the price of loyalty to the regime. In the hands of an autocratic leader, bureaucracy is easy to manipulate and promises to create rends, which might otherwise not be available to opponents. In ethnically divided countries, incorporating rivaling groups into the system of administration is a perfectly rational strategy of not only enforcing compliance and cooperation but also in stressing the symbolic notion of being a regime of the ordinary people. Authoritarian regimes, as recent scholarship into the role of elections and parliaments of authoritarian rulers has shown, are less resting of simple principles of coercion and expulsion than often thought. Their own legitimacy rests not only on conveying the impression of being a regime for all but also their stability rests on strategically incorporating powerful fraction, on whose goodwill they rely and whom they otherwise would not be able to withstand.

In contrast to the revolutionary *Type A* relationship between political and bureaucratic representativeness, who are unrepresentative *per definitionem*, *Type C* uses the sources of its administrative machinery to integrate rivaling forces. The long-term ruler of Yugoslavia, Tito, was well known to have staffed many high positions in public organizations with members of multiple ethnicities in order to secure their say in the administrative process and represent the interests of their group to the center (Trogen, 2001: 383). Gadhafi was known for having created positions for members for regional tribe chiefs, on whom he depended to rule his territory. Large territories or ethnically diverse states often seem to make it necessary to incorporate rivaling forces in order to be able to implement centrally taken decisions. Logics of patronage, Guenther Roth (1968) argues, are at the heart of rulership strategies that are meant to consolidate position and create legitimacy among a selected group of influential societal actors.

Representation seen in this light is a strategy of rulership. It is a means to stabilize power and exert control. Administration is instrumentally useful as it allows on the one hand the creation of positions and on the other hand provides financial, technical or repressive resources that can be deliberately exploited by those who are supposed to represent a specific clan, tribe, region or political party. This type shows that representation can be a feature of political systems, though it must not necessarily be political or based on free and universal elections.

Type D: High Representative Bureaucracy, High Political Representation

Type D stands for high scores on both political and administrative representativeness. Both branches of government serve as representative institutions and are equipped with mechanisms to safeguard this purpose. Elections guarantee a representation of different interests and quotas or affirmative action programs promote the representation of minority groups in the bureaucracy. Bureaucracy is not seen as standing in a purely instrumental relationship to parliament but it is acknowledged that bureaucrats de facto enjoy discretion and leeway to shape decisions when it comes to the implementation of political decisions. This receives strong normative support from advocates of representative bureaucracy and diversity management who share the idea that a bureaucracy that mirrors the composition of the society it serves is more responsive to public interests and will therefore, as Selden and Selden point out, "better serve democratic principles" (Selden and Selden 2001: 308).

Scholars of different political complexion and academic discipline have thought about the link between representation and bureaucracy. Today it is mostly absent in modern democratic thought, in which the prevailing "administration without representation" view prevails.

Comprehensive representation in all branches of government actually dates back to the cradle of modern democracy: Athens. In the cradle of modern representative government, *representation* was understood to encompass both legislative and administrative activities (Alford, 1985). The best established is probably the ancient idea of a lot system that introduces randomness to the determination of leadership in magistrates and council (Manin, 1997). This old Athenian idea of a lot was a pillar in theorizing and securing good governance until, somehow paradoxically, the emergence of modern representative governments. With emergence of representative political institutions, first in the colonies that later became the United States, the idea of the lot as the ultimate democratic mechanism for leadership selection was replaced by a mechanism – election – that was conceived by many, such as Montesquieu or Rousseau, as an aristocratic tool of leadership selection. Somewhat paradoxically, as Manin observes, is the fact that with the rise of the principle of equality, the lot disappears from the scene, both in science as well as in practice.

It is necessary to bear in mind that also after the Athenian model of democracy vanished, theorists of society and politics have viewed bureaucracy as an essential force in society that needs to be kept under tight control and cannot be left to professional bureaucrats. Karl Marx and Friedrich Engels advocate the filling of administrative posts on the basis of universal suffrage (Engels, 1968: 21). In his description of the Paris Commune of 1871, Marx propagated the election of magistrates, an idea the Austro-Marxist Otto Bauer (1923[1965]: 237) also propagated during the revolts in Vienna in 1917 that led to the end of the monarchy in Austria. Local self-government through democratizing bureaucracy was in his view the way to go. Electing magistrates instead of appointing them was in Bauer's view the only way that would lead to true form of self-governance. And also Harold Laski (1921: 243) wrote around the same time in England "that where administrative organization is made responsive to the actual associations of men, there is a greater chance not merely of efficiency but of freedom also".

However, at that time, constitutional theorists such as Hans Kelsen (1920) and Carl Schmitt (1928) viewed the ideas by Karl Marx and Otto Bauer extremely critically. Both reflecting upon the crisis of governing in the Weimar Republic of the 1920s and the post-monarchical system in Austria, dismissed those positions as not being suitable for modern, large, and differentiated societies. Although Carl Schmitt acknowledged the tension between democratic equality and a public service hierarchy that may lead to the evolution of a distinct class – *Standesbildung* – and viewed the Athenian lot system to be the most democratic form of selection magistrates, he considered it inadequate as it would not allow a selection of public servants on the basis of merit and knowledge (Schmitt, 1928: 256, 257). However, Carl Schmitt mentions the possibility of running small-scale municipalities according to such principles. Nevertheless, Schmitt was deeply aware of the tension that may occur when different types of principles of political form are being combined with each other. Schmitt differentiated between three different forms of selecting leaders. Appointing public servants he considered to be problematic or even undemocratic, as appointments are a feature of monarchies. While lots represent the most democratic form, elections he viewed to be, just as Plato, Rousseau, and Montesquieu did, as aristocratic (Schmitt, 1928: 257). Schmitt solved this dilemma by declaring that bureaucracy must depend on the trust of the people and be in line with their will. This is not to say that Schmitt propagated a liberal or pluralistic view of democracy or representative bureaucracy as it is viewed by Laski and Kingsley. He was suspicious of democratic pluralism and rather favored a strong bureaucracy that incorporates the 'spirit' of the people.

Laski's ideas of making bureaucracy more responsive to societal demands has arguably strongly influenced the work of authors such as Subramaniam (1967), Mosher (1968), Krislov (1974), or Meyer (1975), whose research centers around the difference between *passive* and *active representation*. While the former concept refers to a form of *descriptive* representation, *active representation* raises the question to what extent the presence of a distinct group also translates into favorable policies for it. This group of scholars, almost exclusively from Anglo-Saxon countries, views bureaucrats to have a significant impact on parliamentary decision-making. From this flows the normative claim that if bureaucrats shape policies as much or sometimes even more than parliamentarians then bureaucracy should reflect the diversity of the society it is made of. The whole problem is about reconciling the "basic principles of representative government with the powerful roles that unelected civil servants collectively play in the formulation and implementation of public policies" (Dolan and Rosenbloom, 2003: 11). The *symbolic* function is viewed in the passive as well as active promotion of equal opportunity and equality. The civil service may even serve as an example and trigger change in broader society, such as private enterprises, or compensate for inequality and discrimination in other institutions (Krislov, 1974).

From all this derives the normative plea of turning bureaucracy in a mirror image of society. This normative plea for more representation of minorities in the public service seems to be on the rise in many western democracies. Countries such as Canada or the United States actively promote the representation of minority groups in the public service. In the meantime, not only have the United States written the goal of achieving a representative federal bureaucracy into the Civil Service Reform Act of 1978, but years later Bill Clinton called for a government that "looks like America". One central legal measure to achieve the goal of a representative bureaucracy, have been so-called "affirmative action" policies in the United States (Katznelson, 2006; Kellough, 2006). The term affirmative action refers to policies that take gender, race, or ethnicity into account in an attempt to promote equal opportunity. The focus of such policies ranges from employment and public contracting to educational outreach and health programs. The impetus towards affirmative action is twofold: to maximize the benefits of diversity in all levels of society, and to redress disadvantages due to overt, institutional, or involuntary discrimination. Not necessarily a consequence of those policies but probably rather a generic feature of the US political system of interest representation, Aberbach et al. (1981: 23) argue that the "US bureaucracy has been recognized as a channel of representation rivaling Congress and, moreover, one that aggregates interests in a manner that is hardly less comprehensive or progressive". This underscores the idea that bureaucracies may feature strong representative characteristics in democratic systems, even rivaling the traditional *locus* of parliamentary representation.

And students of consociationalism, accommodation, and neo-corporatism (Lijphart, Lehmbruch, Schmitter, Katzenstein) have convincingly argued that the principle of proportionality does not stop – empirically speaking – at the doorsteps of public administration. Instead, it is an important part of a consensus-seeking political culture, for example in the Netherlands, Switzerland, and Austria, in which proportionality goes beyond electoral rules and applies to other areas, e.g. state-owned radio and television, appointments to public office, of the polity as well. Significant areas of the state are subject to the logic of what Gerhard Lehmbruch (1967) called *Proporzpatronage*, which can be translated as a proportional form of patronage. The composition of the national civil service in The Hague, as Lijphart (1976: 128) explains, is contingent upon the blocs in society. Incorporating rivaling societal blocs into the political systems is a prerequisite for political stability but is also often regarded to have caused ineffectiveness.

High political and high bureaucratic representativeness characterizes our fourth type of representation. It calls to mind a number of critical questions about "maximizing" representation across different types of government institutions in a democracy. As advocates of diversity management and representative bureaucracy often call for making bureaucracy more representative, this is often being done in the absence of considering the potential consequences for its democratic sister institution "political representation". We will do so after discussing a number of potential explanatory factors.

EXPLORING VARIATION AMONG DEMOCRACIES

And yet, despite the process of bureaucratization in western democracies, countries seem to have followed different paths. While countries such as Japan, France, and Germany have established over time a professional bureaucracy, which advocates merit recruitment and the absence of representation from public bureaucracies, the United States (and maybe also Canada) stand for the "administration with representation" school.

This account, however incomplete, poses starkly yet another question: "So, why do regimes (including democratic ones) turn towards bureaucracy as a tool of representation while others do not?" The response to that question must await further research, yet, my hunch circles around the following factors: what representation actually then means in an administrative system and to what extent public organizations are turned into representative bodies raises questions about the influence of a variety of institutional as well as socio-cultural factors that range from currently as well as historically existent cleavages, the traditional role the state encompasses in a society (liberal vs. organic) to the institutionalized forms of interest group articulation and mediation.

No single theoretical formula will answer this question. However, a number of shaping factors may be worth hinting at, which appear to be relevant and await further empirical exploration. By means of reviewing those shaping factors, we aim at developing a more differentiated understanding of the forces at work.

State Formation, Democratization, and Industrialization

Timing and sequencing of state formation, especially the link between the establishment of a professional state apparatus and the extension of suffrage, may matter for accounting for the degree to which bureaucracies lean towards representation or not.

In Prussia and Japan, did the rise of the bureaucracy preceded the development of democracy as well as industrialization. As a matter of fact, the state, meaning a highly skilled and professional public sector workforce, shaped the way industrialization happened in both countries (Silberman, 1993). In overcoming not only a strongly agricultural economy but especially breaking the vested interests of the "Junker" – the landed aristocracy – in Prussia, the administrative reforms by Freiherr von Stein and Graf Hardenberg in Prussia and Graf Montgelas in Bavaria, had the twin aim of following England's lead as an industrialized country but also to create a loyal and predictable bureaucracy in times, in which the closely studied French Revolution spread anxious concerns to those monarchs who still carried their heads on their shoulders. Sequence matters to the extent as it tells us about the purpose of a rational and merit-based workforce in the absence of representation and political conflict.

Administrative Traditions and Forms of Recruitment

A second factor that seems to be worth further exploration concerns the influence of national *state or administrative traditions*. By 'pooling diverse streams of experience' as Kingsley (2003: 18) put it, or Mosher's idea of bringing together "different perspectives, knowledge, values, and abilities" (1968: 16) citizens, they both argued, are better served as it improves the quality of governance. This very general argument, which seems to prevail in the representative bureaucracy as well as diversity management literature, provokes the question whether this might not only be true under very specific institutional, historical, and cultural conditions and is therefore difficult to generalize for all administrative systems. Our assumption would be that, when considering the variety of administrative traditions and cultures (Painter and Peters, 2010), the extent to which bureaucracies function actively as representative institutions is not only highly contingent upon different administrative traditions but also on the different roles the public service plays within societies. This idea is being nourished by the distinction between a liberal and an organic state tradition. The former, also labeled as a *public interest state* (Pollitt and Bouckaert, 2004: 53) is generally being associated with Westminster political systems, whereas the latter *Rechtsstaat model* is more representative for the political systems of France, Germany, Switzerland, and Austria. This distinction, especially with regard to administrative system, rests on different beliefs of the role of state in society, the existence of administrative law, and the education and recruitment of public servants.

In the German and French administrative tradition, the state is a transcendent entity, its citizen's members of an organic society. As bureaucrats personify the power and overarching capacity of the state, they take an essential role in shaping or even bringing about society. Their devotion, loyalty, and accountability is essentially a consequence of their specific training as professionals in the practice of law and administration of power. In this context, it seems relevant to remind ourselves of the different career systems that are embedded in the different administrative traditions. In the continental tradition, especially Germany and France, university graduates enter a career at an early age of their life and then proceed through the ranks often within the same organization. Attending specific training programs, as in the case of the ENA in France, is often a prerequisite for entering a civil service career. Obviously, this does not only form a specific expertise but is also the basis for a shared set of values among elite members of the administrative class. Being member of a state elite, especially in France (Suleiman, 1974; Birnbaum, 1977), carries the connotation of being able to take the right decisions for society and all its members. The idea of representation is officially non-existent in these systems, although the idea of "égalité" has prevailed ever since the French Revolution in 1789, also, at least as a principle, in the French civil service. Nevertheless, the idea of representation can be seen to exist in a different, rather indirect form as civil servants perceive themselves, due to their expertise and training, to be able to consider all necessary interests and take justified decisions as a consequence of their competencies and social status. Representation is therefore not so much a binary-coded issue of absence or presence of individuals or groups but rather concerns the institutionalized mechanisms, by which a civil service system legitimizes and institutionalizes distinct forms of dealing with it. This refers especially to the dominant idea of the nineteenth century reform movement to elevate the art of administration to a science that rests on the insights of objective and positive science.

Related to this, is, of course, the more general acceptance of hierarchy and sub-ordinance that legitimizes (to a certain extent) elite circle decisions. This is quite the opposite to the notion of state and bureaucracy in Anglo-Saxon countries, though one should be quick to point out that these are here very broad generalizations, which cannot do justice to each country. Still, one must not go as far as Margaret Thatcher's observation, "there is no such thing as society" (in an interview 1987), but it underlines the importance of the individual in society and its relationship to government. 'Stateless society' (Stillman 2003; Luton 2003) expresses the attitude that the state, especially within the United States, arises from a contract among members of society and is being held accountable by its members. The boundaries between state and society are more distinct in the liberal tradition than in the *Rechtsstaat* tradition. In addition, as the legal foundation of the state is less important compared to the *Rechtsstaat* tradition the training of public servants rests less on law. Representation is important in this administrative tradition as it defines a distinct form of holding government accountable, as being a 'mirror' of society, means actually to be able to reflect all existing values and interest in society.

And yet, this account suggests that there might not be a bureaucracy with representation and one without representation at work but two different logics of representation. One system looks at individuals and the other one represents a certain type of knowledge. Representation through systematic and positive knowledge: This nineteenth century doctrine of a neutral and objective science is central to Max Weber's writing about the rational–legal bureaucracy and supposed to elevate bureaucracy above everyday politics.

Notwithstanding the relevance and recalcitrance of ideas, any explanation that builds on them is confronted with the challenge of making sure that ideas are not only being attributed by us ex post facto but have played a shaping role while the events unfolded. In addition, this explanation might be good in making sense of a general inclination of an administrative system, but may have more problems explaining who gets represented and who does not.

Bureaucracies as Opportunity Structures and "Milk Cows"

Bureaucracies establish opportunity structures. Opportunity structures provide specific configuration of resources and institutions, which allow actors to use them for different means (see Kitschelt, 1986: 58). Controlling those structures means access to resources, while their availability or sheer existence provides incentives for capturing them.

Bureaucracies are easy to manipulate, elections not. In resource-poor countries or strongly non-egalitarian societies, bureaucracies may be viewed by groups as a "milk cow" that provides club goods to some privileged individuals or groups. In addition government positions serve as rents for potential support during elections or in authoritarian regimes as rewards for support during revolutions, for loyalty in times of crisis, for providing resources in repressing opposition or turmoil, or the incorporation of powerful ethnic and regional clans and tribes. This "milk cow" logic seems to be a clear logic of authoritarian regimes but, as noted below, democratic regimes do not always resist making use of administration structure, which is susceptible to legal manipulation.

In addition, public administration serves as a proxy for welfare state services. In the absence of solid welfare state security, large public armies, Russia or also the United States may serves as examples, are used to create jobs, which the market does not provide. In addition, post-conflict situations often feature situations in which marauding and armed gangs fill the streets, terrorize neighborhoods, or set up paramilitary structures, which exist parallel to the old or newly formed ones. The official police force or the army provide structures which can be used to incorporate the members of those gangs. Employment, a regular salary, and status are strong incentives to attract rivaling groups. However, it is not necessarily said that those processes actually translate into stability and functional services

What makes it easy, is that governments, often *par ordre du mufti* create jobs in public administration without consulting parliament. This gives them ample leverage to create rents for distinct groups. Loyalty is being returned on the other hand. The result is eventually not the kind of representation we usually define as "giving voice" but public administration serves as an opportunity structure in the absence of other institutions.

While opportunity structures and club resources help us to understand the incentives, mechanisms, and locus of representation they cannot, as argued in the case of "ideas", explain who gets represented. Social cleavages may serve better to do so.

Social Conflicts

Considering the variation among countries of how representation essentially plays out, we propose that historical and salient social cleavages offer one explanatory factor for further investigation (Lipset and Rokkan, 1967). Lipset and Rokkan understood "social cleavages" as arising "out of a great variety of relationships in the social structure [...]" (1967: 6) but were also clear in seeing that "only a few of these tend to polarize the politics of any given political system" (1967: 6). In other words, we think that there are good reasons to believe that the extent to which a countries' administrative system acts as a representative institution depends on the nature of prevailing social cleavages in a society. The type of cleavage, e.g. ethnic, language, or class polarization, appears to be a necessary though not yet sufficient indicator for the type of representation we find in a given administrative system. And yet we lack systematic analysis across administrative systems that would allow us to move beyond hypothesizing causal relationships but determine to what extent a distinct form of representation can be understood as an expression of manifest or latent social conflicts (cf. Lipset and Rokkan, 1967: 5). The extent to which a country's administrative system is a function of salient social cleavages depends furthermore on the ability of groups to articulate and advocate those conflicts over a significant period of time in the political arena. It is therefore plausible to assume that salient social cleavages play then a role in shaping the representative nature of a country's administrative system, when specific issues, e.g. ethnic conflict, dominate the political agenda. Though social cleavages shape the nature of representation, there is no reason to believe in a deterministic relationship as other factors mediate this relationship.

As noted earlier, social cleavages may direct us to fundamental divisions in society, which can be relevant in understanding the lines of conflict. The answer to who – individuals, groups, regions etc. – seeks representation, is coupled to those societal conflicts, though it cannot explain who is actually being represented. As will be pointed out in the following, this is contingent on institutionalized channels of representation.

Channels of Representation

One of these mediating factors can be seen in the different ways interests are being articulated and political preferences are being transmitted into a political system. One may argue that in the absence of alternative institutions of interest group representation, for example strong multiparty systems or corporatist patterns, and the presence of the "winner takes it all" electoral systems, the bureaucracy serves as an easy to manipulate institution of accommodation.

The ability to organize the interests of a group and translate those concerns into the political arena by actively advocating a group's concerns, seems to be a factor that shapes the way bureaucracies respond to the specific demands of a group. The related, though yet still open question, however, concerns the influence of more general features, such as the type of electoral or interest group system, of a nation's system of political interest articulation. While majority electoral systems often lead to a two-party system, for example in Westminster democracies, the 'winner takes it all' logic makes it difficult for minority groups to articulate their political will in the political arena (Lijphart 1999). This could account for why the absence of proportional representation in the legislature is being (often) balanced by a tendency towards proportional representation in public sector organizations. This, at least, suggests the case of the United States as well as the case of the Canadian political system, though it is contradicted by the United Kingdom (cf. chapters by Andrews and Turgeon and Gagnon in von Maravić, Peters, and Schröter 2013). Political systems, which determine the composition of the legislature by using proportional representation, tend to give more room for smaller parties to be represented with their ideas and agendas and therefore offer a channel for articulating societal conflicts. Does this automatically make representation in public organizations superfluous? Though it may have some explanatory leverage for the case of the United States and Canada, it cannot explain the system of accommodation we find in the Netherlands. We may assume that this is not necessarily the case but it could make us think of alternative mechanisms of representation vis à vis the bureaucracy.

The two different logics of determining representation within parliament are not only related to the number of parties in parliament and the tendency to form coalition governments but also to interest group systems. While consensus democracies, to use Arend Lijphart's (1999) term, do not follow the more antagonistic pluralist logic of interest group articulation of Westminster systems but instead incorporate a few selected interest groups into the policy-making process, which tends to lead to the exclusion of other interest groups, this corporatist style of policy-making (Schmitter 1974) is necessarily more dependent on finding a consensus among different groups. Gerhard Lehmbruch has pointed towards the difference between an individualistic tradition of representation in Anglo-Saxon countries and a more corporatist tradition of representing groups in Continental Europe (1967: 16–17). However, as indicated before, the Continental European way of institutionalizing interest articulation does not necessarily lead to a greater openness for less well-organized groups or newcomers (Lehmbruch, 1967; Katzenstein, 1987b). Corporatist patterns of interest representation are often built around the cleavage of capital versus labor and not, although the Netherlands may serve here again as a deviant case, ethnic groups and newly arrived immigrants. Corporatist patterns rest on century old learning-cycles of consensus seeking, which have translated into a political culture of *amicabilis compositio* (Lehmbruch 1967: 53). It can therefore not serve as an easy-fix.

Nevertheless, the ability of groups to articulate their interests in the political arena, one way or the other, seems to be having an effect on either stabilizing existing institutional solutions or pushing them towards change. However, this form of "corporatist" representation may provide an alternative form of indirect representation of interests to the bureaucracy and could be more relevant in countries such as Germany or Austria. This specific type may provide a functional equivalent to the recruitment of "representatives" in the civil service as we see it in Canada or the United States. At least, the case of the German civil service suggests that the influence of relevant organized interest groups happens directly at the edge of relevant government departments, allowing them to institutionalize the partisan shaping of decision-making processes without being necessarily part of the civil service (Katzenstein, 1987a; Derlien and Mayntz, 1989). Again, immigrant groups or newly formed interest groups have difficulty to access those circles. But this could matter for other countries as well. Lipset and Rokkan (1967) argue that the interest group system constituted a second pillar of democracy in Norway and other Scandinavian countries that enabled segments of society who were not well represented by the dominant Labor Party to influence policy. This representation was important for legitimation of the existing political order. As time and society have moved on, a third pillar of representation, within the public bureaucracy, may become increasingly important. Pluralist systems of interest group mediation may offer similar mechanisms, though they are often less institutionalized.

Institutionalized channels of representation give us hints about the decision-making processes that are being shaped. They are important in figuring out what formal and informal practices shape the politics of representation and may create institutional legacies for future processes.

Summary

Social cleavages, forms of interest mediation as well as administrative traditions are in our view relevant, though not necessarily sufficient to understand why we observe variants of representation in administrative systems. In some instances the social groups who may have something to gain politically and in terms of employment simply do not mobilize, or do not mobilize effectively. This may be from lack of understanding of politics in democratic systems, or because the groups feel threatened in some way. For whatever reason, simply existing may be insufficient for a group to gain representation in representative bureaucracy. There is no 'dearth', as Lipset and Rokkan (1967, 6) pointed out, of well-founded hypotheses but making sense of them systematically and empirically will be a major task for the future, which will hopefully lead us to a more comprehensive understanding of the dynamics, facets, and contradictions of the politics of representation in the public sector.

DYNAMICS AND CONSEQUENCES

While there may be strong normative reasons for using bureaucracy as a tool for representation, e.g. reconciliation of past cruelties, for accommodating societal conflicts, for establishing a strong symbol of equal opportunities, one needs to acknowledge the adverse effects. Despite the strong normative undercurrent in favor of 'more' representative bureaucracy, several issues seem to be noteworthy that shed a more critical light on it.

Functioning: Stability and Effectiveness

Any consociational system raises question about the relationship between stability and effectiveness. This is especially the case of institutionalized mechanisms of power sharing, which have the potential of undermining democracy (Hughes and Sasse, 2001). Does diversity affect the performance of a political system in terms of its ability to adapt to changes in its environment, to implement political programs effectively, and guarantee accountability? This question is especially relevant when it comes to filling administrative positions according to rules of "parity" or "proportionality".

While students of consocational politics, such as Gerhard Lehmbruch (1967) and Arend Lijphart (1979), have pointed towards such a potential dilemma, they have also argued that those polities, which institutionalize proportionality and consensus mechanisms, do not necessarily show inferior performance to majoritarian democracies.

However, the historian Michael Mann (1987: 350) notes that the outfighting of Austro-Hungarian troops in 1917 is a good indicator how detrimental diversity as a strategy of rulership is. The representation of different ethnic groups in the military stabilized the multiethnic empire for a while, however, it also hampered its functional effectiveness when it came to suffering a humiliating defeat in only seven weeks against the Prussian army in 1866 or eventually devastating and final defeat during World War I.

Theda Skocpol describes in her comparative study of revolutions in agrarian societies how the representation of an aristocratic "privileged strata" (Skocpol, 1976: 186) in the bureaucracy, hindered the system to adapt prior to the French revolution and, for example, to introduce a new tax system that would have allowed the state to finance its war machinery and to modernize.

Gerhard Lehmbruch (1967: 52–53) also points towards the problem that imposed formulas of proportionality may lead to less adaptation and flexibility. Lehmbruch reminds us also that in countries such Switzerland the old democratic tradition hampered the establishment of a professional bureaucracy and the proportional staffing of administrative positions is only the logical continuity of incorporating minorities in processes and structures of power and decision-making. This form of *Proporzpatronage* was characteristic for Austria as well and may characterize the highest echelons of public service, army and police, the judiciary as well as public companies.

Studies have shown that those societies, e.g. the Netherlands and Austria that were characterized by strong traditions of proportionality in terms of staffing administrative posts prior to democratization have extended this logic of representation to other elements of the democratic system as well.

Obviously, as patronage may serve the group that profits from it directly, it has significant and detrimental effects for the effectiveness and efficiency for any organization. In addition, questions of accountability arise in a system, in which no one acts independently.

We cannot generalize from these findings. The accounts we have so far do not allow us, for example, to take account of the effects of different organizational characteristics.

Legitimacy: Adversarial Representation

Another issue of relevance concerns a more normative question about what happens in an ethnically or culturally fragmented society, in which the electoral outcome leads to a majority of one ethnic group and formal as well as informal mechanisms of representation make another group dominate the other branches of government.

The central idea of a neutral bureaucracy means that in an ideal-typical situation the interests of parliament match those of bureaucracy. Or, if, again in an ideal-typical Weberian world, the bureaucracy does not have any interests, then it follows the commands of parliament. Irrespective of interests that might be held by individual public servants the idea of *sine ire et studio* shall safeguard the domination of personal interest over public interest. However, if we conceive bureaucracy to function as a representative institution then it would be absurd to consider it to be apolitical. So what happens when a clan, religious or ethnic group forms the majority in parliament but turns out to be a minority in public administration, ranging from judges, to high police and military officers or tax officials? This may be especially of concern if different ethnic groups control different institutions of government. This form of *adversarial representation* has inevitable effects on the efficiency of a system as well as a straightforward system of accountability.

Irrespective of the mechanisms that have led to this situation, the question of representation in this case directly translates into a question of accountability. In addition, any adversarial majority in bureaucracy may block, resist or change any initiative taken by the other group that dominates as political representatives, as those in control of the bureaucratic apparatus control all relevant means of coercion, production, and communication. Now, this might be an extreme case for western democratic systems, though not uncommon in countries of transition.

Cleavages: Manifestation and Politicization

The third aspect I would like to draw your attention to concerns the effects bureaucratic representativeness may have for social cleavages. Although systems of accommodation may have significant effects for introducing stability, it may be naïve to think that those institutions of *amicabilis compositio*, first established out of a logic of replacing the majority principle by such a technical legal instrument for safeguarding minority rights during the *Peace of Westphalia*, may dissolve ethnic fragmentation. Instead, it may rather lead to a manifestation of conflicts, ethnicization of politics, and freezing of preferences. Roeder (1999) and James Hughes and Gwendolyn Sasse (2001) point towards the problem that institutional configuration of managing diversity may lead to a freezing or even polarization of ethnic preferences. Successful strategies of gaining access to state resources (club goods) in the past are prolonged into the future. The Dutch political scientist, Hans Daalder, has the following to say about the effects of the great Pacification in 1917:

> The great Pacification of 1917 was not a response to Dutch pillarization [sequential cleavages], but in many ways its prelude. Only after 1917 did the various Dutch groups develop their strong networks of subcultural interest organization. (H. Daalder quoted by Lijphart 1977: 41)

As those mechanisms to accommodate conflicts are deeply embedded in the political culture of a society, this practice of "balancing" the interests of different ethnic, cultural, regional or political groups can be seen, as in the case of Austria, as a precursor of a later consociational party system (Lembruch, 1967: 26).

In terms of consolidating democratic systems, one could argue that such mechanisms rather petrify social cleavages, as they offer actors some benefit, it also suggests that bureaucratic representativeness may rather help than hamper processes of democratization. One important factor, as Lehmbruch reminds us, is the political culture of *amicabilis compositio*.

BY WAY OF CONCLUSIONS

This comparative analysis of representation strongly reinforces the idea that both theorists of democracy as well as positive scholars can benefit from a more nuanced conceptualization of political and bureaucratic representation under different types of rulership. Our conceptual differentiation between different types of representation, stresses the necessity to focus future research on *Types C* and *D*. As outlined in this chapter, both authoritarian and democratic regimes employ techniques of representation though they do so for different reasons. Obviously, these ideal-types may help us better understand the logic and institutionalization of representation in government, but it shall also encourage us to devote more attention to the dynamics between those types. Political systems are dynamic and therefore also logics of representation. One question future research may want to take a closer look at concerns the transitions from one type to another and the reasons for those transitions. Why do bureaucracies play a more important role at a certain point in time than at another or why do other countries feature at the same moment in history different characteristics? Getting a firm grip on those type of questions makes it necessary that comparativists acknowledge the insights both from public administration as well as comparative politics and bring those subfields back together.

The comparative evidence presented here suggests that bureaucracies take more often the role as anchor of representation than often conceived in both normative political and administrative scholarship. Focusing more on the representative function of bureaucracy that in modern representative governments takes such a pivotal role in shaping policy choices and outcomes, not only helps to elucidate underlying structures and processes of state capacity it helps also to understand the role of bureaucracy in plural and divided societies.

The first and foremost lesson is that professional bureaucracies act as representative institutions, although to a varying degree. Bureaucracies develop or are forced to develop strong ties to the societies they are meant to serve and, depending on the type of political system, meant to control. However, as shown above they do so for different reasons, by different means, and with different outcomes. This is not only, as often-conceived in scholarship, a feature of developing or "backward" societies but at the heart of modern western democracies.

5. Representative bureaucracy in a cross-national context: politics, identity, structure and discretion

Kenneth J. Meier and Tabitha S.M. Morton[1]

INTRODUCTION

Although representative bureaucracy has been studied in numerous countries, one aspect of that literature, the empirical linkage between passive representation and active representation has been based almost exclusively on examples from the United States. Because this passive to active linkage serves as a major normative justification for representative bureaucracy, whether the US findings can be generalized to other countries is an important policy and scholarly question. The purpose of this chapter is to elucidate the theory of representative bureaucracy to set up a template for how studies could be implemented in a variety of national contexts. The focus will be on the concept "identity", a term that includes individual characteristics such as race, ethnicity, and gender; characteristics that are difficult for an individual to change in the short run and that are often highly visible.[2] The current effort draws from two prior theoretical efforts (Meier, 1993c; Keiser et al., 2002) that attempted to specify the theoretical relationships precisely and extends this work to a cross-national context.

DEFINING REPRESENTATION

The literature on representative bureaucracy distinguishes between passive and active representation. A bureaucracy is representative in the passive sense if the bureaucracy has the same characteristics as the population on the variables of interest (e.g. race, ethnicity, social class, gender, etc.; see Mosher, 1968). In fact, passive representation is sometimes called symbolic representation because it defines representation as "standing for" (Pitkin, 1967). While much literature is focused on passive representation and its determinants, the concern of this chapter is when, and under what conditions, passive representation generates active representation.[3]

Person A actively represents person B if A pursues actions that are in the interests of B; in short, A represents B if A acts as B would act if B were in the same position with the same information that A possess. Passive representation, therefore, is a characteristic while active representation is a process. Active representation does not guarantee that B's interests will be served; only that A will attempt to do so. A could fail in the effort to attain the outcomes of representation.

Unfortunately, in empirical application the definition of active representation gets muddied. Operationally most scholars define active representation as a set of bureaucratic outputs or outcomes that benefit B so that active representation is claimed when passive representation is positively correlated with a specified set of outcomes. That is not a correct conclusion since a specified set of outcomes can occur for a variety of reasons other than active representation by the bureaucracy. This issue will be directly addressed in the section on the microfoundations of representative bureaucracy.

REPRESENTATION AND THE POLITICS OF BUREAUCRACY

Although representation is frequently not considered a bureaucratic function, at one level it is important to recognize that all bureaucracies represent in some fashion. Many bureaucracies represent the interests of the legislature; sometimes, such as in the case of Japan, the bureaucracy and the legislature are so intertwined that the difference between them is unclear (Kato, 1998). In other cases (e.g. France), the bureaucracy is designed to represent the broader interests of the state (Meier and Hawes, 2009). In still other cases, bureaucracies are established to represent the interests of specific groups or clients, such as farmers, workers, small businesses, etc. Bureaucracies can even represent an abstract concept such as the public interest, environment protection, human rights, or the idea of the European Union.

Although bureaucratic representation is ubiquitous, not all representation is encouraged by political principals; in fact, the representative bureaucracy literature tends to focus on representation that is discouraged, or at least ignored, by electoral institutions. In part, this reflects the difference between scholarly questions that are interesting and those that are banal. Simply put, the idea that a bureaucratic agent will do what a political principal wants done is just not interesting. That is a very predictable, Adam-Smith/principal-agent world. The more interesting cases, and the focus of much research, are when a bureaucratic agent acts on behalf of individuals not specifically designated by law or policy. As a result, the representative bureaucracy literature focuses most of its attention on cases where the bureaucracy acts for individuals or groups who are disadvantaged.[4]

GENERALIZING REPRESENTATIVE BUREAUCRACY TO OTHER BUREAUCRATIC THEORIES

The theory of representative bureaucracy contends that because bureaucrats share ascriptive identities with citizens, i.e. the same race, gender, or religion, they also share values that can play a role in bureaucratic decisions. Traditional Weberian theories of bureaucracy cast a role/an identity for a bureaucrat as a neutral implementer of decisions in an impartial manner based on rules and written records. This too can be considered a value, thus making "Weberian bureaucrat" another type of bureaucratic identity. Contemporary rational choice theories of bureaucracy consider bureaucratic incentives as the key variable in determining bureaucratic decision-making (see Downs, 1967; Niskanen, 1971). In fact, goal conflict (read value differences) is the key causal variable in the theory. Humanistic views of bureaucracy, on the other hand, tend to incorporate more normative incentives such as the values that affect decisions. The common thread in all of these theories is that they specify a set of values, an identity, or set of identities for the bureaucrat, and contend that you can predict behavior by using these values. In this sense, representative bureaucracy is no different since it holds that ascriptive characteristics influence values. To illustrate the general nature of the theory of representative bureaucracy and to also introduce a framework for determining when bureaucracies might represent in a cross-national context, this paper presents three assumptions and the eight factors that either facilitate or hinder the translation of passive representation into active representation.

THEORY OF REPRESENTATIVE BUREAUCRACY: ASSUMPTIONS

Assumption 1. Bureaucracies Exercise Discretion

Bureaucracies exercise policy discretion in two ways. First, in many cases bureaucracies or individual bureaucrats participate in the policy formation and adoption process (see Rourke, 1984; Carpenter, 2002). They do so by providing recommendations and specific program expertise, as well as lobbying for provisions in law and policy. Second, during policy implementation bureaucracies have ample opportunities to influence the direction of policy by rulemaking, adjudication, program operations, or enforcement (Sowa and Selden, 2003; Sapat, 2004). Because 50 years of scholarship on policy implementation has demonstrated that only rarely can a policy be crafted that does not rely on bureaucratic discretion (Hill and Hupe, 2002), the ability of bureaucrats to either influence the original policy or to structure the day-to-day operations can have dramatic impacts.

The degree of discretion itself varies at different levels within an organization as well as across organizations. Policy discretion linked to representative bureaucracy has been found at the street level in schools, police forces, and firefighters (Meier and Stewart, 1992; Meier and Nicholson-Crotty, 2006; Ashworth and Andrews, 2010), at mid-management levels in child support enforcement (Wilkins and Keiser, 2004), and at upper levels in schools and federal contracting decisions (Theobald, 2007; Smith and Fernandez, 2010). In each case, bureaucratic discretion worked to alter policy implementation to allow outputs and outcomes favored by a particular group to occur.

Assumption 2a. External Political Actors Will Seek To Limit Bureaucratic Discretion

Legislatures and elected executives frequently seek to limit or structure discretion either by establishing specific legislation/policy, creating reporting requirements, providing for post-audits or scrutiny processes, and other means. This often occurs due to reasons of credit claiming or blame shifting, as elected officials attempt to manipulate their public images in order to prevent backlash from unpopular policy outcomes, maintain their current offices, or advance their political careers. Although the political science literature has generated a modest set of studies on what is termed the "legislative delegation" question (Huber and Shipan,

2002), for the most part that literature is flawed by its reliance on statute length as a measure of discretion.[5]

A more promising cross-national approach to bureaucratic discretion, therefore, might be to rely on Hood's (2002) categorization of the "civil service bargains" that delineate the role that top level bureaucrats and legislators play in the governance process. These bargains are a set of expectations about where and when bureaucrats should exercise discretion; that is, they define bureaucratic roles (read identity) in the governance system. These bargains are salient to the study of representative bureaucracy in the cross-national context because they are not linked both to who has discretion in public policy and how this discretion varies across time, across countries, and across organizations.

Assumption 2b. Upper Level Bureaucrats Will Seek To Structure or Limit the Discretion of Lower Level Bureaucrats

Many processes and structures of organizations are also designed to guide the decisions of lower-level bureaucrats and thus put some limits on their discretion. Standard operating procedures, specific job descriptions, and hierarchical reporting requirements restrict overall bureaucratic discretion, and also limit the ability of identities to become salient and thus lead to active representation. These procedures and structures can also be viewed as potential bureaucratic identities that compete with ascriptive traits for attention when the bureaucrat makes implementation decisions.

The efforts to restrict discretion, however, need to be qualified to make an important point. Neither elected officials nor upper-level bureaucrats will try to completely eliminate discretion. First, eliminating discretion, as Downs (1967) demonstrates, is costly in terms of transaction costs and monitoring costs. Efforts to limit discretion are frequently countered by subordinates who seek to evade these restrictions on their discretion. The result is an escalation of the controls and corresponding evasion that displaces the time needed to achieve agency goals. Second, it is irrational for a political principal to completely eliminate the discretion of a bureaucratic agent. Doing so robs the political principal of the agent's expertise and superior knowledge and also restricts the flexibility of the agent to react as conditions change. This in turn hinders the agent's ability to implement policies that maximize the benefits and services available to clients (or the benefits to the political principals). So while there will be significant efforts to channel and structure bureaucratic discretion, there are also strong incentives to retain discretion at all levels of the organization.

Assumption 3. Bureaucrats Engage in Rational Utility Calculations

When bureaucrats exercise discretion, we expect them to make decisions consistent with their values. This does not mean that a bureaucrat will necessarily benefit from a decision in a tangible way. The payoff might be in terms of satisfaction with the decision, a belief that the decision will benefit the bureaucrat's career, or even the vague feeling that the public interest is served. Our contention is not that the bureaucrat is synoptically rational, but rather boundedly rational (Simon, 1947) in that the bureaucrat seeks to maximize the values that are salient to the bureaucrat at the time of the decision. In some cases the decision process might even be one of satisficing; the important point, however, is that bureaucrats engage in a systematic decision-making process that includes their own values.

Representative bureaucracy, as a result, is a way to tap into some of the values held by the bureaucrat. We have ample evidence that attitudes vary by race, ethnicity, gender, and a variety of other characteristics linked to representative bureaucracy. In essence, this means that a bureaucracy that mirrors the population on a set of demographic characteristics is likely to hold some values that are similar to those of the public. By maximizing his or her own values, a bureaucrat also furthers the values of the public that he or she passively represents. In this sense, passive representation is an indicator of bureaucratic values; and, thus, the theory of representative bureaucracy is consistent with principal-agent theory or other theories of bureaucracy that include bureaucratic preferences. The only difference is which preferences (identities) are emphasized. As an illustration of the utility of this notion, Meier and O'Toole (2006) use representative bureaucracy to indicate policy ideal points and then to assess the efficacy of political control of the bureaucracy. They illustrate that in many cases what is accepted as political control is not control, that is, getting the bureaucracy to do what it would not have done otherwise, but rather congruence between legislative preferences and what the bureaucracy would have done on its own.

KEY VARIABLES IN THE STUDY OF REPRESENTATIVE BUREAUCRACY

A variety of factors need to come into congruence for passive representation to generate active representation. These factors are quite likely to vary across national contexts, meaning that cases of representative bureaucracy are going to be highly dependent on the factors and situations of the specific polity. In essence, this argument recognizes that all bureaucrats have multiple identities – citizen, government employee, agency employee, engineer, female, minority, etc. Organizations seek to reinforce some of these identities (often those in line with the organization's culture/mission) while suppressing others. Those identities linked to representative bureaucracy are only a few among many, and whether these identities become salient is likely to vary across bureaucrats and even for a single bureaucrat vary over time. This section discusses the factors likely to influence which identities become salient and, therefore, when passive representation might translate into active representation.

Bureaucratic Discretion

Bureaucratic discretion must overlap with the issues/values that are salient to the identity in question. Many issues that bureaucrats deal with are not related to the relevant identity. An African-American bureaucrat in the US National Aeronautics and Space Administration, for example, would rarely face issues relevant to his or her African-American identity. This is evident in Keiser et al.'s (2002) discussion of how a person's determination of an issue as "gendered" is likely to trigger a pattern of behavior consistent with active representation. They suggest three possible ways to determine if an issue is gendered, and that these three possibilities can be used with any identity if one simply substitutes the identity in question for gender.

First, an issue is gendered if the issue benefits women as a class, such as equal pay or women's health issues. Second, within a given national context, an issue is gendered if the issue has been defined politically as a women's issue; in the United States child care is a women's political issue in contrast to some nations, such as Sweden, that more broadly define child care as a societal issue. Third, an issue is gendered if the gender of the bureaucrat changes the relationship between the client and the bureaucrat such that the client does something different. Meier and Nicholson-Crotty (2006), for example, demonstrate just this pattern for women police officers and the reporting of sexual assault crimes (see also Dee, 2004, on same race teachers). Sexual assault victims were more likely to report an assault in jurisdictions with more women on the police force. By applying these same three criteria to the identity of interest in the national context being studied, therefore, the analyst can pinpoint the cases where policy outcomes are likely to be congruent with passive representation.

Agency Mission

Agency mission greatly influences whether discretion is relevant to the identity in question. In some cases the agency has an advocacy mission; this is particularly the case of clientele agencies that deal with farmers, labor, business, veterans, etc. In many nations a visible agency is concerned with gender issues and might even be represented at the cabinet level. Although advocacy on behalf of ethnicity, race, or class is not common, at times units within organizations are concerned with diversity issues, such as eliminating hostile work environments in order to maximize the potential contributions of employees.

In addition, from a governance perspective, many programs are now implemented by non-profit organizations that frequently advocate for clientele who do not normally benefit from government services. For example, there are several non-profits, like the Insight Prison Project, the Art of Living Organization, and the Lionheart Foundation that work with prisons to provide inmates with the tools and guidance they need to reintegrate into society as productive citizens. The Art of Living Organization operates cross-national; with organizations in 151 different countries.

In contrast, Van Gool's (2008) work on untouchables and Indian bureaucracy is especially relevant to the idea of how an agency's mission can prevent the linkage of passive representation to active representation when the agency's mission is not explicitly advocacy. Because the policy outcomes he studied were used by elected officials to build patronage support rather than represent the interest of the disadvantaged, untouchable bureaucrats had little policy discretion that was relevant to their social origins. As a result, the value maximized by the bureaucrats was more likely to be the personal status gained as the bureaucrats rejected their caste identity to pass for another caste, rather than any outcomes that might benefit the untouchables.

Socialization

Socialization, both government-wide and for individual agencies, can work to limit or, on rare occasions, facilitate the translation of passive to active representation. All civil service systems seek to create a unique identity for employees as public servants. In some cases, such as France, the socialization is reinforced by common educational patterns (Rohr, 1995). Hood's (2002) work on the civil-service bargain is a good outline of the general roles that various civil service systems try to instill. Individual agencies also socialize their employees; this is part of the normal process by which organizations encourage employees to adopt the organization's goals as their own (Barnard, 1938; Downs, 1967). Socialization patterns in most cases run counter to the identities that concern scholars of representative bureaucracy, that is, they reinforce values related to agency goals rather than the individual identities of the bureaucrat. Socialization can include training programs, standard operating procedures, incentives for promotion, and even the history of the organization. Much of the orientation, policies, and procedures of the US Food and Drug Administration, for example, can be linked to a decision about thalidomide in the 1960s (see Quirk, 1980).

While all agencies and public services socialize employees, the extent of socialization varies a great deal. We should expect that as the degree of socialization increases, the less likely there is to be a link between passive and active representation, except in the unusual case that the agency's mission is linked directly to the identity in question. Although these cases may be rare, we should expect to see favorable policy outcomes for that particular group.

Hierarchy

Hierarchy is a means of control; it can be used to limit discretion and, thus, dampen the translation of passive representation into action. Meier and Bohte (2001) demonstrate that representational outputs are enhanced in more decentralized organizations (Keiser et al., 2002 present similar findings with different data). Selden and Sowa (2003) show a corresponding result for state government agencies in the United States. In more decentralized agencies, bureaucrats are allowed greater discretion, thus permitting them to implement policies that better represent minority interests. This finding not only emphasizes the significance of bureaucratic discretion and hierarchy to representative bureaucracy, but perhaps also decentralization's ability to increase the salience of ascriptive identities over bureaucratic prescribed identities.

In addition, a more decentralized organization can allow for different segments of an agency to develop their own sense of organizational culture, procedures, and norms. Such an agency may be more welcoming to diversity and innovation, thus making it more appealing to a broader set of individuals. This diverse set of bureaucrats may have a better sense of the clientele's interests because of their shared identities as well as be more willing to actively represent the interests of these groups, since they do not have to adhere to the control mechanisms or top-down procedures often found in more hierarchical organizations.

Stratification

The relationship between stratification and representation should be positive. Logic suggests that as individuals move up the hierarchy in a bureaucracy that they will have a greater ability to affect agency outcomes; and, thus, as passive representation increases at the top of the bureaucracy, active representation should also increase. Most of the initial empirical work, however, found that street-level representation not higher level representation was the key (see Meier and Stewart, 1992). More recently, however, some findings indicate that representation at the top of the organization is important. Theobald (2007) shows that Latino superintendents, the key decision makers for school districts, are able to allocate more funds to bilingual education. Smith and Fernandez (2010) demonstrate that U.S. federal agencies with more minorities in top management positions also allocated a larger percentage of contracts to minority-owned businesses. Keiser et al. (2002), in their study of gender and schools, discovered an interaction effect; while top-level women were not directly associated with better performance by female students, the impact of female teachers was substantially larger when women were well represented in management.

Two reasons explain the less consistent findings for top-level managers. First, minorities are rarely well represented at top levels of an organization and at the same time are underrepresented at lower levels. Most organizations promote from within, and the pool of potential top-level managers can be found among mid-level managers. This bottom up causal sequence means that top-level managers do not have to advocate minority interests; they can leave those tasks to mid-level and street-level personnel.[6] Second, organizations have elaborate reward systems that generally favor individuals who adhere to organizational norms (Teodoro, 2010). Individuals who adopt a role of representative at lower levels may be perceived as not accepting the norms of the organization and, therefore, be less likely to be promoted to top level positions.

Critical Mass

Management theorist Rosabeth Moss Kanter (1993) contends that women will not be able to influence the organization until they attain a critical mass of at least 15%. Her logic is that many individuals will be reluctant to take chances or advocate something out of the ordinary unless there are others with similar views and interests. Such an impact is especially likely to be the case in hierarchical organizations and those that engage in a great deal of organizational socialization.

While the argument has intuitive appeal, Kanter provided no evidence that such a threshold for a critical mass actually existed in practice. The most systematic assessment of the notion of critical mass has been done on US schools. That work consistently shows that street-level active representation does not need a critical mass. Teachers appear to be able to influence student assignments, discipline, and performance even when there are only a few passive representatives in the organization. For the management level, a critical mass is needed, but the level is closer to 25% than the 15% that Kanter hypothesized. These results held for both racial minorities (Meier and Stewart, 1992) and women (Keiser et al., 2002). Whether this different threshold is the result of a mis-specification theoretically or whether the needed critical mass differs in different types of organization is unclear and awaits additional empirical studies.

Professionalization

Professionalism is a major alternative source of identity and values for a bureaucrat. Professions provide not only training but approaches to deal with problems and opportunities for associating with other professionals, who, in some cases, may be viewed as the bureaucrat's critical audience. Teodoro (2010) contends that professionalism provides an external source of motivation, values, and rewards that may impede the formation of the passive to active representation link. In general, professionalism will limit representative bureaucracy because professions in the twenty-first century rarely seek to explicitly incorporate values linked to gender, ethnicity, or social class. To an electrical engineer, there is little training that might be linked to his or her ethnicity.

At times, however, professionalism will reinforce advocacy and, thus, support the development of active representation. The public health profession is an excellent example of one that contains a normative commitment to helping disadvantaged public health clientele in dealing with bureaucracy or other problems. Other professions that rely on emotional labor (Guy et al., 2008) or empathy such as teaching, social work, etc. might also facilitate the transformation of passive representation into active representation because professionals in these fields may feel ethically obligated to advocate on behalf of disadvantaged or marginalized clients.

Bureaucrats who are professionals may also be more secure in their jobs because they are more difficult to replace due to their unique skill set as well as the great demand from the public for these professionals.

Certain professionals like teachers and public health practitioners, therefore, may be more willing to engage in representation because they know their positions are relatively safe. Such professionals are often awarded a great deal of discretion because of their expertise thus giving them more opportunities to advocate for groups that share their particular identities.

Issue/Policy Salience

General policy salience may also play an important role in determining which identities become important to a bureaucrat. Policies that are salient to a particular clientele may encourage the clientele to "lobby" the bureaucrat to implement the policy in such a way that it falls in line with their interests. They may approach a bureaucrat who shares their identity, assuming that the bureaucrat will find the issue salient as well and, thus be sympathetic to their interests. This in turn may lead to active representation because a specific identity has been triggered within the bureaucrat by the policy as well as the targeted group.

One such example may be in the case of Arizona SB 1070, one of the strictest anti-immigration laws passed in the United States. Due to the salience of the policy to his racial identity, a Latino police officer may be less willing (or likely) to implement those provisions of the law that permit bureaucratic discretion. In addition, he may be "lobbied" by other Latinos or civil rights organizations, which see him as someone who can protect and advocate on behalf of their interests and contribute to nullifying the policy by not enforcing its provisions. In this way, the interests of Latino clients may counter the bureaucrat's professional bureaucratic identity as a neutral implementer of laws, thus increasing the occasions/circumstances that the passive to active link of representative bureaucracy occurs.

STUDYING REPRESENTATIVE BUREAUCRACY ACROSS NATIONS

The three assumptions and the eight variables trace out the basic parameters of the theory of representative bureaucracy. This section illustrates how that theory could be applied in a variety of national contexts. Doing so requires the knowledge of both the politics and the bureaucracy of the country or countries to be studied because the cases of representative bureaucracy are likely to be specific to the national context.

The first step in any study of representative bureaucracy is to determine which identities are likely to become salient and when are they likely to generate representation, that is, what demographics are politically salient? The salient identity could well vary from country to country and even within a country across time. Ethnicity/race is clearly the prime candidate for representative bureaucracy. Ethnic cleavages are a fundamental part of the political landscape in countries such as Belgium, the United States, and many others. At times these ethnic cleavages are linked to indigenous populations such as in many South American and North American countries, and at other times the ethnic cleavages also reflect language or religious differences (Quebec, Belgium, Lebanon, etc.). Immigration plays an interesting role in representative bureaucracy in that the process of political and economic incorporation is rarely ever smooth and can be a key issue particularly during economic downturns as the vote for far right parties in recent times indicates (Kestila and Soderlund, 2007).

Other potential characteristics for representative bureaucracy include social class (India, Thailand), region (Korea), and gender (numerous countries). In most cases these cleavages are also strongly linked to political issues about equity such as the Cholla province issue in Korea or the economic status of poor, rural areas in Thailand. This variance is consistent with Keiser et al.'s (2002) contention that gendered issues will vary across nations depending on how the role of women is defined both socially and politically in the specific nations.

Politics will define the identities that are salient. Recent work on Africa, for example, shows that over a period of time politics and how politics favors some groups rather than others has a dramatic impact on ethnic identification (Posner, 2006; Habyarimana et al., 2009). Ethnicity in this view can be endogenous to politics. As a result, the analyst needs to pay significant attention to national politics because politics in essence will define when representative bureaucracy is likely by determining which identities become salient, and what identities will be associated with dissatisfaction with current policy.

Just as national politics and history shape salience so does the history and politics of the organization. The infamous Tuskeegee syphilis experiment has made US health agencies very conscious of the racial implications of medical research and has generated specific guidelines on benefits across racial groups. Similarly the political history of the US Equal Employment Opportunity Commission led to first the downplaying of gender and then a greater focus on it after the Clarence Thomas hearings.

ISSUES IN REPRESENTATIVE BUREAUCRACY

Four empirical and normative issues in representative bureaucracy have a great deal of potential for cross-national assessments. These are investigating the microfoundations of the theory, linking representation to issues of performance, probing the relationship between bureaucratic and legislative representation, and addressing whether representative bureaucracy will create a biased bureaucracy. Each issue in turn merits further discussion.

The Microfoundations

The empirical literature on representative bureaucracy has found many correlations between passive representation and bureaucratic outcomes but has not gone down to the micro-level to determine exactly how these relationships come to exist. In terms of the theoretical literature, this means with few exceptions (see Selden, 1998; Bradbury and Kellough, 2008), the empirical literature deals with collective representation not dyadic representation. Specifically, the literature asks if an institution (bureaucracy) represents a collection of individuals sharing a trait. It does not probe whether a specific bureaucrat represents a specific individual. A fair challenge to the literature to date, as a result, is that it has not demonstrated active representation; it has only demonstrated a correlation between passive representation and some bureaucratic outputs or outcomes that benefit the specified group. Theoretically, the literature has identified four potential causal paths that could generate this result (see Meier et al., 1999) and form the microfoundations that generate this aggregate result.

First, active representation may occur directly – the bureaucrat acts for the client and in the process benefits the client. Second, the representation might occur indirectly because the presence of the minority bureaucrat influences other nonminority bureaucrats to change their behavior. In this case, a bureaucrat does something different, but it is not the bureaucrat who shares the representative trait with the client. Third, the representation might occur through changes in the policies and procedures of the organization. The bureaucratic representatives are likely to play a role in the discussions in the organization and whether or not policies or procedures have institutionalized biases in regard to the represented clientele. The bureaucrat, therefore, represents by advocating for changes in the standard operating procedures of the organization. All three of these processes include some aspects of active representation in the sense of the adoption of a representation role by the bureaucrat

(Selden, 1998). Finally, in the fourth causal path, the client changes his or her behavior as the result of the characteristics of the bureaucrat. In the education context this is termed the "role model" effect, but the process can occur outside the education arena (see Meier and Nicholson-Crotty, 2006).

While the microfoundations of representative bureaucracy are empirical questions, they have varying normative implications. In general, the first causal path is most likely to generate objections of favoritism in regard to the client; this normative concern declines with causal paths two and three and disappears completely in the fourth causal path. In the last instance the organization is merely taking advantage of the coproduction of public goods and services rather than making any changes in decisions. The basic fact, however, is that we know almost nothing about the microfoundations of representative bureaucracy. To date, the literature has only produced evidence that passive representation is correlated with bureaucratic outputs and outcomes, and we still have little concrete evidence that bureaucrats are actually engaging in active representation.

Bureaucratic Performance

The relationship between bureaucratic representation and performance was first examined in a study of representative bureaucracy and education in Texas (Meier et al., 1999, 2001). Those articles examined cross-group tradeoffs, that is, whether an increase in minority teachers negatively affected the performance of nonminority students. As part of the analysis, a bold, aggressive hypothesis was put forth that representative bureaucracies would be more effective than non-representative bureaucracies. The hypothesis was supported theoretically by the work of Gary Becker (1974) who argued that discrimination in employment would create inefficiencies for an organization. The authors suggested that an unrepresentative bureaucracy would reveal management's preferences for certain types of employees and those preferences would likely result in reduced organizational performance. The empirical study found that Anglo students (nonminorities) were not negatively affected by minority teachers, indeed, they actually experienced higher performance with minority teachers than did minority students.[7]

The relationship between representative bureaucracy and organizational performance was taken a step further by David Pitts and his coauthors. Relying on private sector research that indicates more diverse organizations are likely to generate a greater range of ideas and consequently perform better, Pitts (2005) finds that as the bureaucracy more closely mirrors the clientele in terms of ethnic composition, performance does increase. A subsequent analysis (Roch et al., 2010) shows that schools with more representative teaching faculties tend to shift from punitive disciplinary policies to more corrective or ameliorative disciplinary policies. The implication of this change in policy is that the organizations are more likely to get positive results in terms of performance.

LEGISLATIVE AND BUREAUCRATIC REPRESENTATION

Representation is often not perceived as a bureaucratic function; in contrast legislative bodies exist for the purpose of representation, yet it is possible that a group could be represented in both institutions. How the two types of representation combine, however, is theoretically ambiguous. On the one hand, one might theorize a positive relationship because the bureaucratic representatives will have political allies to protect them as they represent clients and because the legislative representatives can rely on sympathetic bureaucrats to implement their policies. On the other hand, because legislatures see representation as their prime function, they might be reticent to permit bureaucracies to engage in the same process and thus weaken their own claims as legitimate representatives. Daley's (1985) survey of US state legislators offers support for the latter position as he found that legislators supported all forms of efforts to make bureaucracy more responsive to the public except for representative bureaucracy.

Because many countries, particularly in Latin America (Htun and Jones, 2001), have passed constitutional provisions that mandate representation for specific groups (generally gender quotas), we have an interesting natural experiment on the linkage between the forms of representation. Will such political structures facilitate the representation of the bureaucracy, or will it result in restrictions on the policy-relevant discretion of the bureaucrats?

The two institutional forms of representation also suggest that an interesting question is the causal relationship between the two. Does an increase in bureaucratic representation result in a subsequent increase in legislative representation or does an increase in legislative representation translate into a change in bureaucratic representation? Some empirical work on gender in Latin America suggests that legislative representation is preceded by increases in top-level bureaucratic representation (Escobar-Lemmon and Taylor-Robinson, 2005). Work on school systems in Florida (Meier and Smith, 1994) and Texas (Meier and O'Toole, 2006), however, indicate that the relationship between the two forms of representation is reciprocal.

Representative Bureaucracy and Bias

Lim (2006), in an assessment of issues involving representative bureaucracy, raises the question as to whether or not increased representation will add biases to a neutral process. This is based on the Weberian notion of bureaucracy as a neutral instrument implementing the will of the sovereigns. Changes in decisions or outcomes as a result of representative bureaucracy, therefore, are then perceived as biasing the system.

There are reasons to be skeptical of arguments that representative bureaucracy generates favoritism or bias in otherwise neutral processes. The argument is based on a naïve view of structures that is frequently endorsed in the formal literature. This literature views government structures, including bureaucracies, as ways to solve collective action problems and, thus solely as efficiency enhancing (see Shepsle, 1979). An alternative view of structures, however, is that a wide variety of structures can solve any collective action problem (Knight, 1992). The specific structure adopted obviously generates greater benefits to those setting up the structure than the alternative structures. This view holds that all structures contain biases, and by implication all bureaucracies generate disparate treatment. The real question, therefore, is not whether representative bureaucracy generates favoritism or biases, but whether representative bureaucracy generates less equitable results than unrepresentative bureaucracy. Given the types of clientele that scholars of representative bureaucracy are interested in (generally the have nots), a reasonable hypothesis is that representative bureaucracy is positively associated with more equitable results. As an illustration, educational bureaucracies are perhaps those that generate the most equitable results in general, but the numerous studies of representative bureaucracy in schools all show that representation compensates for existing inequitable outcomes. In short, representative bureaucracy is likely to counter the existing biases of bureaucracy rather than adding new biases.

CONCLUSION

Three themes of this chapter in regard to representative bureaucracy should be reiterated. First, politics defines representative bureaucracy by determining what identities become salient and when they do so. As a result, scholars must consider the political context of the country they are examining in order to determine if, in what circumstances, and to what extent passive representation is linked to the active representation of interests. Second, scholars must understand that regardless of national, regional, or local context, discretion is the key factor in creating the linkage from passive to active representation. Bureaucrats must be able to maneuver and manipulate policies in order to generate the policy outcomes favored by a particular clientele. Finally, scholars should acknowledge that all representation is channeled within structures. By considering the government and organizational structures, scholars can determine if biases have been ingrained within the bureaucracy, as well as if representative bureaucracy can mitigate these biases thus creating more equitable outcomes and outputs. By taking these three points, as well as the assumptions and issues of representative bureaucracy into consideration, scholars should be better able to determine the role that this process plays in a cross-national context, therefore allowing for a deeper understanding of bureaucracy and the role it can play in a democratic state.

NOTES

1. We would like to thank Vicky Wilkins and Ling Zhu for comments on an earlier draft.
2. Some representative bureaucracy characteristics might not be visible such as sexual preference (Theilmann and Stewart, 1996) or caste (Van Gool, 2008). Visibility creates the more interesting dynamic because identities are determined both by the individual and by others who impose them via stereotypes.
3. This chapter does not deal with the determinants of passive representation. The extent of passive representation is a political characteristic worthy of study on its own since it represents, in part, the openness of the political system to all groups. There is a well-developed literature in this area that is addressed in the other chapters.
4. For clientele agencies if the groups are not disadvantaged, it is difficult to tell whether this is a case of representative bureaucracy or if it is merely the implementation of legislative preferences. The focus on the disadvantaged allows some to contend that representative bureaucracy can make up for some of the shortcomings of legislatures or other electoral institutions (Long, 1952).
5. One can easily illustrate the problem with statute length as a measure of limited discretion by comparing the extensive length of the state of Texas law on regulating the price of property and casualty insurance with the very short law in Wisconsin. The political science literature would hold that Wisconsin bureaucrats have more discretion than Texas bureaucrats in regulating insurance prices. In fact, the opposite is true since the Wisconsin law prohibits the state from regulating insurance prices.
6. Another possibility might be the collinearity makes it more difficult to find significant results and because there are fewer individuals at the top level, that influence will be less apparent.
7. The location of the study, Texas, a state with a large immigrant population suggests that these results might occur as the result of a segmented labor market. Children of immigrants are likely to have relatively limited occupational aspirations. As a result, many talented

individuals in the second generation of immigrants will opt to become teachers since such role models already exist in the community. In subsequent generations, one would expect that children of teachers would have occupational aspirations on a par with other middle-class children.

6. Political patronage, machine politics and ethnic representativeness in the public sector

B. Guy Peters

INTRODUCTION

Whether being discussed by scholars or by practitioners in Western countries, the prevailing assumption about managing personnel in the public sector is that public administration should be politically neutral. The Weberian ideal of the career public servant recruited on merit and capable of acting *sine irae ac studio* with both superiors and clients pervades discussions of public bureaucracies. This model is assumed to produce the most capable public servants and also to provide for the greatest possible equality in the recruitment, promotion, and retention of public servants. Further, the equality implied in the merit system can be justified in democratic terms, with all citizens having equal opportunity for public employment.

While the model of political neutrality and merit recruitment has a powerful normative standing, we should not assume that it is necessarily the best means of attaining all the goals of personnel management in the public sector. In particular, we should not assume that merit-based recruitment will necessarily produce the most representative public bureaucracy. The problems with merit-based recruitment are especially evident when there are significant numbers of minority group members who are new to a country or who may have been excluded from government for other reasons, e.g. caste or racial discrimination. Further, it is not just overt discrimination in the public sector that may influence representativeness but also the more subtle influences of the educational system and the examination systems.

The usual mechanisms for coping with the absence of adequate representativeness produced through merit recruitment are to institute programs such as affirmative action or quota systems. These legal mechanisms may indeed produce some improvement in representativeness (see Pitts, 2005). Those programs also depend heavily, however, upon individuals generally accustomed to implementing merit-based personnel systems, and generally committed to those merit system values, being willing to deviate from them in order to attain other social goals through public personnel policies. Many of these officials may perceive that they are in reality undermining the civil service to which they are committed if they actively pursue goals of greater diversity achieved by altering the normal standards for recruitment.

In addition to the legal means of fostering recruitment there have been other mechanisms that have often produced a more diverse public sector, albeit through means that might be considered extremely undesirable on normative grounds. In a number of instances the use of political machines and patronage politics have had the effect of opening government employment to groups who might otherwise be excluded, or at least of expanding the proportion of minority group members recruited to the public sector. While the public positions involved generally have been far from the top of the administrative hierarchies they nonetheless are public sector jobs, and especially for groups in society who might otherwise be excluded these positions represent a means of opening up the public sector.

The argument of this chapter is that, despite a number of serious normative and practical problems, patronage and political machines at some times and in some ways may perform some important democratic functions. Especially when considered as a complement to the more conventional forms of managing the civil service (Helmke and Levitsky, 2004; see below) then these more personalistic and politicized mechanisms for recruiting public sector employees may make governments more open and even more transparent than merit-based systems of recruitment.

PATRONAGE POLITICS AND THE PUBLIC SECTOR

As already noted, patronage and politicized forms of managing bureaucracies are generally considered negatively, and in general this is an accurate characterization of forms of managing personnel that do not depend so much upon objective criteria for assessing personnel. But more politicized versions of personnel may have their place in governing. This version of personnel management can be seen clearly by the role that machine politics has played in a number of settings as a means of controlling local governments and with that also controlling public employment. Machine politics depend upon political parties that control both the political and administrative structures of a government and utilize their control over public employment as one of several means of providing benefits to citizens in exchange for their political support.

The tendency is to think of patronage always as being illegal, but we should remember that in all political systems there is some level of legal and legitimate patronage designed to permit the political party or parties in government to provide more direction to government and to control policies. The degree of institutionalized and legal patronage differs markedly across countries, even among western democracies. For example, in the United States the president has over 4000 positions that he controls.[1] At the other end of this continuum the Prime Minister in the UK has only a few hundred positions in his or her gift, but even in that case there is some capacity for the executive to control some appointments.

Clientelism provides another example of the use of non-merit-based recruitment of personnel for public administration. Rather than being based on political parties clientelism tends to be structured more around individual *patrons* who use their positions in government to provide employment for their clients in exchange for political support of various sorts. This style of governing tends to be found in less modernized systems where political parties may not be sufficiently developed for machines to be effective. Indeed, a strong patron–client system may inhibit the development of effective political parties (Warner, 1997) with the patrons more interested in preserving their own powers (often with a territorial foundation) than with developing political power bases that extend more broadly. Again, although these relationships do tend to perpetuate personalized forms of governance and may inhibit political and social development, they may not be illegal per se.

In both of these cases there is an exchange relationship between a public official or a political party and an ordinary citizen. This exchange involves trading political support – voting, campaigning, even campaign donations etc. – in return for material benefits and especially for jobs. The jobs may be in the private sector, as when a patron is also a powerful economic actor, but most often the positions have been in the public sector. In the case of the western countries mentioned above most of the patronage positions tend to be in the upper levels of the public bureaucracy and are held by people who generally would not have difficulty in finding other positions.[2]

THE MERIT SYSTEM AND REPRESENTATIVENESS

Although there are a number of normative and empirical arguments on behalf of merit civil service appointments, this system may not necessarily promote greater representation within the civil service. Merit recruitment generally depends upon passing various examinations, and for upper level positions generally involves having attended university or other institutions of higher education. Both for ethnic minorities and for individuals from lower economic classes these formal requirements of the merit system of recruitment may constitute a significant barrier to successful entry.

In general, members of ethnic minorities tend not to attend universities in the same numbers as do members of the majority population. This pattern may be because of overt discrimination on the part of the universities (subtle or unsubtle) or it may be because of financial barriers,[3] or it may be because of difficulties in passing entry examinations. And there may be cultural restraints within their own communities that militate against even talented members of minorities pursuing higher education.

Some of the same barriers may operate to prevent members of minority groups from doing well on the examinations used to accept members into the civil service. Language itself may be a barrier to passing examinations for immigrants or members of groups that speak dialectical versions of the dominant language. And even if language is not an issue, examinations often have a cultural element that biases them against minority groups, immigrants, and women. These cultural biases may be exaggerated when the examinations involve an interview as they often do for upper-level positions in the civil service.

Merit systems may also not be particularly effective at managing the careers of members of minority groups. Although these systems are designed to deal with all employees fairly and equally, the criteria of performance in civil service systems may be somewhat subjective. At the very bottom of the hierarchy measuring performance may be relatively easy, but the further one goes up the hierarchy the more difficult that measurement becomes. At that level performance measures may depend upon cultural and social values that tend to disadvantage members of minority groups. Hence, merit systems may again not be the best friends of members of those minority groups, despite their normative appeal on other dimensions.

The above having been said, however, there are instances in which merit systems have been successful in recruiting members of minority groups, albeit often at lower level positions. For example, the US civil service and the US Postal Service have been an important source of social mobility for African-Americans and more recently for Hispanic Americans. Most of the positions obtained by the minority group members were not at the apex of the system, but they were reasonably stable and well-paid positions.[4] And the public service in Canada also has been important in integrating some elements of the francophone community into the broader national governance system.

NON-MERIT APPOINTMENTS AND REPRESENTATION

If merit systems are not necessarily the best things for producing representativeness in the public sector, then perhaps there may be something to be said for the non-merit systems mentioned above. These personnel systems may not have the strong normative commitment to equity or equality found in the merit-based systems and hence may be able to consider representativeness more directly, or at least may not be constrained by legal or moral commitments to formalized merit principles.

In both the party patronage system and in clientelism the individuals in positions of power may have incentives to provide public sector employment for minority group members. This incentive is perhaps clearest for the political machine with its patronage. The primary motive of the political machine is to remain in power. Leaders of machine not only have their own political positions as a function of retaining control of the reins of power, but they may be able to utilize that control for much greater financial gains. Although some political machines do have policy ideas and ideologies, even in those cases maintaining political power is the only means of putting those ideas into effect.[5]

Machines

For the machines to remain in power they must have votes. Votes from minority group members or from new immigrants count just as much as do votes from the majority community. The members of minority groups, and especially new immigrants, may have fewer political attachments than do more established members of the society and therefore may be more readily mobilized by the political machines. The exchange relationship involved is quite clear. The vote in essence bought public jobs, access to other public benefits, and therefore produced the means for economic survival and for integration into the broader social, economic and political communities of the city or perhaps a larger geographical region.

The urban machines in the United States were a quintessential example of this pattern of integration and minority employment. In the nineteenth century workers for the machine would meet immigrants at the docks or the train station and begin the process of involving them in the process. Robert Merton (1957) described the latent functions of these machines as substitutes for social welfare programs, but employment was very much a part of the process of coopting the immigrant groups into the political machine. And to some extent public employment became identified with certain immigrant groups. The Irish were the stereotypical policemen, while many Italians became sanitation workers, and many Jewish immigrants went into teaching and into white-collar jobs.[6]

An interesting variant of this process of using political machines to integrate minority groups into the political process is when the minority groups come to dominate the machine or establish their own machines as sources of countervailing power to the political establishment. The Irish political machine came to dominate Boston politics, producing in the end powerful national figures such as John F. Kennedy and Tip O'Neill.[7] More recently, African-American political movements, or machines, have come to dominate politics in cities such as Atlanta and New Orleans, and to some extent Detroit.

In other cases political machines may be more clearly identified as criminal and/or authoritarian. In these cases the political machines may depend less upon building political coalitions with migrant or minority populations, but instead would rely upon coercion or extreme forms of corruption in order to maintain their control of the political system. Even in these cases, however, the machines often provide opportunities for minority group members…

Other Patronage Systems

Although the nexus between political power and votes may be less direct than in machine politics, other forms of patronage may also have the effect of increasing the representativeness of public employment. When political leaders have the opportunity to make a number of political appointments they are of course looking for partisan loyalists, and also for good policy advisors, but they also have to consider the political consequences of their personnel choices. Appointments to patronage positions can be used to send signals to minority group members that the political party in charge is indeed open to them and is providing relatively good public sector jobs to members of the minority community.

Although political leaders must be concerned with the quality of the appointments they are making, they have the opportunity to make appointments that would not be constrained by merit system routines. The machine based model of patronage tends to provide primarily blue-collar jobs in the public sector, while patronage coming at national levels tends to be more white-collar positions that will pay better. In addition these positions may be means of breaking negative stereotypes of minority group members and women and functioning as a means of opening employment for these groups more broadly in the economy. Thus, patronage appointment may offer opportunities for enhancing representativeness that more formal merit system appointments do not provide.

Again, if we take the American case as an example, some early appointment of women in major positions in government functioned as a beginning toward greater gender equality in public and private hiring.[8] The first African-American cabinet member was appointed in 1966, and cabinets now have to have some representation of African American, Hispanic, and Asians. This implicit requirement for representativeness is true whether the administration is Democratic or Republican. Likewise, many sub-cabinet positions are now also filled by women and minority group members. At the end of the George W. Bush administration approximately 27 percent of the patronage appointments were members of recognizable minority groups, something that might not be expected from a conservative administration.

Clientelism

The role of clientelism in promoting greater representativeness in public employment is less clear than those for the two versions of patronage discussed above. The patrons in a clientelistic system are searching for political support, just as are the leaders of political machines or political leaders in government making patronage appointments. They need votes and other modes of political support just as much as do the other political leaders. The difference is that *patrons* in clientelistic systems may have fewer options for whom they will give their patronage to than do the other leaders.

Clientelistic systems tend to be geographically defined. The patron tends to have their power base in a specific region and as already noted may not be interested in, or capable of, extending that influence. In some political systems there are important regional disparities that create a need for representativeness just as ethnicity or class may. For example, in Italy the south tends to be poorer than much of the remainder of the country and its population may have fewer alternatives in government without the strong clientelistic patterns. Likewise, in many countries the capital city tends to dominate educational, economic and government opportunities, so that bringing in employees from the more remote areas offers another form of representativeness.

Although primarily expressed in regional terms, clientelism can also be seen as increasing the class representativeness of public employment as well. Local patrons tend to have many of their exchange relationships with the working class or the peasantry. Thus, to the extent that public sector jobs are being created for clients, they will tend to go to these less affluent and less socially connected individuals.

There are notable cases in which clientelism and political machines tend to converge to produce dominant party systems. The domination of Mexican politics by the Institutional Revolutionary Party (PRI) for decades (Fox, 1994) is perhaps the clearest example, but in Europe the domination of the Christian Democrats in Italy was also a powerful example. In the latter case, as described above, the clientelistic party did also serve to provide employment opportunities for parts of the country that might otherwise have had fewer opportunities. In the Mexican case, however, the party did not have to be as concerned with issues of representativeness in general (see Pardo, 2013) in part because the federal nature of the political system provided public employment opportunities within the local regions.

SUMMARY AND CONCLUSIONS

In the best of all worlds' merit systems for recruiting public employees would produce a representative public sector. Unfortunately, we do not live in the best of all worlds and most merit-based recruitment systems do not generate that type of equality of opportunity for members of the society. Rather, merit systems often tend to privilege the dominant ethnic and religious groups, the more affluent, and at least historically males. Merit systems also have tended to favor inhabitants of the 'center' of the country as opposed to the peripheral regions. While these advantages offered to some groups in the society are not necessarily provided out of any particular desire to exclude others in practice they do exclude and they do favor.

This chapter has argued that more purposive mechanisms for selecting personnel for the public sector may produce more representative bureaucracies. This possibility of representativeness may, however, be purchased at a high price. Democratic systems, and many non-democratic systems, have emphasized the importance of using merit criteria for public servants in an attempt to produce a fair recruitment process and also to attempt to attract the 'best and brightest' to work in the public sector. Those are themselves laudable goals for personnel management, and inevitably there may be some tradeoff between several significant goals for managing public personnel.

NOTES

1. This number has been increasing as presidents and political parties attempt to drive political control further down into the public bureaucracy (Light, 1995).
2. Even here, however, holding a public sector position in the right organization can be a valuable career step. For example, a Wall Street lawyer may want to spend a year or two in the Securities and Exchange Commission in order to gain contracts with the regulators and to understand the regulatory process better.
3. Even if tuition is free, there may be financial barriers. Families may need the income from their university-age children, or may not have the resources to support the prospective student with room and board.
4. These positions were especially important for African Americans during the period of segregation in Southern states. Jobs in the federal civil service and the post office were some of the few white-collar jobs then available to African Americans in these areas. Further, even in segregated schools there were positions for African American teachers on the public payroll.
5. For example, the Long machine (beginning with Huey and continuing with Earl K.) in Louisiana had a strong populist agenda. This was both a means of maintaining its political power but also appears to have been a relatively sincere commitment to those values that created benefits such as a system of public hospitals for the public.
6. These, of course, became stereotypes but had a good deal of validity as once an ethnic group had established a foothold in an occupational grouping they tended to bring along others from their community.
7. Just as the Long Machine was immortalized in literature in *All the King's Men*, the Boston Irish machine appeared thinly disguised in *The Last Hurrah.*
8. For example, Frances Perkins was appointed Secretary of Labor by Franklin Roosevelt in 1933, the first woman in the cabinet.

7. Migration and urban governance: challenges for democratic legitimacy?

Tassilo Herrschel

INTRODUCTION

Over the last years, the governance of cities has attracted considerable attention, primarily in the context of globalization and a competitiveness agenda (Begg, 2002). As part of that, implicitly, cities have largely been viewed as more or less black boxes, competing with each other, and defining policies as complete entities. Yet globalization and internationalization and, in a European context, "EU-ization", have not just provided a stage for this competitiveness agenda, but have created an underlying dynamism for many cities through migration, be that intranational (rural urban migration or suburbanization) or international – within the EU or across continents. In Western Europe, rapid post-war economic development resulted in labor shortages attracting considerable numbers of workers from less developed countries within Europe and beyond. The subsequent changes in the composition of the population have been particularly evident in the old industrial and manufacturing centers, such as the Ruhr region in Germany, or the West Midlands and Yorkshire, in England. Much of this legacy, reinforced by the recent, albeit different "waves" of immigration, raised the topic of integration and multi-culturalism, and the search for "best" policy answers, as a major political agenda at national and European level (Miles and Thränhardt, 1995), Implicitly, this placed public policy in the driving seat of this debate, shaped and implemented by governments as part of a liberal democratic agenda.

Research and public debate have so far addressed the relationship between governance and migration essentially from an integrationist perspective, depicting migrants in a predominantly passive role as "recipients" of, and respondents to, public policy. This view reflects the first dominant paradigm of "political quiescence", i.e. passivity, among immigrants, in the European literature on immigration. Migrant workers were considered to be apolitical and inherently apathetic (Martiniello, 2005). Not surprisingly, as both Marxist and non-Marxist commentators observed, given the near absence of political rights, migrants felt little inclination to engage in democratic political processes. The question then is, however, how representation is defined – merely as the formal version through electoral processes alone, following official, institutionalized avenues of representation, or also informal participation and engagement. This is less predictable and structured, following instead, and building, networks linking people with shared interests and agendas – all outside formal institutional politics. The latter is highlighted by the World Bank, when it argues that, "In most societies, democratic or not, citizens seek representation of their interests beyond the ballot as taxpayers, as users of public services, and increasingly as clients or members of NGOs and voluntary associations. Against a backdrop of competing social demands, rising expectations and variable government performance, these expressions of voice and participation are on the increase" (Harriss, 2005: 1041). Much of this approach focuses on national governments setting national conditions for multi-culturalism and integration (Fukuyama, 2006) closely linked to immigration policies. Yet with the growing focus on subnational levels of governance in competitiveness, the local arena has also gained growing attention as an important place for interaction between indigenous and migrant populations, where democracy becomes accessible to popular concerns.

Here, "governance" refers to regulation and policy-making that embrace other than state actors as an expression of "governing". These actors are linked through policy-specific networks that may reach across institutional and administrative boundaries and, also across different spatial scales. The term "multi-level-governance" (Bache and Flinders, 2004) refers to the interplay between several political–administrative levels. Depending on the number of actors and agencies, a sense of overcrowding ("overcrowded policy making") may emerge. At the same time, new forms of governance are understood as a way to improve decision-making by including more stakeholders and by replacing top-down-politics by networks of various public and private agents.

But local democracy is more than "enabling" institutionalization and regulation. It also includes the important dimensions of legitimacy and representativeness of governance institutions, and policy-making processes as well as policy outcomes. Ultimately, it is about ownership of policy results by the whole of the local demos. But has local governance been able to address the interests and democratic needs (and expectations) of migrant groups, and to integrate them with the local electorate? Can established *dirigiste* policies, based on an instrumental view of "integrating" migrants in a conventional governmental understanding, still fit the growing shift towards governance, which goes beyond institutional structures and mechanisms and embraces informal, involvement?

With actor networks, informal linkages, and virtual spatialities playing an increasingly important part in framing policy-making processes (and outcomes), can a conventional approach to integration policies, be effective? Can this shift offer different opportunities to migrants to access existing structures and mechanisms of governance, such as through informal contacts, which may appear less "forbidding" than formal institutional arrangements? Yet, informality may also make it more difficult for outsiders to join existing policy-making and democratic networks, as they are less visible and may be exclusive. Under such conditions, what is the likely scope for migrant groups to adopt a more *active* role within "their" localities as local citizens and shape local political agendas in a policy-making capacity, rather than waiting for "*being* integrated"? "Democracy not only constitutes a formalized system of impartial procedures and conventions, routines and norms [but through] political participation also reflects exclusionary practices long well-documented in, for example, the housing and labour markets" (Dahlstedt and Hertzberg, 2007: 177). This raises questions about the reality of Foucault's observation that power penetrates and permeates all levels of society (Marshall, 1997), as it depends, inter alia, on the definition of "power" and its manifestation in politics. And here questions of participation, legitimacy, accountability, and representativeness come into play as key ingredients of (local) democracy (EC, 2001). The exercise of power is thus not restricted to the narrow confines of formalized decision-making organs and their interrelationships, but, conceptualized under the broader term of governance, embraces a host of other actors and agencies which are embedded in, and an expression of, civil society, built on a "social field" (Dahlstedt and Hertzberg, 2007).

Martiniello (2005: 2) distinguishes among four dimensions circumscribing nature and degree of the integration of immigrants:

1. the political rights granted to immigrants by the host society, that is their statutory (theoretical) scope to get involved;
2. degree of identification by immigrants with the host society, circumscribing a sense of participation and "being part of" the host society (which is likely to define the wish to get involved);

3. the adoption of democratic norms and values by the immigrants, that is the realization of, and subscription to, established ways of doing things. Again this contributes to a sense of belonging and thus entitlement (or requirement) to engage;
4. degree and form of political participation (institutionalized, such as party memberships, etc.).

Yet it is not only, so the argument here, about merely "signing up" to existing structures and their representations and agencies, but also, and in particular, about forming and shaping these as part of an engagement and "taking ownership" process, And here informal and ad hoc arrangements, forms of organization and mobilization offer an important avenue for political engagement and participation.

SCOPE FOR PARTICIPATION THROUGH FORMAL AND INFORMAL ARRANGEMENTS

This chapter considers questions of democratic participation in, and thus the shaping of, local governance in localities experiencing a dynamic change in their population through immigration. In particular, the focus is the scope for, and extent of, active engagement by an immigrant population at the local level, as a prelude to ultimately shaping governance institutions in accordance with specific agendas and expectations and ways of doing things, rather than a mere passive form of "being integrated" as a top-down policy objective. It is thus essentially about the ownership – or, rather, the obtaining of such ownership –, of local democratized structures through participation (Halfmann, 1998) and their practical expression in "governance". The argument here thus seeks to draw on the two conceptualizations from within both debates on urban governance and migration-centered integration studies, and the formation and operation of civil society (Calhoun, 1993). Given the focus on urban areas by migrants – specifically economic migrants – whether outside of Europe (developing countries), or within Europe in such cities as in Marseille, Leicester, London, Berlin or Antwerp (OSI, 2010a, b), questions about the impact of migration-driven changes in the composition of urban populations on the governance mechanisms and arrangements in those places seem opportune and timely.

While there is some work on how government affects migrants, e.g. in service delivery and effecting integration (Miles and Thränhardt, 1995; OSI 2010a), there is little on the *inverse relationship* between governance and migrants. How does the changing composition of a local population impact democratic government or governance, concerning participation (Huth, 2006), representation (Özmal, 2008) and thus legitimacy. Could it lead to an "atomization" of society through hyperdiversity (Cooke, 2008) or superdiversity (Vertovec, 2006) in the wake of growing multiculturalism and the emergence of societal subdivisions? While such questions have been addressed in discussions of civil society (Yeoh and Huang, 1999; Odalm, 2004), there is little on the interdependence between migration and structures and operations of subnational governance (Huth, 2006).

This leaves considerable uncertainty, given the growing range of actors as government changes to governance, as well as an increasingly important role of informal linkages and connections between actors, be they institutions or personalities. On the one hand, this opens opportunities for innovative ways of connecting to existing governance arrangements outside the formal structures. And here, experiences and culturally embedded ways of doing things brought with the migrants may add new dimensions to existing practices and conceptions of community engagement with state authorities. On the other hand, the very informality, viewed as a defining characteristic of "new" governance, may produce invisible divisions and access routes to political processes and decision makers, distinguishing between being "inside" and being not so.

A weakness in the network approach, seen as underpinning new forms of governance, is a tendency to map, network connections between governmental levels, or between public and private sectors, while paying less attention to the varying "weight" of different interests and their abilities to either gain influence, or resist the danger of becoming marginalized. Some networks and some network members will be more powerful than others, and this can change over time and with shifting policy agendas. There is also the effect of personalities, lending additional weight to the position and impact of individual "nodes" of a policy network, with attendant uncertainty and temporality. Institutional hierarchies are being supplanted by network forms of governance and negotiations between interests of different actors – be these localities, organizations, or social groups and individuals. This broadening of the range of potential actors delineates the concept of governance. While the concept of government concentrates on hierarchies and formal decision making processes and structures, with clear and fixed allocations of responsibilities, governance points to horizontal networks of influence, intergovernmental negotiation and cooperation, and the blurring of public and private boundaries in negotiating and defining policies. Governance can be seen not as a means of control but as an "attempt to manage and regulate difference" (Kearns and Paddison, 2000: 847). There is thus a distinct managerial undertone. The concept is applied at both city and regional levels, and focuses on challenges of identifying and negotiating shared interests as the basis of – temporary – cooperation between actors. And governance covering a territory is the sum of such negotiated collaboration and the linkages among actors.

Debates on urban governance revolve around its inherent dynamics, i.e. its functional relationships and policy networks between actors at local and city–regional level. For some commentators, networked forms of governance open new progressive possibilities for urban and regional governance. Amin and Graham (1999), for example, see progressive aspects of "reflexive" networks, consciously adapting to external challenges. Rather than following hierarchically imposed rules and policies, new strategic directions for cities and regions could emerge from within. Such new political capacities may compensate for the widespread disaffection from traditional politics (Clark and Hoffman-Martinot, 1999). Citizens may become more attached to, and involved with, governing regimes that can deliver in consideration of, and response to, interests and requirements by immigrant groups.

Such governance networks create a different spatiality than the one with the conventional notion of space as a contiguous territory defined by a surrounding boundary. This means that new arrivals to a city are not automatically included based on their new residential location. Instead, they find themselves facing clearly selective provisions for accessibility to the system and thus scope to become part of it. Some may succeed, others may remain excluded and thus marginalized. This follows the distribution of social and communicative linkages. As agendas are achieved, or they change, so do once established policy networks and thus the inclusion or exclusion of actors. And with that change, accessibility to, and participation in, urban governance and its institutions, also change. The picture is thus one of flux in the scope for engagement and ownership of governance structures and ways of working.

"LOCALIZATION" OF GOVERNANCE AND DIFFERENTIAL LOCALIZATION OF REPRESENTATIVENESS VIS-À-VIS LOCAL AND NATIONAL CONDITIONS

Cities, especially of the metropolitan scale, have increasingly gained in importance as foci and drivers of economic development and competitiveness at national and international level. Using a somewhat broad and generalized understanding of "city", such an urban focus is propagated as the most effective approach to economic development policies (Cox, 1997; Raco, 1999; Porter, 2000; MacLeod, 2002; Swyngedouw, 2004). The beginnings of a more urban-focused perspective can be seen in the late 1980s when the EU undertook a series of studies of European cities. This work located cities in regional contexts but also sought to analyse specifically urban factors that made some cities more successful than others (Parkinson et al., 1991). Urban analysis drew on different academic traditions to regional studies and in particular sought explanation of relationships between government and other actors as part of "urban governance" and the attempt, for example, to build "growth coalitions" to maximize local development potential and opportunities, including "boosterist" urban policy (Harvey, 1989).

Governance with such an inherently cooperative arrangement allows a combination of both – maintaining existing governmental structures with their associated clearly defined portfolios of power, responsibility and, crucially for effective policy making, finances, and, simultaneously, engaging in varying, goal-driven, informal arrangements which define belonging through being represented by the participating actors. They may join or leave without having to surrender powers or being tied in institutionally with high exit barriers. Instead, networks and linkages between actors, whether institutions, organizations or individual persons, define hierarchies of relevance and influence in terms of defining and setting a policy agenda. Their main feature is an absence of "formalized alliances and programs" (Harvey, 1989: 114), and the underlying driver is, essentially, a local self-interest, the pursuit of which makes collaborative policy coordination seem opportune at the time. Kantor (2008) distinguishes between different types of political coordination in a liberal market democracy, based on the diversity of actor interests and the macro-political (primarily national) context. The degree to which shared and agreed policy agendas can bundle otherwise diverse actor interests, and to which macro-political (that is primarily national) contexts allow policy responses to be formulated, coordinated and collaboratively implemented, are affirmed as key factors at the metropolitan scale.

The increasingly pivotal role attributed to cities as centers of mobilizing political processes is also reflected in their importance as platforms for the formation and operation of civil society vis-à-vis governance institutions. This includes addressing the diversity of a globalizing society, including various immigrant groups, and finding mechanisms of engagement, participation and stake holding in society (Martiniello, 2000). In turn, this involves providing institutional avenues for doing so as part of state-led integration policies, but also, and this is the main focus here, proactive engagement by various groups of an urban population in the pursuit of more influence and shaping local policies and ways of governance. The urban arena provides such opportunities at a scale that allows more immediate communication, political experimentation and a greater sense of scope for engagement in democratic processes than the seemingly more remote and abstract national level. This process shapes urban political space as an interplay between four main variables: mechanisms of politics, civic-ness, and society; principles of democracy "in practice"; spaces to express collective identity and sense of belonging; and arena for the competing claims for responsibility between state (government) and citizens (Jenson, 2005).

Drawing on the concept of political opportunity structure (Tarrow, 1988; Koopmans, 1999), the argument brought forward here revolves around actors' interpretations and, with their growing experience, reinterpretations, of the scope and value, i.e. opportunity, of engaging with governance, and acting on this. And this contrasts with resigning to exclusion as a response strategy, and/or establishing competing alternative mechanisms. How are decisions to engage articulated in the different contexts set by European cities, and how, in turn, do these choices reshape metropolitan governance? This has vital consequences for the integration of migrant groups in European cities, and increasingly for their other residents, as evidenced, for instance, by how migrants influence policies and governance on religion, education, or the allocation of public housing (García, 2010).

Pushing the regional and also national level of governance more into the background in favor of the urban arena, translates into a parallel rescaling of citizenship. While raising questions about national identities and cohesions, and the relative importance of different, multi-scalar, levels of identities and, by extension, citizenship. This raises questions about their compatibility and interrelationship. Citizenship as sense of belonging and identity, but also as practiced political engagement, is thus showing signs of becoming unhinged from its traditionally dominant tie to the nation-state, and being re-interpreted and translated into smaller and thus more cohesive (if separate) entities within a multi-cultural environment. This localization (or urbanization) of citizenship may be expected to correlate more closely with the increasingly diverse nature of civil society in urban areas as the main destination points of immigration. And this, in return should offer better scope for "getting involved" in governance than at the more distant national level.

The engagement of migrants with governance is structured by five main dimensions, reflecting particular local and national conditions and contexts: (1) determination by supra-/national regimes of residence, employment and civic rights of migrants (Geddes, 2003); (2) incorporation of migrants into formal politics vis-à-vis different traditions of openness and "path dependent" developments of political institutions in European nation states (Garbaye, 2002); (3) re-evaluation of the representation of migrants, and involvement with local governance, through both formal politics and informal linkages and connections (Clarke, 2006), including as part of urban development projects and through migrant associations as fora for articulating interests and agendas (Andrews, 2009); (4) variation of formal and informal governance linkages, including the nature of institutions and the degree of bureaucratization (Oberti, 2000); (5) perceptions of political opportunities for migrants resulting from changing city policies, e.g. Amsterdam's diversity policy shift (Uitermark et al., 2005). Contents and practice of urban policy can signal a welcome to, or "deflection" (Light, 2006) of, migrants, depending on the reality and/or projection of barriers and hurdles to engage and participate (Blanc and Beaumont, 2005).

Two main avenues to engage with urban governance are available: conventional formal representation through political parties and thus government mechanisms (and democratic mechanisms), and, increasingly so, representation and engagement through informal links and non-institutionalized bodies. The growing shift towards the latter, that is informal, network-based, relational "new" forms of governance principles (Imrie and Raco, 1999; Blomgren Bingham, 2006), however, makes such engagement less obvious to access, predictable and transparent. Informal links, by their nature, depend on networks and the nodes, i.e. actors, which connect these linkages. Finding access to those is less structured and predictable, and also more variable and changeable. Networks, by definition, are inherently more selective in who is in and who is outside of it than simple, area-based inclusions, where access is based on belonging to a territory alone, rather than on "making it" into a network.

"LOCALIZATION" AND THE CREATION OF (*PERPETUAL*) MARGINALIZATIONS

Increasingly, governance is moving away from territory-based relationships between places to less formalized, more topically selective and temporal arrangements, based on networks between actors and "their" localities (Hajer and Wagenaar, 2003; Provan and Kenis, 2008). Variations in such connectivity among places and actors circumscribe the scope for participating in a network of competitors, as they shape and reflect variations in comparative attractiveness. Different degrees of connectivity also shape the scope for access to, and participation in, policy-making networks. This difference creates new, hierarchies of connectivity and access to, and relevance in, decision-making processes. The outcome is the emergence of networks constructed of variably dense and relevant connections, and thus with differing reach and political weight.

The new relational, network-defined spatialities, fragmented by a multitude of linear spaces, i.e. "corridors of communication", reflect a growing trend towards a "*perpetual marginalization*" among increasingly virtual and non-contiguous policy-making spaces (Allen et al., 1998; Heeg et al., 2003; Herrschel, 2009). Such constructs operate at the regional scale and function as a dynamic, continuously re-adjusting, framework for the location and connection of locally rooted nodes of political interaction and communication. The underlying (actual or perceived) pressure to seek maximum competitiveness may thus essentially reinforce "atomized" variance and inequalities in opportunities. These can be found in multiple intersecting and overlaying networks, nodes and linkages between actors and decision makers – be they localities, agencies, or individuals. Yet this fragmentation undermines the coherence of regional spaces. And this may well contradict the perception of "new regionalism" (Keating, 1998; MacLeod, 2002) as a mechanism to connect individual spaces to a larger entity, actual or imagined.

Inevitably, and unsurprisingly, these dynamics and shifts in the perceived democratic legitimacy as a result of a changing voter base, shape the framework for, and dynamics of, urban governance (Pierre, 1999; Stoker, 2000). Such shifts include the roles of actors and their influence. New alliances may be created, established ones terminated, and actors gain or lose in influence. The result is a shifting balance between being included in, excluded from, or simply ignored by, policy networks and their actors, creating new peripheralities and exclusions. Networks and their characteristics and functioning have attracted attention from both sociologists and economists, although both approach the topic quite differently. While economists have focused on networks from a strategic, managerial business perspective, driven by an economic rationality, sociologists have focused more on personality and the circumstance within which actors are situated and, subsequently, make their decisions (Burger and Buskens, 2009). Communication links – physical, informational, and social – emerge historically, and, if leading to a successful network, may develop their own dynamics, shaping objectives and behaviors. The result may mean greater cooperation and a sense of shared purpose, or the opposite, abandoning existing links because they served their purpose and interests "have moved on".

A network thus shows two dimensions: it depends on the power, influence and effectiveness of participants and, in return, shapes an actor's scope for effective policy making. The main drivers of such linkages are on the one hand integrated, systemic conditions and, on the other, more ad hoc and personality-based social characteristics as an interpersonal network (Law and Hassard, 1999). The question then is, how responsive to changing conditions and circumstance a network is, and what scope there is for actors to join and leave as objectives and conditions change. Will those shaping the network allow newcomers to join and, potentially, "upset" the established balance of power, "control" of the mechanisms of governance, and ways of doing things within it? With attention directed to the virtues of informal relationships in metropolitan governance (Kantor, 2008), it is the societal–political dimension of accepting and reinforcing "core" and "margin", i.e. inclusion and exclusion, that needs to be considered at least as much as geographic location and representation in a locality. The emerging, and changing, virtual mosaics of varying degrees of inclusion and participation across an urban area will inevitably create new, virtual boundaries and borders, inclusions and exclusions with the political process and avenues of representation and participation. It is in this context of new scalar and territorial variability and fluidity that active versus passive citizenship may be distinguished.

MULTI-SCALAR CITIZENSHIP AND DEMOCRATIC REPRESENTATION

In Europe, since the Maastricht Treaty of 1992, citizenship has been rescaled to embrace three levels: (1) a supranational European citizenship, entitling citizens of an EU state to participate in the local elections of another EU country where they live. This implies a (2) local citizenship, and (3) the conventional national dimension of citizenship derived from the concept of the nation state. The traditional hegemony of the national-scaled political community has thus been opened (and, effectively, weakened) by recognizing, and providing for, the creation of communities at other scales both above and below the national level. This opens questions about spatial references for the development of senses of belonging, and loyalties, and thus, by extension, scope and willingness to engage with the adopted new host society and its institutions and mechanisms of democratic representation. Establishing more explicitly the local level, especially cities, as arena of civic engagement and, eventually, integration, reduces the perceived distance between the individual and institutionalized governance. The local level appears more accessible and responsive to individual engagement and expressions of concerns and interest. This much emerged from a recent international comparison of urban civic engagement among immigrant groups (OSI, 2010b).

Actual engagement will much depend on "inventing truly participatory, empowering and democratic forms of local governance" which draws on communication across society and with institutions (Blanc and Beaumont, 2005: 409). And this, in turn, is circumscribed by the capacity of residents to do so within the confines of internal (local, societal, group-specific) and external (national, international, wider society) conditions and barriers. Centrally defined, top-down implemented programs and initiatives, including those aimed at "bringing about" integration, are more likely to achieve the opposite: an increase in the distance between the local population, including the immigrants, and the (national) state (Blanc and Beaumont, 2005).

With the importance of the local dimension, variations in local forms and practices of governance, including the range of actors and established traditions of local civic engagement, matter just as much as general attitudes to local democracy. Koopmans (2004) found that cities with a more liberal tradition tend to offer greater opportunities for practicing citizenship, including involving immigrants. And such local engagement may well, as a next step "up the governmental hierarchy", also shape national politics. International comparisons (OSI, 2010b) show that differences, and similarities, do exist *within* as well as between countries and cities, down to neighborhood level. They also highlight differences in involvement between established and immigrant populations. Such variations are caused inter alia by national differences in attitudes to political engagement, institutional preparedness to engage with the public, and, partly a willingness by resident groups to engage. One potential drawback of the growing localization – especially urbanization – of governance is fragmentation of civil society (García, 2006). Locally varying identities and perceptions of "the state", and society, become more varied, as they focus increasingly on local agendas, rather than a wider national narrative. And the question then is to what extent this localization can and does reflect local differences in cultures and variations in society, including the presence of immigrant groups, as against a simple "handing down" of national agendas. Is there evidence of locally responsive mechanisms of democratic engagement emerging as a variation of national structures and practices? And if so, what are the implications for the validity of existing theoretical explanations of governance and policy making (Rogers and Tillie, eds, 2001)?

Cities offer a particularly interesting platform for analysis of the increasingly more prominent multi-scalar nature of the relationship between the local and the national levels of civic-ness and governance. What is the relationship between emerging new administrative geographies and forms of institutionalization of urban governance and of local forms of civil society? The practical reality of local democracy and participation faces a number of uncertainties and challenges, especially for engagement of immigrant groups with little experience in democracy. Many see engagement with a place as merely temporary, serving more as an incidental background to temporary employment. There may thus not be a clear sense of commitment to the locality and its community, and thus desire to engage and participate. Migrants may feel somewhat insecure, for lack of confidence and experience, to engage with the local *demos*, its politics and forms and mechanisms of representation. By the same token, existing local social support systems are more likely to facilitate scope for migrants to engage more independently with the host locality than would be likely at the more distant national level. As García (2006) points out, social groups differ in their skills to organize politically and develop collective capacity to devise engagement strategies and mechanisms. This could lead to differential interest representations, leading to variable qualities of democracy in response to whose voices are heard, and made to be heard, in the public sphere at the expense of those who fail to find such representation of interest. Representativeness would thus be selective and partial, clearly placing the onus on immigrant groups to reach out and engage in order to gain voice. And here the "enabling role" of the state comes into play, needing to provide "opportunity structures", that is avenues for engagement, by somewhat leveling out the political–democratic playing field.

The new type of informal governance, including its virtual forms, is thus likely to predispose communities to more or less active engagement. In this respect, Schultze (2003), referring to the relationship between national and EU-level governance, distinguishes between policy-takers and policy-makers, whereby the former category is subdivided into two sub-types with varying degrees of "taking": the "managerial", hierarchically organized and entirely top-down implementation of policies with little in terms of consultations, and a more moderately "mostly" "top-down" version of "consultative governance". These contrast with "participatory governance" and its emphasis on grass-roots, bottom-up activity in combination with top-down flows of governance. The German model of multi-level governance, based on the "principle of counterflow" in the way in which policies are framed and implemented, is a good example of this two-way approach (Herrschel and Newman, 2002).

In principle, these distinctions may be equally applied to the relationship between national and subnational tiers of government. Applied in this way, such a distinction offers a helpful differentiation between varying forms of governance arrangements in cities, and with them conditions for local democratic participation as the underpinning of urban citizenship as an integral part of multi-level citizenship (García, 2006). And this, in turn, requires studying citizenship across all those levels in order to gain a more realistic understanding of the complexity of integration as a fundamental process of shaping civil society in a multi-level setting.

In a further elaboration of the different types of community responses to, and engagement with, local policy and governance, Blake et al. (2008), distinguish between those "players" inside the system and those who are not. The latter are considered "non-players". Between them and the active players, there are varying stages of "in betweenness" and aspiration about gaining access to the policy-making and governmental system, that is the "hopeful players". In other words, there is a distinction between players, not yet players and non-players of the mechanism of governance. Once "inside", some players are more satisfied and ambitious than others, seeking to expand their influence and become "powerful players", i.e. key nodes in the policy network. The main platforms and mechanisms of facilitating access and participation are both formal routes, such as local councilors, local parliamentarians, council officers, and political parties, and informal routes, including civic fora, pressure groups, partnerships between different actors, and other forms of non-governmental political engagement. It is here that the nature of governance matters – conventional institutionalized with clear structures and thus recognizable "access points", or informal, network based with less evident access points and, instead, a reliance on personal relationships and linkages. Gaining access and becoming an insider, depends on the particular agendas pursued by such policy networks, and thus their interest in co-opting certain types of actors. Being resident in a particular city is not in itself a sufficient condition for inclusion. Fitting into the prevailing agendas and their policy networks, is what matters. And these, of course, may change over time as a result of learning processes and shifts in public discourse, but also in response to the actors themselves. Thus, while "new governance" is inherently more difficult to locate and thus access, it varies with the type of actors gaining access. It is thus more than merely fitting into a set framework, as modulating and modifying the existing system of governance by changing the range of actors and their relations. As a consequence, while the hurdle to gaining access may seem higher, the "reward" is potentially greater, as it allows changes to the whole system of governance, its operation and policy prioritization.

Evidence from various European cities about democratic participation in local democratic processes among immigrant Muslim groups (OSI, 2010a) points to the importance of trust in encouraging engagement, coupled with assumptions about the impact of engagement on the framing of policies. Generally, it emerged that local governments and institutions are trusted more than those at the national level. Some of this may result from local politics and government being not such a big step away from engagement in local community groups, whether religious or not. These provide a form of rallying point for immigrants (and existing residents alike) and serve as a platforms and "training ground" for civic engagement to form and frame policies and political agendas. It is here also that a "conditioning" of local institutions and politics by an immigration-driven changed local society may occur, as community groups are extended into wider local agencies.

In central England, the old medium-sized industrial city of Leicester, is predicted to be the first English city with a majority non-white population by the end of this decade (Herbert, 2007), "Muslim and ethnic minority immigrant groups are reported to generally seem to have settled well into the political and civic landscape of Leicester" (OSI, 2010a: 205). Politically, these groups have been represented by ethnic-minority members of local government (councilors) since 1973. From the then single councilor, the number has now increased to 17 (a third of the total number). This suggests greater visibility and representation at the local level, with corresponding greater impact on local policy-making agendas and ways of doing things. Yet, at the national level, engagement seems more hesitant, leading to distinct differences between immigrant and non-immigrant groups. "The difference in the levels of trust between Muslim and non-Muslim respondents in relation to Parliament is striking. The qualitative data from London focus groups found criticism of politicians as incompetent, career-minded and out of touch with people because they were "not genuine enough to deal with the issues". "The skepticism towards mainstream politicians, irrespective of whether people were Muslim or not, reflected the idea that to enter mainstream politics one has to compromise one's views and beliefs for the party line" (OSI, 2010a: 205). It is the difference in the degree of trust in national representation that suggests a continued sense of being "outside" of, or no more than peripheral to, national narratives and society. Yet there seems to be a generational gap emerging, reflecting a learning and de facto integration process: "young Muslims have greater confidence in their ability to affect local change than the older generations. This appears to coincide with growing levels of education and familiarity with political institutions" (OSI, 2010a: 209). Yet, there are signs that cultural differences translate into a degree of separation between avenues and mechanisms of engagement, although this separateness, in turn, seems to produce a more confident and trusting civic engagement, one which seems more "at ease" with the political process and the principle of representativeness. Thus, referring to a survey among Leicester's population, it emerged that "respondents involved in own-ethnic/religion civic organisations are significantly more likely to trust their city councils than those involved in mixed organisations" (OSI, 2010a: 209).

CONCLUSIONS: "NEW" URBAN GOVERNANCE, IMMIGRATION, AND DEMOCRATIC REPRESENTATION: BETWEEN LOCAL CONDITIONS AND SOCIAL PRACTICES

This chapter discussed the relationship between immigration and urban governance against the background of questions of democratization and participation in a multi-level governance setting. Starting off from the growing role of cities as arenas of both civic involvement with governance and changes to the very *demos* as a result of city-focused immigration, the suggestion has been of a multi-scalar civic-ness. This stretches across local, national, and supra-national (European Union) tiers of civil society, and its interaction with governance structures and practices has been of particular interest. There have been discussions in the literature about "integration" of immigrant populations as part of a multi-cultural agenda, but such has mostly focused on questions of providing "integrating" in the sense of "allowing" such to happen. The underlying notion has been one of an essentially passive immigrant population that needed to be "incentivized", or "trained up", to engage with civil society and processes of democratic representation. The onus has thus been on them to engage.

However, this is only part of the picture. The engagement by immigrants may give existing structures and practices a new shape and way of working, giving immigrants a much more active role, especially so at the local level. They may shape the democratic practices and institutional workings, so that these reflect the particular cultural and social interests and ways of doings things of these groups, rather than merely permitting them to raise tentatively their civic voice. And the scope for a more comprehensive, integrational process of representation varies between localities in reflection of the particular societal structures, established political practices and institutional arrangements.

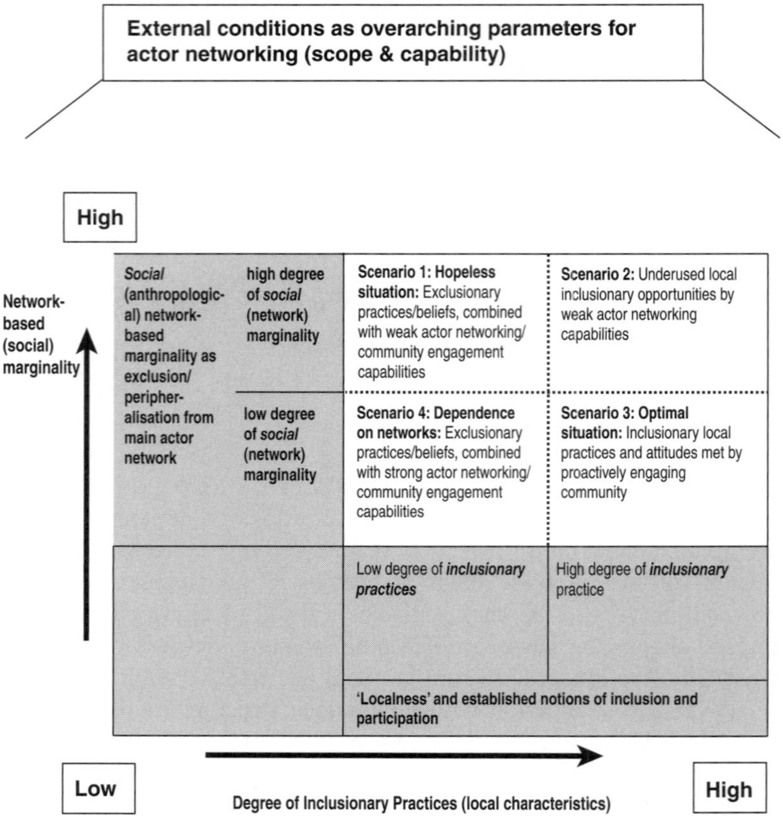

Figure 7.1 Scenarios of intersecting local practices of inclusion and network-based marginalization over time

Figure 7.1 provides a schematic presentation of the intersection between the two main variables shaping the integration of immigrant groups – local democratic and social processes and structures. This included in particular the varying nature of governance as an increasingly informal, actor network-based arrangement, where finding access to such informal networks gains in importance over the following of strict institutionalized avenues of representation and civic involvement. And while this shift provides for greater fluidity, responsiveness and variability, it also means a more selective and often less transparent way of working, making it more difficult for outsiders to gain access and become part of such networks. By their very nature, they are much more stringent in their inclusionary and exclusionary effects respectively than territory-based definitions of belonging. Living in a certain area not necessarily means an automatic representation and gaining a democratic voice, simply through spatial belonging. A more proactive approach is required for individuals to acquire access to networked governance. By the same token, as in the argument here, individuals representing immigrant communities may have a potentially greater effect on their representation by being able to use the network to this effect. So, much will depend on the networking abilities of individuals. And this is more variable, unpredictable and time-limited than fixed, albeit cumbersome, structures and mechanisms of conventional government.

8. Civic leadership and local politics in multi-cultural cities

Robin Hambleton

INTRODUCTION

For centuries, if not throughout human history, cities have grown and changed as a result of migration and immigration. A consequence is that all cities are, to some extent, multi-cultural or multi-ethnic.[1] However, in recent years, as a result of the rapid movement of peoples across national frontiers, many cities have become even more multi-cultural than in the past. Given the pace of population change now taking place in some urban areas, Jill Gross and I suggested that it may be helpful, at times, to use the term "dynamic diversity" – a phrase we used to describe a startling transformation in the diversity of the population of a locality in a relatively short space of time (Hambleton and Gross, 2007: 218). Thus, in recent years some immigrant "gateway cities" have experienced remarkable population shifts. For example, in Toronto, Canada, almost 50 percent of city residents are foreign born – according to the 2006 census the residents of Toronto come from 208 countries or regions and speak 140 languages or dialects. In major cosmopolitan cities, like London and New York, it is now the case that literally hundreds of different languages are spoken. For example, a study of the languages of London's schoolchildren found that over 300 languages are now spoken in the capital (Baker and Eversley, 2000). This increase in urban diversity poses important challenges for city leaders and public managers and for the systems of representation in urban governance.

The debate about whether this increase in multi-culturalism is "good" or "bad" for the people living in cities is complex and contested. In simple terms we can suggest that, on the "upside", supporters of multi-culturalism argue that it enhances the quality of life in a city. The "newly arrived" introduce fresh energy and ideas, and bring progress in science, arts, culture, and economic development. Indeed, it can be argued that the vibrancy and excitement we experience in the modern city is, as often as not, a direct consequence of the diversity of the city. Different kinds of people living and working together in close proximity can stimulate creativity and provide cities with a "diversity advantage" (Florida, 2002; Zachary, 2000; Wood and Landry, 2008; Saunders, 2010).

There is, however, evidence to support the argument that there is also a "downside" to diversity in the sense that immigrants are often treated unfairly. Indeed, it is often the case that the "newly arrived" are ruthlessly exploited. Davis (2006), for example, argues that current patterns of Third World urbanization take us "back to Dickens", with a spectacular growth of slums containing literally millions of poverty-stricken, unregistered rural migrants – residents without any legal or political rights. City leaders in western democracies do not face migration challenges on this scale, but there is no room for complacency. While many migrants and immigrants to western cities prosper, others encounter racial discrimination and are often the poorest in the city.

This chapter aims to describe the main challenges now facing those charged with governing modern multi-cultural cities. It also offers tentative suggestions, drawn from the pioneering practice developed by a number of innovative cities, on how to improve the quality of local governance in multi-cultural cities. A caveat is due at the outset. Cities are geographically and culturally specific – they exist in different economic, political, socio-cultural and legal contexts. It follows that we should guard against generalizing too freely about how to lead and manage multicultural cities across the world. Having said that, it is hoped that the discussion that follows identifies ideas that can be used to stimulate fresh thinking on how to promote diversity and equality in cities.

Following a short section looking back at the evolution of social scientific research on the multi-ethnic city, the chapter discusses two general themes that are currently shaping debates about urban democracy: (1) the shift from government to governance, and (2) the need to develop stronger forms of civic leadership to combat "place-less" power. The next three sections focus on specific themes relating to diversity and equality: (1) the importance of developing a local approach to understanding race and ethnicity, (2) building empowered communities, and (3) urban policies and practices to accommodate diversity. A concluding section offers some reflections and pointers.

SOCIAL RESEARCH ON THE MULTI-ETHNIC CITY

We now have more than a century of social scientific research documenting the experience of "new arrivals" in cities.[2] Many studies have shown that migrants and immigrants often find themselves in conflict, sometimes violent conflict, with the established population (Bollens, 2003). On occasions, this discord stems from competition for urban services and jobs, but friction also results from huge gaps in understanding between host communities and newcomers.

In his classic, intellectual history of urban planning in the twentieth century, Hall (1988) devotes his final chapter to "The city of the permanent underclass". He notes that problems associated with migration and immigration have been a continuing source of concern to social reformers. He refers, for example, to the pioneering work of W.E.B. Du Bois, one of the greatest of America's early sociologists. In 1899, Du Bois studied the black population of Philadelphia's seventh ward and showed how the biggest single group, numbering nearly 48 percent, were the "hard-working labouring classes". Above them were the 25 percent described as "comfortable", the 4 percent in "good circumstances", and the 4 percent who were "well-to-do". He advised his mainly white readers that there was "no surer way of misunderstanding the Negro or being misunderstood by him than by ignoring manifest differences of condition and power in the 40 000 black people of Philadelphia" (Du Bois, 1899: 310). In practice, while the great majority of the African Americans in Philadelphia were certainly not the degenerate, criminal, slum-dwellers of the rumor mill, a small minority of young black men did commit a significant amount of street crime – for example, "snatching pocketbooks" – and became the focus of public attention and resentment.

Du Bois, in his sophisticated analysis of social attitudes and behavior, anticipated a host of urban sociological studies – from the "discovery" of the "underclass" by the Chicago School of sociologists of the 1920s through to modern socio-psychological research on our attitudes to race examining "why we hate" (Levin and Rabrenovic, 2004). Attitudes and perceptions are clearly critical, as evinced by a recent major survey of multi-ethnic American communities by Putnam (2007). This suggests that residents of all races in ethnically diverse neighborhoods tend, at first, to "hunker down":

> Diversity does *not* produce "bad race relations" or ethnically-defined hostility [...] Rather, inhabitants of diverse communities tend to withdraw from collective life, to distrust their neighbours, regardless of the colour of their skin, to withdraw even from close friends, to expect the worst from their community and its leaders, to volunteer less. (Putnam, 2007: 150–151, author's emphasis)

Putnam has been unfairly criticized for emphasizing the "downside" of diversity. What his research shows, however, is that, in the longer run, successful US immigrant communities have overcome the initial "hunkering down" phase by creating new, cross-cutting forms of social solidarity and more encompassing identities.

A unifying theme in scholarship on the multi-ethnic city, including work in the expanding field of "intercultural studies", is that race relations are complex, dynamic and socially constructed (Ben-Tovim et al., 1986; Landis et al., 2004). Particularly important for this chapter, is that there is a growing body of literature suggesting that the negotiation of intercultural understanding occurs – if it occurs at all – *at a very local level*. Cities may well be sites of ethnic conflict, but it is also the case that urban neighborhoods provide opportunities to build intercultural understanding.

FROM URBAN GOVERNMENT TO URBAN GOVERNANCE

In this section, we explore the movement from "government" to "governance" – a shift that appears to be taking place in many countries. The phrase "urban governance" is now very familiar in both public policy and academic debates about cities and city regions, but this has not always been the case. Back in the 1970s and 1980s, analysts would be more likely to talk of "local government" and/or "urban management". A number of scholars have contributed to the urban government/urban governance debate. Stone (1989), in his classic study of governing coalitions in Atlanta, influenced a generation of urban scholars. And Di Gaetano and Klemanski (1999) made an important early international, contribution to the field of urban governance, with their comparative study of power in selected cities in the United States and the UK. Over the last decade or so the literature examining the shift from urban government to urban governance has grown significantly (McCarney and Stren, 2003; Denters and Rose, 2005; Hambleton and Gross, 2007; Davies and Imbroscio, 2009; Peters, 2011).

But what do these terms mean? For the purpose of this discussion *government* refers to the formal institutions of the state. Government makes decisions within specific administrative and legal frameworks and uses public resources in a financially accountable way. Most important, government decisions are backed up by the legitimate hierarchical power of the state. *Governance*, on the other hand, involves government *plus* the looser processes of influencing and negotiating with a range of public and private sector agencies to achieve desired outcomes. A governance perspective encourages collaboration between the public, private and non-profit sectors to achieve mutual goals. Whilst the hierarchical power of the state does not vanish, the emphasis in governance is on steering, influencing and coordinating the actions of others.

Moving to the local level, *local government* refers to democratically elected authorities. *Local governance* is broader – it refers to the processes and structures of a variety of public, private, and community and voluntary sector bodies at the local level. It acknowledges the diffusion of responsibility for collective provision and recognizes the contribution of different levels and sectors. This argument suggests that approaches to leadership and public service management that may have served societies well in the past will need to be updated to meet the needs of changing times.

Elsewhere, I have argued that to contrast two "schools" – the pro "government" school and the pro "governance" school – runs the risk of presenting a caricature of a more complex political debate (Hambleton, 2007). However, for the purposes of our discussion here, this juxtaposition will suffice. A key theme in these debates concerns the degree to which elected city governments are able to exercise democratic control over what happens to their cities and the people living in them. Some scholars argue that locally elected politicians can do little to shape the fortunes of their city – for example, Peterson (1981) argues that cities must serve powerful economic interests if they are to prosper. Others take the view that "place-based" power can be significant (Savitch and Kantor, 2002; Heinelt et al., 2006).

The move to "governance" approaches is important for our discussion of the multi-cultural city as it raises questions about the effectiveness of local democracy. Several studies – in, for example, the UK and the United States – have shown that the new kinds of partnership created to advance collaboration between different stakeholders in the city lack transparency. Worse than that, it would seem that urban "public/private partnerships" and "special authorities" are becoming increasingly undemocratic and authoritarian (Davies, 2007; Judd and Smith, 2007). We can, then, raise a concern about the degree to which elected local authorities are able to have a decisive impact on the life chances of their residents, whether or not the residents are long established or newly arrived. Certainly we need to recognize that powerful global economic forces limit the power of the local state and partly explain the continuing existence of major inequalities in cities.

STRENGTHENING CIVIC LEADERSHIP

We now turn to our second theme of civic leadership, which is used here to refer to all leadership activity that serves a public purpose in a given locality. Civic leadership is "place-based" leadership – meaning that those exercising decision-making power have a concern for the communities living in a particular "place". Some of the most powerful decision-makers in modern society are "place-less" leaders in the sense that they are not concerned with the geographical impact of their decisions (Ranney, 2003). Following Stiglitz, who draws on Putnam, I take the view that an unfettered market, especially in the context of globalization, can destroy communities (Stiglitz, 2006). There is now a substantial body of literature on "social capital" and the role that it plays in fostering a caring society (Putnam, 2000; Gilchrist, 2004). There are different kinds of social capital and sometimes this capital can be used to exclude groups – the creation of social capital will not necessarily reduce socio-economic inequalities. However, with the right kind of civic leadership, of which more in a moment, it may be possible to encourage the bridging of social ties between different social groups.

Civic leadership is inspirational and collaborative. In previous work, I have defined leadership as "shaping emotions and behaviour to achieve common goals" (Hambleton, 2007: 174). This implies a wide range of activities aimed at generating both new insights and new ways of working together – it prizes respect for the feelings and attitudes of others as well as a strong commitment to collaboration.

Civic leaders are found in the public, private, and community/voluntary sectors and they operate at many geographical levels – from the street block to an entire subregion and beyond. Three kinds of civic leadership can be distinguished:

> *Political leadership* – referring to the work of those people elected to leadership positions by the citizenry. These are, by definition, political leaders. Thus, all elected local councilors are political leaders, although we should acknowledge that different councilors carry different roles and responsibilities and will view their political role in different ways. Also we should note that countries vary in their local electoral arrangements. Some have directly elected mayors and some have separate elections for politicians who are charged with governing particular services – for example, some countries have elected school boards and/or directly elected police chiefs.

Managerial/professional leadership – referring to the work of public servants appointed by local authorities, central government and third sector organizations to plan and manage public services, and promote community wellbeing. These officers are *not* elected – rather they are appointed to their positions because they bring professional and/or managerial expertise to the tasks of local governance.

Community and business leadership – referring to the work of the many civic-minded people who give their time and energy to local leadership activities in a wide variety of ways. These may be community activists, business leaders, voluntary sector leaders, figures in religious organizations, higher education leaders, and so on. Particularly important here is the potential contribution to civic leadership of an independent and engaged voluntary and community sector. In multi-cultural cities the role of immigrant community leaders is particularly important.

These roles are all important in cultivating and encouraging public service innovation and, crucially, they overlap. The areas of overlap between these different realms of leadership can be described as "innovation zones" – areas providing many opportunities for innovation – see Figure 8.1. This is because different perspectives are brought together within these zones and this can enable active questioning of established approaches. If mishandled processes of dialogue in these spaces can become "conflict zones" with little listening taking place. This is where civic leadership can play a vital role – in shifting the focus to learning and innovation and away from dispute and fear (Kahane, 2004).

This framework is elaborated elsewhere (Hambleton, 2009; Hambleton et al., 2009; Hambleton and Howard, 2012). For our purposes an important point to note is that inspirational, civic leadership can emanate from any of the three realms of leadership. Elected politicians can exercise a critical role but so, too, can community leaders operating outside the state. It is also the case that appointed officers – for example, an inspiring city manager or service director, a neighborhood manager or area police officer – can set the tone of local leadership. The role of managers and professionals in local civic leadership is often undervalued. Officers can work closely with political figures and community stakeholders to bring about transformative change. In particular, street-level workers can play a key role in promoting dialogue over time that stimulates creative solutions to local problems. In the US context, Nalbandian (1991) has emphasized the importance of professional managers identifying, understanding and working with the values of their

Figure 8.1 Realms of civic leadership

local communities. And, in more recent work, he has shown how professionals can play a crucial role in promoting community involvement and, what he describes as, "civic discovery" (Nalbandian 2007: 197) – of which more in a moment.

The UK Coalition Government, formed in May 2010, advocates the development of a "Big Society" (HM Government, 2010a, b, 2011). The central idea is to encourage communities to help themselves, rather than rely on a continuing expansion of state-run services (Norman, 2010; Tuddenham, 2010). In theory, this approach could promote an outpouring of local activism in British society. But three weaknesses in the Coalition Government's approach can be identified. First, there are fears that the better off will be more successful in taking advantage of the opportunities for community-led initiatives that are opening up. Society may, therefore, become more unequal as a result. Second, some observers detect an anti-state philosophy in the approach the government has adopted thus far. They claim that the truly massive cuts in public spending that are now taking place in Britain are politically motivated rather than economically necessary. Third, the implications for local civic leadership, for the measures needed to make a reality of the "Big Society" notion in local communities, including multi-ethnic communities, have not been thought through.

This brings us back to the importance of promoting in, each locality, an authentic process of "civic discovery". For Nalbandian (2007), the task is not just to close the gaps between those striving to improve administrative effectiveness, and those concerned to express passions and feelings derived from the lived experience of the city. It is to create bridges of deliberative thought and action that engage traditional democratic values – representation, efficiency, social equity, and individual rights – with conflicts in values that lie at the root of many difficult issues faced by local communities. Fortunately, there is considerable evidence of experience with public deliberation that new approaches to locality leadership can draw on (Fischer, 1993; Roberts, 2004; Cornwall, 2008). We will return to this theme shortly, but first, we examine the value of adopting a very local approach when trying to comprehend life in the multi-cultural city.

UNDERSTANDING RACE AND ETHNICITY: A LOCAL PERSPECTIVE

In the spring and summer of 2001, civil unrest erupted in three northern cities in England – Oldham, Bradford, and Burnley. These were not the first urban race riots in Britain – the first example of this kind of disturbance took place in Bristol in April 1980, an event that was to be followed in 1981 by a series of urban riots in London, Liverpool, and elsewhere (Scarman Report, 1981).[3] The 2001 troubles provided a shocking reminder of the existence of racism and cultural intolerance in Britain and led to a further round of research and analysis (Ouseley Report, 2001). In his insightful study of ethnicity in the multi-cultural city, Amin (2002) notes that, while much of the UK debate about racial and ethnic relations was taking place at a national level, the really important negotiations of difference were taking place at the very local level. This very local dimension still tends to be neglected in current debates, and I draw directly on his analysis in the discussion below in an effort to illuminate the street level dynamics of local politics in the multi-cultural city.

First, Amin notes that there was no shortage of heated public discussion in the UK following the 2001 riots. There was alarm at the scale of urban deprivation and ethnic segregation in these poor industrial cities, growing Islamophobia, and widespread criticism of the national allegiances of British Muslims. This reached fever pitch after the terrorist attacks on the World Trade Centre in New York City and the Pentagon in Washington DC on September 11, 2001. Racist organizations, such as the

British National Party (BNP), took advantage of the situation to stir up resentment in white working-class communities. Amin notes that, while there was a good deal of excellent research available to inform national public policy debates, there was rather less evidence available on the daily negotiation of ethnic difference – on the micro-politics of everyday social contact and encounter. His study set out to fill this gap. It examines the forces behind entrenched ethnic suspicion and examines the dynamics of deprivation, segregation and changing youth cultures (Back, 1996).

An attractive feature of this study is that Amin does not just examine the causes of the urban riots, he also attempts to outline the possibilities for urban "interculturalism". One line of thought that he examines in depth has its roots in republican urban theory. Here the argument goes that the city needs to provide visibility for different groups and opportunities for encounter between strangers – in cafes, parks, streets, shopping malls, squares, community projects, and so on. He states:

> The political implication is that the gains of interaction need to be worked at in local sites of everyday encounter. But there is no formula here other than perhaps the engineering of [...] interaction between adversaries or provision for individuals to broaden horizons, because any intervention needs to work through, and is only meaningful in, a situated social dynamic. (Amin, 2002: 969)

A connection can be made here between this analysis of ethnic relations and the notion of "innovation zones" set out in Figure 8.1. The innovation zones in this model can take many different forms and need to be suited to local circumstances. However, a key aim is to create safe settings within which people can hear the views of others who differ from themselves and explore new possibilities. In Amin's terms such zones can create moments of cultural destabilization, offering individuals the chance to break out of fixed relations and fixed positions and, through this, learn to become different through new patterns of social interaction. Amin draws on an array of other research on multi-culturalism, including work in Leicester by Vertovec (1996), to advocate multiple modes of minority representation at the interface with local government:

> This is a democracy based on widespread bottom-up organization that, in addition to supporting multi-cultures, yields checks, balances, and overlaps between associations and a local state, thus nourishing a common public culture. (Amin, 2002: 974–975).

From this brief discussion we can surmise that what elected local governments actually do can make a great deal of difference to the way multi-culturalism is experienced in a city. Is the representative bureaucracy creating new political spaces that strengthen ethnic minority engagement or not?

BUILDING EMPOWERED COMMUNITIES

The objective of enhancing community empowerment – defined broadly – can be advanced by developing sound arrangements for both "representative" democracy and "participatory" democracy. A high quality approach to both these aspects of democracy is needed if community empowerment, including the empowerment of ethnic minorities, is seen as an important objective (Taylor, 2003; Gaventa et al., 2007; Cornwall, 2008).

Representative Democracy

If we take "representative" democracy first we can note the importance of: encouraging a diversity of people to stand for public office; having representative structures that are clear to citizens; securing a respectable turnout in local elections; ensuring elected politicians (whether mayors, aldermen or councilors) are well supported in exercising their various representative roles; having a sufficient number of politicians to represent the different communities in the city; and for the decision-making arrangements within the city governments to be sufficiently decentralized to enable politicians in different areas of the city to be responsive to the varying needs of different localities.

A key issue, discussed elsewhere in this volume, concerns the voting rights of immigrants (see chapter by Herrschel). We can note that, in some countries, immigrants have few political rights and this can work against efforts to bring about social integration at the local level. In France, for example, immigrants have, over the years, been politically marginalized. This process of exclusion undoubtedly contributed to the civil unrest which took place in the poor suburbs of Paris and a number of other French cities in 2005, 2006, and 2007 (Meier and Hawes, 2009). Sadly, it seems little has been done to rectify matters (Chrisafis, 2010). This is troubling as research on the degree to which ethnic minorities engage in local elections suggests that immigrants do participate if sensitive policies designed to reach out to excluded groups are pursued – Copenhagen provides a notable example (Gross, 2007).

These concerns relating to the quality of representative local government are, of course, familiar to policy makers, local government politicians, officers, and community activists. An excellent review of the changing roles of New Zealand councilors is, for example, provided by Drage (2008). This analysis explains how it is important for New Zealand councilors to be supported in developing new skills as community leaders – and we have referred to some of these in the discussion of civic leadership above – and, at the same time, to assist councilors stay connected to their communities. Her study examines themes that are relevant to debates taking place in a number of countries.

In 2006, the UK Government established a Councillors Commission to review the incentives and barriers to people standing and serving as councilors (i.e. local politicians). Chaired by a very experienced councilor – Dame Jane Roberts – the Commission reported in December 2007 (Councillors Commission, 2007). The "Roberts Report" rejected calls for full time professional councilors – with Dame Jane arguing in at least one interview that "Councillors need to be reasonably normal human beings". Research carried out for the Commission found that most councilors in the UK are white, male and retired, and a key theme in the Roberts Report concerns the need to reach a better balance across class, age, ethnicity, and gender in the makeup of the typical council. Again, it seems likely that this study provides insights that could be useful to other countries.

Indeed, in the US context, Checkoway (2009) argues for both "descriptive representation", which aims to replicate the socially descriptive characteristics of the population, and "substantive representation", which emphasizes the behavior of representatives (whatever their ethnic background). In adopting this approach he is following the helpful distinction made by Mosher (1968) between passive and active representation. A bureaucracy that is passively representative has a composition that mirrors the population – in terms of race, social class, ethnicity, religion, gender – it is there to serve. A bureaucracy is actively representative if it advocates the interests of a given segment of society. Meier and Hawes (2009) provide a thoughtful analysis of the interplay between these two conceptions of representation.

In Chapter 6, Peters examines the way some ethnic groups have been able to secure positions in city government by means of the patronage system and this has been a significant factor historically. A striking feature of US urban politics in the last 40 years or so is the growth in the number of African American and Hispanic politicians. This is partly because suburban white flight has left many American cities with majority African American and Hispanic populations. But it is also because inspirational leaders from ethnic minorities have come forward to run for office and have become role models for younger would-be politicians. For example, the following African Americans made significant breakthroughs by becoming the first black mayor in the following cities: Coleman Young, Detroit, 1973; Maynard Jackson, Atlanta, 1973; Harold Washington, Chicago, 1983; and Kurt Schmoke, Baltimore, 1987.

Participatory Democracy

Turning to the theme of "participatory" democracy we can, again, record that there have been significant advances in local governments across the world.

The movement towards "New Public Management" in the 1990s, which took different forms in the different countries where it was tried out, sometimes resulted in a narrowing of thinking in relation to community involvement. In many instances public service providers were encouraged, even required, to redefine service users as "consumers" or "customers", not "citizens" with democratic rights.

Previous research on neighborhood management and community involvement in the UK suggests that, to be effective as instruments of community empowerment, community boards (and similar innovations, like area committees and neighborhood forums) must have significant decision-making power (Burns et al., 1994; Taylor, 2003, 2007). This research has also shown that there is no contradiction between enhancing the representative role of local politicians and community empowerment – successful models blend the two approaches. For example, participatory budgeting, in some versions at least, can achieve this creative mix of representative and participatory democracy (Wainwright, 2003).

If we accept the argument advanced earlier that a successful approach to multi-cultural challenges needs to pay attention to the *very local* lived experiences of residents, we can surmise that innovation with neighborhood management and/or government offers a promising way forward for social inclusion. An interesting example of a neighborhood approach is provided by the Quartiermanagement (QM) program set up by the Berlin Senate in 1999. Initially focused on 15 neighborhoods, most of them with a high migrant population, this program introduced local consultation processes designed to increase the shared ownership of policies. QM areas are served by local teams of officers and control a "resident fund", a form of participatory budgeting. The evidence suggests that the QM approach has increased participation by migrants and immigrants significantly (Eurocities, 2010a).

Urban Policies and Practices to Accommodate Diversity

City governments have, over the years, taken steps to respond to the changing needs of diverse population groups living within their boundaries. This can be quite a challenge because, as mentioned in the Introduction, many cities have been faced with a very rapid influx of large numbers of newcomers from foreign lands. It is fair to say that this "dynamic diversity" has come close to overwhelming local public service bureaucracies in some cities. In response to these challenges, Eurocities, a network of more than 140 major European cities, set out to develop a new strategy for accommodating diversity and this resulted in the organization agreeing the *Integrating Cities Charter* in 2010. This Charter seeks to build a positive two-way engagement between newcomers and established residents. The Charter states:

> The greatest challenge we face is polarization and conflict between newcomers and established residents when integration fails [...] Our vision of integration is one where all city residents can develop their full potential and have an equal chance of a life in safety and dignity [...] This Integrating Cities Charter harnesses our duties and responsibilities as policy-makers, service providers, employers and buyers of goods and services to provide equal opportunities for all residents, to integrate migrants, and to embrace the diversity of the population that is a reality in our cities. (Eurocities, 2010b)

In this section we draw on the study prepared by Eurocities to underpin the Charter (Eurocities, 2010a). We discuss briefly the three main strategies that progressive cities are using to promote diversity and equality in their cities: (1) cities as policy makers and service providers, (2) cities as employers, and (3) cities as buyers of goods and services. There are some overlaps between these categories but, as revealed by the Eurocities report, these headings can provide a helpful way of benchmarking performance in relation to diversity and can stimulate fresh thinking in relation to what European cities call their "local integration strategies" (meaning their efforts to embrace diversity, create equal opportunities and harness the benefits of a diverse population).

Cities as Policy-makers and Service Providers

The first point to stress is that cities need to be committed to welcoming diversity and advancing equality. However, even when policy commitments are in place, there can be a gap between the commitment and the day-to-day practice carried out at street level. The Eurocities report has numerous suggestions on how to tackle this "implementation gap". These include:

requiring heads of departments to translate commitments into explicit guidelines for each staff position; introducing equality impact assessments to ascertain compliance with anti-discrimination policy commitments; recording the experience of service users with a migrant background; consulting citizens with a migrant background; and adapting a variety of services to the needs of populations with a migrant background.

The Eurocities report expresses some concerns about the preparedness of city bureaucracies to respond to the diversity agenda:

> In some cities, the lack of a coherent system to register and treat complaints about discrimination is another challenge [...] cities do not always have the information that would allow them to assess how accessible their services are [...] This in turn means that the development of services cannot be based on a solid analysis of the needs. (Eurocities, 2010a: 10)

However, the main purpose of the report is to identify examples of promising innovation. It notes that the City of Amsterdam publishes a "State of the City" report every 2 years. The data gathered to underpin these reports allows the city to understand if citizens with a migrant background have similar experiences to others. It also highlights the relatively successful Quartiermanagement (QM) program in Berlin, referred to earlier. It is encouraging to note that local governments across the world are now working in a variety of ways, often with local voluntary bodies, to adapt policies and practices to the needs of the multi-cultural city. Local, national, and supranational governments have created web based resources that can support these innovation efforts.[4]

Cities as Employers

A second way in which cities can respond to multi-cultural challenges is by using their power as employers. There are various elements to such a strategy. An important one in many multi-cultural cities involves attempting to employ a workforce that reflects the diversity of the population it serves. This is not only desirable from the point of view of social justice, it also enhances public service effectiveness as service providers can build up a better understanding of service user needs. The Eurocities report makes it clear that national legislation is critical in this area. In some countries cities are actively encouraged to achieve this "mirror effect" between those working in and those being served by public services. In other countries the national legislation may actually prevent this – for example, some European countries do not allow non-EU nationals to be employed by public bodies. To advance this approach cities should adopt creative approaches to recruitment – for example, advertising positions in outlets read by ethnic minorities – and should monitor the ethnic profile of their employees.

A second strand in relation to cities as employers is to increase the intercultural awareness of city administration staff. Efforts are taking place in some universities to develop courses relating to "intercultural competencies" and many city halls have their own in-house training programs (Landis et al., 2004; Benavides and Hernandez 2007). However, there appears to be considerable uncertainty about the precise nature of intercultural skills and this has hindered the development of indicators that can be used in staff recruitment and promotion. Clearly, it makes sense to draw in experts with a migrant background to provide intercultural training and development.

Other steps can also be taken – for example, cities can record the experience of treatment of staff with a migrant background, build diversity and equality principles into job specifications, review the composition of interview panels, and encourage and support diversity "role models".

Cities as Buyers of Goods and Services

The third route to reform identified by the Eurocities report is to use diversity and equal opportunity principles in the public procurement process. This is an area of policy that is not highly developed and, in some countries, there may be legal obstacles to this approach. First, the city needs to discover "diversity information" about the firms they contract with or may contract with. Defenders of this strategy argue that a city stands to gain benefits in economic growth and social cohesion if it can ensure that migrant-owned businesses have equal access to public contracts. For example, Leeds City Council in the UK examined the council's supply chain and its workforce in 2009 and the survey findings have helped the city assess how open and transparent its procurement practice is. The city has also developed a guide for prospective contractors to help them comply with their equality duties under the law and with the council's policy in this field.

REFLECTIONS AND POINTERS

This chapter has suggested that ethnic diversity is increasing in modern society, particularly in urban areas, and that this has important implications for the civic leadership and local governance of cities. This final section highlights three sets of reflections or pointers for further consideration. But, before that, we should revisit the notion of "place-less" power. It has been suggested in this chapter that some of the most powerful leaders in modern society are "place-less" leaders who care not a jot about the impact of their decisions on particular communities. Ranged against these distant figures are place-based leaders – leaders who *do care* about the social consequences of their decisions for communities living in particular localities. Indeed, the main normative conclusion flowing from the analysis presented in this chapter is that place-based power – the power of localities to shape their own futures rather than serve place-less interests – should be strengthened. But what if citizens don't care about the place they live in? What if they are "here today, gone tomorrow"?

This is not a fatuous point. Within the literature on the so-called "creative class" it has been suggested that a young, well-educated group of people has emerged – perhaps 150 million worldwide – who might be thought of as modern urban nomads. These highly mobile individuals "participate in a global technology system and a global labour market, both of which allow them to migrate more freely among the world's leading cities" (Florida, 2008: 30). These "place-less" citizens, so the argument goes, are unlikely to develop a commitment to any particular locality and cannot be expected to engage in place-based decision-making. In some respects this suggestion reprises an argument that has been familiar in the literature of urban planning for over 40 years. Webber (1968: 146), in a prescient essay, argued that the "enlarged freedom to communicate outside one's place-community that the emerging technological and institutional changes promise, coupled with an ever-increasing mobility and ever-greater degrees of specialization, will certainly mean that urbanites will deal with each other over greater and greater distances".

To argue for a strengthening of place-based power is, however, not to contest the view that a growing number of citizens are active members of communities and networks that are international, if not global. There will be many in this fortunate group who enjoy meaningful, regular and highly productive relationships with people who are thousands of miles away. My point, however, is that most of these people still live somewhere. There are, I would argue, very few people who care not a jot about the place where they live. The highly paid, cosmopolitan nomads have some kind of interest in the place where they reside, even if they are not going to be there very long. More important, the argument about the emergence of place-less citizens does not speak in a compelling way to the daily, lived experience of the vast majority of the world population – particularly when one considers the lives of children and older people.

Place matters in social life, not just as the context and the substantive focus of much activity in civil society, but also as a source (in part at least) of identity for many people, and even as a source of ontological security, or selfhood, for some.

What lessons or pointers emerge from the analysis presented in this chapter? First, it is clear that place-based leadership matters. As part of this, it is evident that elected politicians can exercise a critical role in setting the tone for race relations in a city or, indeed, a country. President Obama of the United States provides an inspiring example of this kind of leadership. When campaigning for the US Presidency, he gave a remarkable speech on race relations on March 18, 2008, in Philadelphia which saw "both sides of the race debate" (Wolffe, 2009: 178). In his speech, which reduced thousands to tears, he set out the choice that continues to present itself to all civic leaders:

> For we have a choice in this country. We can accept a politics that breeds division, and conflict, and cynicism [...] Or, at this moment, in this election, we can [...] talk about the shuttered mills that once provided a decent life for men and women of every race, and the homes for sale that once belonged to Americans from every religion, every region, every walk of life. This time we want to talk about the fact that the real problem is not that someone who doesn't look like you might take your job; it's that the corporation you work for will ship it overseas for nothing more than profit. (Obama, 2008)

Barack Obama captured the mood of the nation and went on to win a spectacular victory in the national election later that year.

In this chapter it, has been suggested that, given the growth of "place-less" power in our rapidly globalizing world, it is becoming increasingly important to strengthen *place-based leadership*. This is because "place-less" leadership disregards the concerns of communities living in particular localities, and it rides roughshod over the rights of local people. A conceptual model for thinking about civic leadership in a given locality has been put forward – see Figure 8.1 – and this outlines three realms of civic leadership. This model suggests that inspirational, civic leadership can emanate from any of the three realms – elected politicians, paid public servants, or from civil society.

But are there limits to place-based leadership? The answer is "yes". It is important to recognize that the argument should not be taken to the extreme. Untrammelled "place-based" power can work against good race relations. For example, if neighborhoods are granted massive authority to rule their areas we can be sure that the rich and selfish will be quick to ensure that people who differ from themselves are excluded. Indeed, as documented by Davis (1992), Minton (2009), and others, the growth of privatized "gated communities" is a worrying international urban trend. The creation of privatized communities with high walls and security guards could be described as an example of "place-based" leadership. In this case the residents of the fortified enclaves strive to secure the success of their "place" in what they consider to be an increasingly hostile urban environment. This is *not* what I am advocating when I argue for a strengthening of "place-based" leadership. Rather, following Frederickson (2005), I am suggesting that politicians, professionals and community activists should be guided by "instincts of appropriateness" and what is understood to be right and fair.

Second, the institutional design of local governance arrangements matters. Structures, constitutions and decision-making processes are not the whole story when it comes to defining "good governance", but it is misguided to believe that they are irrelevant. Institutional design can either hinder or promote effective and accountable civic leadership, public involvement and place shaping (Hambleton and Sweeting, 2004). Thus, governance arrangements can foster inclusion of excluded voices or do the opposite. A warning note has been sounded about the shift from government to governance. Privatized forms of urban governance, sometimes advanced in the name of "public–private partnership working", can erode the corrigibility of decision-making. A risk with these models is that, "behind closed doors" local leaders become servants of "place-less" leaders to the disadvantage of their communities.

The discussion of representative democracy and participatory democracy within cities has suggested that these are not mutually exclusive approaches. On the contrary, they need to be pursued together if urban democracy is to respond to the needs of ethnic minorities. Moreover, given the importance of very local matters in shaping the quality of life, it would seem that the design of governance arrangements at the neighborhood level is a particularly promising avenue for development. Many cities have introduced, and/or are introducing, new systems of neighborhood governance, often involving local participatory budgeting, in an effort to ensure that decision-making is more responsive to the needs of different communities of interest and place. These efforts should be assessed and lessons shared.

Third, it seems clear that public service innovation – defining it, understanding it, developing practical ideas on how to promote it – is a very important topic now, not just for urban government and governance, but also for all those concerned with public services as a whole. There is light-weight thinking in this area and more than a little lofty rhetoric. Scholars can play an important role in advancing thinking about public service innovation and helping public service leaders move beyond performance management regimes that seem to be increasingly outdated. The emergence of major, new challenges for governments – notably climate change and the economic recession – give added weight to this argument.

The civic leadership model advanced in this chapter advocates a *political*, as opposed to a managerial, approach to public service innovation.[5] It has suggested that the overlaps between the different realms of civic leadership can provide "innovation zones" in which new ideas can be explored and tried out. In the multi-cultural city it goes without saying that it is imperative that the creation and design of these new spaces for interaction are shaped by local people. This will require risk taking by both political and managerial, public service leaders.

These three sets of pointers have important implications for leadership development programs at local, regional and national levels. For much of the time countries are investing in a "silo" approach to public leadership analysis and development. Civic leadership development, if it is supported at all, tends to be handled separately within each of the three realms of civic leadership set out in Figure 8.1. A consequence is that breakthrough educational practice linking leaders from the different realms of leadership together in a shared process of social discovery is sorely under developed in universities and elsewhere.

The civic leadership conceptual framework presented in this chapter highlights the dynamic interplay between those operating in different realms. Effective "place-based" leadership involves actors from the different realms – people with different backgrounds and experiences – building new kinds of relationship. Moreover, this chapter has suggested that successful innovation often involves the empowerment of local communities in intriguing new ways. It follows that the public service innovation agenda is enmeshed in important ways with the revitalizing local democracy agenda. Inspiring place-based leadership is needed to ensure that public service innovation and community empowerment can thrive.

City leaders now operate in a world of shared power and this requires new approaches. The leadership challenge for modern city leaders is to steer a path between two evils. They need to ensure that communities are not exploited by distant, "place-less" decision-makers and, just as important, they need to guard against the development of self interested neighborhoods that become "no go" areas for people with the "wrong" skin color or cultural background.

ACKNOWLEDGMENTS

The author wishes to thank the following experienced local government officers for their advice and comments: Ceta Ramkhalawansingh, Manager, Diversity and Community Engagement, City of Toronto; and Michael Keating, National Advisor for Equalities and Cohesion, Local Government Improvement and Development, UK.

NOTES

1. A note on definitions. In this chapter I use terms in the following way: 'multi-cultural' and 'multi-ethnic' to refer to groups of people comprising individuals from several cultures and/or ethnic groups (including individuals who ascribe themselves to more than one group); the term 'diversity' (in a social, cultural, and demographic sense) to refer to a society made up of individuals from different national, racial, or ethnic backgrounds; and the term 'equality' to refer to an absence of discrimination motivated by nationality, race and/or ethnic origin, gender, sexuality, or age.
2. It is true that immigrants sometimes relocate to rural areas in the country they have moved to – this could be to secure employment in agriculture (e.g. crop picking). However, the vast majority of immigrants set out to start a new life in a foreign city. This is partly for economic reasons and partly because it is in the city that they are more likely to be able to find others with a similar ethnic background.
3. The Scarman Report was, in many ways, the UK equivalent of the US Kerner Report (1968) into civil disorders that took place in American cities.
4. A good starting point is provided by the Eurocities initiative: www.integratingcities.eu.
5. Many writers and consultants advocate a managerial approach to public service innovation, often built around the use of new communication technologies (Tidd et al., 2005). These approaches can play a role in improving service responsiveness, but radical change requires political, rather than managerial, thinking because significant shifts in power are necessary.

9. From plutocracy to diversity: the (de)construction of representative bureaucracy theory

Bas van Gool

INTRODUCTION

This chapter traces the origin and evolution of a small body of argument, speculation and research in public administration and political science known as representative bureaucracy theory. It documents its transformation, over almost seven decades, from a descriptive Marxist theory of bureaucracy to an empirically grounded set of normative arguments that public organizations should be "diverse", or look like the population they serve.

Though scientists like to believe so, the development of a science, or a body of literature, is never the piecemeal process by which facts, theories and methods accumulate and add to an ever-growing stockpile of scientific knowledge. "An apparently arbitrary element", as Thomas Kuhn observed almost 50 years ago, "compounded of personal and historical accident, is always a formative ingredient of the beliefs espoused by a given scientific community at a given time" (Kuhn, 1970). The *parcours de route* of representative bureaucracy theory amply illustrates his point.

Kuhn stressed the arbitrariness produced by elements *internal* to the scientific enterprise – traditions of research, training, and evaluation. The evolution of representative bureaucracy theory, however, appears to have been largely influenced by political, economic and social developments *outside* it. In fact, many of the big "isms" of the past century – communism, fascism, Marxism, McCarthyism, racism – directly or indirectly fed into the initial formulation and subsequent directions of representative bureaucracy theory and research and helped define what was to be studied and why.

This chapter is further organized as follows. Section two deals with J. Donald Kingsley's initial formulation of representative bureaucracy theory in his 1944 book on British bureaucracy and traces the heavy influence of the Marxist political theorist Harold Laski on Kingsley's argument. Kingsley, an American, wrote for an American academic audience which failed, initially at least, to be enthused by his work. Section three accounts for this cold reception in the early Cold War. Section four discusses the subsequent rise of a new, Americanized version of representative bureaucracy theory from the late 1960s onwards. This belated response coincided with what John Skrentny has called the "minority rights revolution", which shaped the normative commitments, conceptual apparatus, and research focus of a new generation of representative bureaucracy scholars. Section five reconstructs the rise of the "passive-to-active" stream in the second wave of representative bureaucracy scholarship and explains the remarkable shift from widespread skepticism over active representation to its embrace in the 1990s.

LASKIAN ROOTS

Now almost forgotten, Harold J. Laski (1893–1950) was one of the most influential political theorists, publicists and public speakers of his time. Laski taught at Harvard, Montreal, and the London School of Economics and wrote prolifically on a wide range of subjects for a vast intellectual audience across the globe. Laski was also active in leftist politics and served for many years as a member of the Executive Committee of the British Labour Party. In this and his other capacities he had the attention and ear of prominent contemporary and future leaders in Britain, the United States, the Continent, and the countries of Asia and Africa. After successive ideological commitments to pluralism and Fabianism in the 1920s, Laski finally developed his own brand of Marxist socialism in the 1930s. It exercised great appeal, especially among young people and students, who flocked to him in large numbers (Deane, 1972; Kramnick and Sheerman, 1993; Newman, 2009).

One of these was J. Donald Kingsley, a young scholar from the United States (PhD, Syracuse University) who spent 2 years in Europe in the 1930s on a scholarship from the Social Science Research Council. Kingsley's research culminated in a book on the British civil service. The book went on to become a minor classic in public administration and marked the start of the study of "representative bureaucracy", after the book's title (Kingsley, 1944). In its preface Kingsley confessed to a heavy debt to his friend and teacher Harold Laski. There was, wrote Kingsley, "scarcely a section which has escaped the impact of his ideas."

These were not gratuitous words. Kingsley's book *breathed* Laski's thought, particularly Laski's theory of the state. After advocating less state (in his pluralist days) and more state (in his Fabian days), Marxist Laski – who inspired Kingsley – had come to view the state as an inherently biased institution and a major obstacle on the road to faith, reason, and civilization. In essence, Laski's theory was quite simple: the basic factor in any society is the way it earns its living – the economy – since all societal relations are built upon it. For the economy (and society) to be sustained, it must be protected by the force of law. The instrument for the enforcement of law is usually the state, which acts through persons – the government – with the formal right to exercise sovereign power. In capitalist societies, in which the instruments of production are privately owned, the struggle for state power is by definition a struggle between *classes*; between those who own those instruments – capital – and those who are denied access to these and suffer continuous disadvantage – labor.

The state is never neutral in these struggles. It is always a *captured* state, biased to the interest of capital. The state puts its supreme coercive power at the service of this dominant class and its laws are so designed as to protect the prevailing class order. The state, in other words, is "the executive instrument of the class in society which owns the means of production". This class will not surrender the advantages of state control unless it is compelled to do so. This also goes for capitalist societies with democratic institutions. "Capitalist democracy", as Laski called it, can only exist as long as it does not threaten the "essential implications of capitalism". If it does, the dominant class is bound to use its state power, and violence, to suppress it (Laski, 1935; Deane, 1972: 154).

Capitalist democracy in England, according to Laski, provided an exemplary illustration of his "realist" account of the state. He berated the "eulogists" who attributed the continuity and success of representative government in Great Britain to "some special British genius for the difficult art of self-government". The real explanation, argued Laski, was rather more mundane. That democracy had thrived in England (a society "divided into the two nations of rich and poor") was simply because members of the governing class controlled its major institutions and "because the rules and habits in which they have confidence are those which do not disturb the social order they dominate" (Laski, 1938: 23). This thesis was central in Laski's *Parliamentary Government in England* (1938). In each of the chapters of this book he detailed the class logic in the operation of a specific British state institution. In the lengthy chapter on the civil service Kingsley's heavy debt to Laski becomes most apparent. Kingsley's main theoretical argument in *Representative Bureaucracy* is in fact a carbon copy of Laski's argument in this chapter.

Just like Laski, Kingsley argued that Britain was "only superficially a democracy" and had remained "essentially plutocratic". Plutocratic tendencies, Kingsley/Laski observed, were particularly prevalent in the civil service. Though a string of administrative reforms had gradually broken up the aristocratic monopoly over bureaucracy,[1] the British civil service continued to reflect "the basic inequalities of the social structure and the prevailing temper of the nation" (Kingsley, 1944: 141). "The opportunity to compete for appointment even to the Clerical Class", Kingsley calculated, "is restricted to about ten per cent of the youth of the nation, while the Administrative Class is drawn from a reservoir of considerably less than one per cent" (ibid.: 143). Also, "the fact that the service classes are linked to various rungs of the educational ladder means that each is drawn pretty largely from a distinct stratum of society [...] to a remarkable degree each Service class is also a social class – a caste – and the Service hierarchy pretty accurately mirrors the economic and social hierarchies outside" (ibid.: 148).

This mirroring effect did not surprise Kingsley. Like Laski, he assumed that administrative arrangements *always* tend to reflect the character of the social structure of a nation; that bureaucracy always represents the dominant class in society in terms of social derivation and social philosophy (cf. Meier, 1975; Bendix, 1945–6). Since British society was dominated by what Kingsley called "the middle class", it was "inevitable" that the bureaucracy, also, was dominated by this very class and that the composition of the bureaucracy resulted in a power structure which mirrored, or "represented", the power structure of society.

The mirroring effect, Kingsley argued, was not only inevitable but also, obviously, quite *useful* to the governing classes. It implied that they did not have to bother too much about bureaucracy's inevitable tendency towards autonomy and self-control. By way of being a mirror image of society British bureaucracy was namely "so constituted" that it could "be trusted to function within the framework of the common desires of the governing classes" (Kingsley, 1944: 186, 187). The reason why the bureaucracy had not been known to use the exceptional opportunities for sabotage offered by its administrative system, was because bureaucracy was *representative* of the powerful in society (ibid.: 16). "In England today", Kingsley wrote, "the bureaucracy is responsible because it is concerned with being so; and that concern is a reflection of its representative character" (ibid.: 274).

Kingsley thus put the famed impartiality of the British civil service in a new perspective. Impartiality, he argued, was not an inherent trait or virtue of the people who manned the British civil service but, rather, a conditional favor, in that it *presupposed* a "harmony of outlook" between civil servants and political executives. Without this basic agreement administrative discretion, said Kingsley, was bound to result in sabotage (cf. Bendix, 1945–6: 76): "[T]he essence of bureaucratic responsibility in the modern State is to be sought, not in the presumed and largely fictitious impartiality of the officials, but in the strength of their commitment to the purposes that the State is undertaking to serve [...]. The view of the Civil Servant as a disinterested assembler of facts simply will not stand examination" (Kingsley, 1944: 274–275; cf. Laski, 1938: 317). Hence, the essence of administrative impartiality was *loyalty* produced by common background, outlook and shared values, *not* civil service professionalism. British bureaucracy could *seem* neutral because its neutrality served the interests of the dominant class (MacMahon, 1946; Moulin, 1971).

Representative bureaucracy in terms of the dominant class served as an effective instrument of political control and thus ensured social harmony. Kingsley, in fact, considered representative bureaucracy the *only effective* instrument of political control. "By no other means", he claimed, "can an elaborate administrative machine be operated. By no other devices can the bureaucracy be controlled. Neither parliaments nor cabinets are adapted to the requirements of detailed or pervasive supervision" (Kingsley, 1944: 186).

Kingsley was apprehensive about British bureaucracy selectively catering to middle class interests and values. He considered the caste-like character of the civil service "antipathetic to political democracy" and "potentially of grave danger to the State". A caste-like civil service, he felt, hampers the "superior insight and wisdom" produced by "the pooling of diverse streams of experience" which defines "the superiority of the democratic Civil Service over its totalitarian rivals". He deplored the far-reaching and disastrous consequences of the linkage between civil service recruitment and education for civil service mentality and its outlook and orientation. "Snobbish" public school education, he felt, inculcated values such as conformity, valuation of good form and gentlemanly behavior over intelligence, conservatism, thirst for power (*fanatique du pouvoir*), formal and specialized education, particularly in subjects comprising "the medieval curriculum" (ancient languages, theology, pure mathematics). Public school education thus produced an "aristocratic contempt for useful knowledge", "amazing ignorance" of "the most elementary social conditions and problems", "a failure to penetrate the problems of those in other strata of society", and "a failure to see the world as a whole" (ibid.: 152–157). "An English gentleman", Kingsley quipped, echoing Laski's harsh vilification of this class (Laski, 1931, 1930), "is a bundle of specifically qualified reactions, a creature who for all the emergencies of life has his behaviour marked out for him in advance" (Kingsley, 1944: 157).

In order to stimulate the needed "interpenetration of class experience" and to overcome the lack of imaginative skepticism, experience, and passion for constructive innovation of the gentlemanly class, Kingsley's mentor Laski proposed "an infusion of lower grade ability into the upper hierarchy" (Laski, 1938: 336). He had no illusions about its materialization, however. Those who governed the civil service belonged to the same class that ruled the House of Commons, went to the same schools and universities, frequented the same clubs, and had the same ideas as those who owned the instruments of production. How could they feel any inclination to question the assumptions of the existing administrative system (ibid.: 16–17)?

Laski's defeatism was reinforced by his interpretation of the great political and economic developments of his time. The 1930s were the time of the Great Depression and the rise of fascism, of Hitler in Germany and Mussolini in Italy. To Laski, there was an intimate connection between the two. In his view the Depression was a sign of the demise of capitalism, and fascism the inevitable and dangerous political response to it, "the institutional technique of capitalism in its phase of contraction", as he called it (Laski, in Deane, 1972: 162). Declining profits necessitated the ruling class to use its suppressive state power to reduce wages, destruct trade unions, crush opposition parties, prohibit strikes, and abolish free elections. Fascism, according to Laski, inevitably appeared on the scene to rescue capitalism and destroy both socialism and democracy (Deane, 1972: 340–345).

In order to prevent fascist rule in England Laski advocated a "popular front" of Labour and the communists (along the lines of the Komintern) and remained just short of calling for a proletarian revolution. This pitted him against the Fabian gradualist Labour party leadership which believed that the ruling classes would continue to uphold democracy and that a socialist society could be established if only Labour gained control of the government. Laski thought this dangerously naïve. The capitalist class would never cooperate in the liquidation of the regime of private property and was bound to sabotage a new Labour government and its programs (ibid.: 203–204). After all, how could a new class possibly "use the institution of the class it proposes to dispossess to effect that change in residence?" (Laski, in Deane, 1972: 210).

Kingsley heavily drew upon Laski's above analysis and predictions when he argued his case for the practical impossibility of reform of the caste-like British bureaucracy. It could not be "readily disposed", he wrote, because "the conditioning factors are embedded deeply in the social structure of the nation" (Kingsley, 1944: 163). The Labour party, once in power, would surely experience the tangible limits of its vaunted neutrality (ibid.: 278–279).

A COLD RECEPTION

Kingsley's book was published in the United States in 1944 and addressed an American academic audience. In the first two decades after its publication *Representative Bureaucracy* was hardly noticed, however. It sparked the usual dutiful book reviews (Bendix, 1945–6; MacMahon, 1946) and a few passing comments by scholars writing on related issues (Long, 1952; Van Riper, 1958). Sociologist Alvin Gouldner borrowed the term "representative bureaucracy" in his *Patterns of Industrial Bureaucracy* (1954) but gave it an altogether new meaning (Gouldner, 1954: 24). Gouldner's study was typical in that none of these sporadic early engagements with Kingsley's book directly addressed its core argument.

It is not difficult to see why this was so. America in the late 1940s and 1950s was no place for Marxist analyses à la Kingsley and Laski. The uncertainty of the post-war economy, Soviet expansionism in Europe, and the USSR's entry to the nuclear club had brought a fear and paranoia for the alien ideology of communism which, as soon as the war was over, replaced fascism as the "ism" to oppose. US governments in the 1940s and 1950s conducted large-scale investigations and persecutions of Americans with suspected ties to Marxist organizations. Suspects were subjected to ideological interrogation by specially formed boards in loyalty and security hearings where they enjoyed but little protection. Normal court procedures did not apply, doubts as to loyalty were typically resolved in favor of the state. In America, these practices became known as McCarthyism, after the fanatical senator who chaired one of such boards (Badash, 2000; Price, 2004).

Academics were among the most prominent targets of McCarthyism (Schrecker, 1986; Price, 2004; Bellah, 2005; Badash, 2000). As educators they could influence opinion and as scientists they had power (they knew nuclear secrets, for example). University employees were made to sign anti-communist loyalty oaths. Those who refused were dismissed. Importantly, McCarthyism also impacted academics' work – the questions they asked, the theories they employed, the answers they gave, and the language they used. In the social sciences, where flirtations with communism and Marxism had been fashionable only a decade earlier (remember Kingsley), scholars quickly learned the art of self-censorship. Some adopted crypto-Marxist approaches (using Marxist analysis but not openly citing Marxist scholars), most abandoned Marxist approaches altogether. "As red-bating witch-hunts spread a generation of social scientists learned not to overtly think under the rubrics of Marxist critique" (Price, 2004: xiii).

The McCarthy era shattered Harold Laski's reputation as a political theorist. Denounced as an apologist for Stalinism and "the greatest communist propagandist of our time" (by McCarthy himself), his "crude Marxism" came to be considered a threat to national security. His work, influential and well-regarded only years before, became too hot to handle.[2] The parallel rise of positivism emboldened a new generation of scholars to further discredit Laski's brand of normative political philosophy as "mystic", "ideological", "unscientific", and "unimportant" (Lamb, 1999: 335; Kramnick and Sheerman, 1993: xiv). Coincidence or not, the early years of the Cold War also marked the end of J. Donald Kingsley's stay in academia. He went on to pursue an administrative career. And though he continued to write essays and reports (Kingsley, 1951, 1956, 1957, 1958; Rucker and Kingsley, 1961) he never returned to the topic of his 1944 book.

REPRESENTATIVE BUREAUCRACY AND THE MINORITY RIGHTS REVOLUTION

After Laski's discreditation (and death, in 1950) and Kingsley's departure from academia, "representative bureaucracy" seemed destined for oblivion. Interest in it gradually picked up by the end of the 1960s, however. Like the cold reception that preceded it, this renewed interest was intimately connected to the political currents and debates of the time.

Political scientist Samuel Krislov was among the first revivalists of representative bureaucracy. In *The Negro in Federal Employment* (1967) he dedicated a full chapter to it. The first few sentences of his book capture the mood of the moment:

> For over a decade our nation – our civilization – has been consciously engaged in a quest for social justice far-reaching enough to satisfy the most visionary dreamers of the American dream. That task has proven to be a conglomerate one; the effort to end legal and spatial segregation of our nonwhite citizens has in turn engendered a drive toward their dispersion by social class and occupation, toward an end to poverty-by-skin-color […]

> equal opportunity has become a litmus test for our entire society. Our progress toward it is being watched as a crucial indicator of the possibility of harmonious interrelations among different races (Krislov, 1967: 3).

"The quest for social justice" for "our nonwhite citizens" was a reference to the civil rights movement, which arose in the 1950s to represent disenfranchised blacks and press Congress to eliminate discrimination in all realms of life. The movement gained a major victory in 1964, when President Johnson signed the Civil Rights Act. The act outlawed discrimination in education, housing, public accommodations and employment on the basis of race, color, religion, sex, or national origin. The civil rights movement soon petered out afterwards, but not so the civil rights project. Much of its subsequent course, like Krislov's book, centered on the issue of discrimination in employment and the question how to combat it. Outlawing discrimination, after all, is not eliminating it. The solution which emerged in the early 1970s – "affirmative action" – provided the controversial policy frame within which the near-dead study of representative bureaucracy gained a new leash of life.

The Civil Rights Act presented some difficult problems for the newly created public watchdog agencies tasked to prevent and address charges of employment discrimination. They were severely understaffed and could not cope with the complaints of discrimination which came pouring in after the act's passage. The act explicitly forbade only *intentional* acts of discrimination, giving watchdog agencies the almost impossible job of discerning and proving employers' intentions. Moreover, the agencies' enforcement powers were quite limited. Thus condemned to do an impossible job badly they quickly came under mounting political pressure of disillusioned civil rights leaders to *do* something (Skrentny, 1996). Organizational survival was at stake.

In an effort to solve their problems the agencies introduced affirmative action. Instead of reactively handling individual cases they started to proactively monitor and target whole firms and organizations, even whole industries and areas. The bases for these interventions were not complaints of discrimination but *indications* of it. "Underutilization" (having fewer minorities in a particular job class than would reasonably be expected by their availability) was the primary indication. Watchdog agencies developed racial reporting systems (which had been taboo until then) to collect the needed statistics on employment practices and patterns. Employers who showed underutilization of minorities were given goals – quotas – and timetables so as to bring the percentage of their minority workforce in line with the total work force in the immediate labor area (Skrentny, 2002; Sowell, 2004). The courts upheld the agencies' new policy of affirmative action – despite the fact that it dissociated discrimination from any idea of intentionality (Sabbagh, 2003). Arguing that a facially neutral employment practice could nevertheless be discriminatory in its application or effect, they developed the doctrine of "disparate impact": employment practices may be considered discriminatory if they have a disproportionately "adverse impact" on members of a minority group.

First conceived by federal watchdog agencies in the early 1970s to eliminate employment discrimination for blacks, politicians and administrators then rapidly extended affirmative action to "groups" they considered to be *like* blacks ("nonwhite", that is, to use Krislov's terminology) and, hence, "disadvantaged". Thus arose America's present-day "minorities" – Latinos, Asian Americans, and American Indians. Equally rapidly, affirmative action expanded beyond employment, to business ownership and university admissions (Skrentny, 2002). Many firms, not quite sure where things were heading but anxious to avoid costly litigation, developed affirmative action programs of their own (Dobbin, 2009). The growth and expansion, between 1965 and 1975, of non-discrimination and affirmative action legislation and practices for "racial" minorities and – a little later – women, was so sudden and rapid that John Skrentny has called it America's "minority rights revolution" (Skrentny, 2002).

The operational, administrative language of the politicians and bureaucrats who crafted the minority rights revolution and its signature policy, affirmative action, was a language of *representation*, of (unjust) underrepresentation and (ideal) proportional representation. Given the issue prominence of employment discrimination, the primary objects of representational policy concern were organizations, both private (firms) and public (*bureaucracies*). No wonder that a number of political scientists and public administration scholars came to theoretically conceive of their professional interest in the political and policy developments of that time as one in "representative bureaucracy".

The theoretical discourse of these new students of representative bureaucracy was largely structured by the twin concepts of "passive" and "active" representation (Lim, 2006), introduced by Frederick Mosher, in 1968, to distinguish between two meanings of bureaucratic representation. Passive representation refers to "*the source of origin* of individuals and the degree to which, collectively, they mirror the total society". It can "be statistically measured in terms, for example, of locality of origin and its nature (rural, urban, suburban, etc.), previous occupation, father's occupation, education, family income, family social class, race, religion". Active representation, in contrast, concerns *behavior*, whereby the administrator "is expected to press for the interests and desires of those whom he is presumed to represent, whether they be the whole people or some segment of the people " (Mosher 1968: 12).

Mosher's conceptual distinction allowed for the emergence of two quite separate streams of second wave representative bureaucracy research that continue to attract contributors to this day. The first – "passive" – stream examines the passive representativeness of existing bureaucracies and the factors affecting it. Passive-studies invariably take their normative and substantive cues from the policy theories and categories of the American minority rights revolution. In fact, since they rely on data gathered through the new racial reporting practices mentioned earlier, they would not have been possible prior to this revolution. Typically framed as "Where do we stand now?" or "Why aren't we where we were supposed to be (and what can we do about it)?" – studies, they routinely underwrite the symbolic significance of bureaucratic representation; conceptualize representativeness in terms of minority identity (or its constituents, race and ethnicity) and gender; only scrutinize American bureaucracies; equate adequate representation with proportional representation, and construe underrepresentation and "manifest imbalances" as problematic (cf. e.g. Rose and Chia, 1978; Smith, 1980; Sisneros, 1993; Kim and Lewis, 1994; Riccucci and Saidel, 1997; Greene et al., 2000). Passive-studies are heavy on statistics and low on theoretical debate. The underlying *problématique* is taken for granted and presumed self-evident; remaining debates center on technical issues of statistical methodology (cf. e.g. Nachmias and Rosenbloom, 1973; Guyot, 1993, 1998; Guajardo, 1996; Kellough, 1998).

Both theoretically and in terms of its evolution, the second – "passive-to-active" – stream of research has proven more interesting. Scholars in this stream "transplanted", "transferred", and "adapted" the Marxist Laski–Kingsley theory of representative bureaucracy "to the United States". Echoing the going concerns and beliefs of the minority rights revolution, they imbued it with "more egalitarian notions", placed "less emphasis on social class and more emphasis on race and gender", and turned it into "essentially a normative theory" which claimed that representative bureaucracies – "recruited from all segments of society" – will produce policies and policy outcomes that "reflect the interests and desires" of people of "diverse demographic backgrounds" and that are therefore "generally responsive to the desires of the public" (Meier, 1993: 2; Selden, 1997: 5; Rhys et al., 2005: 491).

The logic proposed to account for this effect was quite akin to the logic that the Laski–Kingsley theory had held to be applicable *only* to dominant classes: persons of different backgrounds undergo different socialization experiences which form the sources of their enduring values, preferences and biases. Bureaucrats, also, are susceptible to these biases and preferences when they exercise the discretion inherent to bureaucratic position (Van Riper, 1958; Kingsley, 1944; Hindera, 1993; Meier, 1993; Selden, 1997). Bureaucrats recruited from a particular group will therefore tend to make administrative decisions that reflect the interests, needs and desires of that group (Meier, 1993; Selden, 1997). Put differently, passive representation, once established, will lead to active representation which, in turn, will produce "democratic" and "responsive" policies.

Having thus reformulated the original theory of representative bureaucracy, scholars in this stream set about subjecting it to "empirical verification" (Meier, 1993: 2).[3]

SAVING AFFIRMATIVE ACTION THROUGH ACTIVE REPRESENTATION

Once raised, the passive-to-active hypothesis was met with strong and widespread skepticism (at least initially). Major criticism was threefold:

1. The new theory presupposed far more leeway for bureaucrats to use their administrative positions for representative purposes than they might actually possess. Couldn't existing controls of bureaucracy – executive hierarchy, legislative oversight, judicial review – be expected to do a reasonably good job at *preventing* officials from using their office for partisan ends? (Meier, 1975) Wouldn't (and shouldn't) public agencies – which, after all, are *supposed* to be impartial – bring intensive pressures and sanctions to bear on would-be active representatives in order to make them "lean over backwards" and *avoid* the appearance of impartiality (Herbert, 1974; Mosher, 1968)?
2. The theory vastly overestimated birth-group values' enduring influence on individuals, especially so on individuals from disadvantaged and stigmatized backgrounds (the very groups newly incorporated by the theory). Wasn't it more plausible to assume that socialization *continues* throughout bureaucrats' lives and that job, office and agency socialization are at least as important in shaping bureaucrats' values, beliefs and interests as their childhood training (Meier, 1975: 529; cf. Downs, 1967; Subramaniam, 1967; Mosher, 1968; Meier and Nigro, 1976)? Besides, also given the likely risks involved, what good reasons could bureaucrats from disadvantaged and stigmatized backgrounds have to *continue* representing the

values and sympathies of their birth-groups? Weren't they far more likely to *shed* these, to "internally play down their racial roots", "ferret out feelings of sympathy for their racial group", "shuck off the accoutrements of their racial origin", and to use their relatively privileged administrative positions to *escape* their past, and "assimilate"? (Thompson, 1976: 213; cf. Subramaniam, 1967; Mosher, 1968; Krislov, 1974; Peters, 1989; Béteille, 1991).

3. The theory failed to explain the last (and normatively crucial) step in its logic, that is, "the process by which a representative bureaucracy becomes responsive to sectional *as well* as general interests" (Subramaniam, 1967: 1014). If the various passively represented groups all have different and conflicting interests and if their members in the bureaucracy would mainly advocate group interests – as the new theory postulated – wouldn't the result be a "divided", "balkanized", and "ineffectual" bureaucracy rather than a responsive one? (ibid.; Mosher, 1968).

Much of the above criticism was speculative and open to empirical refutation. A string of empirical studies undertaken in the 1970s and 1980s to explore the passive-to-active hypothesis did little to weaken the critics' case, however. In fact, fully in line with their arguments, these studies found demographic variables to be poor predictors of bureaucrats' attitudes (Meier and Nigro, 1976; Rehfuss, 1986) and decisions (Dresang, 1974) and most group-identified bureaucrats to be shunning group advocacy roles (Henderson, 1979). As Dennis Dresang summed up his findings: "Classifying people according to their circumstances of birth or language is […] not grouping them according to any criteria necessarily related to administrative behavior or attitudes […] an ethnic group cannot rely on representation in the bureaucracy as a resource for effectively pursuing group interests" (Dresang, 1974: 1613, 1617). Thus burdened by heavy criticism *and* unilaterally disconfirmatory evidence representative bureaucracy theory seemed once again destined for oblivion.

However, beginning in the early 1990s, a growing collection of empirical studies began to confidently suggest that there *was* a link between passive and active representation after all, even (indeed, *especially*) for minorities and women. Minorities and/or women, these studies reported, *do* derive tangible and substantive benefits from passive representation, including more housing loans (Selden, 1997), better education (Meier and Stewart, 1992; Keiser et al., 2002), better protection against employment discrimination (Hindera, 1993; Meier et al., 2005), more effective handling of rape crimes (Meier and Nicholson-Crotty, 2006), more child support (Wilkins and Keiser, 2004), and more bureaucratic attention for ingroup-related policies (Saidel and Loscocco, 2005).

This remarkable shift from skepticism to enthusiasm regarding the likelihood and occurrence of active representation can be traced to developments in American politics after the minority rights revolution of 1965–75. As we have seen, the antidiscrimination and affirmative action laws and policies of the minority rights revolution formed the backdrop for the renewed interest of American scholars in representative bureaucracy. These laws and policies had been introduced rapidly and without any serious lobbying pressure or opposition; partly because they were crafted almost surreptitiously, outside the political limelight, by Congress staffers, bureaucrats and human resources managers, mostly "mainstream Euro-American males and minority advocates, wearing suits, sitting at desks, firing off memos, and meeting in government buildings to discuss new policy directions" (Skrentny, 2002: 5). But fierce contention over the new policies arose soon after their smooth adoption. The primary bone of contention in this counterrevolution was affirmative action. The ensuing debate over it significantly shaped the trajectory of American domestic politics and continues to this day (ibid.).

John Skrentny has conveniently captured the basic arguments of both sides. According to its opponents, affirmative action is unmeritocratic, creates a vested interest in race through its color-consciousness, leads to reverse discrimination and represents an un-American guarantee of unequal results instead of equal opportunity (Skrentny, 1996). "Civil rights and the road to success and dreams", opponents argue, "should be free of any government-sponsored discrimination" (Skrentny, 2002: 343). To its defenders, affirmative action is a compensation for past injustices, a guarantee of a fair share of the economic pie, and a civil right, guaranteed by the Constitution (Skrentny, 1996). In their view, "an attack on affirmative action is an assault on the core meaning of civil rights and equal opportunity [and] tells minorities that they are not wanted, which is tantamount to racism" (Skrentny, 2002: 343).[4] In American politics, an anti-affirmative action stance is associated with the political right, a pro-affirmative action position with the left, though not neatly and exclusively so. Public opinion on the issue has tended to lean towards the right, anti-affirmative action position (Skrentny, 1996; Morning and Sabbagh, 2005).

Affirmative action received its first real blows under the Reagan administrations (1981–89). In his first presidential campaign, Reagan had rallied against affirmative action and "bureaucratic regulations which rely on quotas, ratios, and numerical requirements". Though, once in office, he never put an end to affirmative action, he drastically curtailed its administrative enforcement. He cut staffing and funding of the watchdog agencies mentioned earlier, reduced the pressure on employers to hire minorities, significantly reduced the sanctions imposed on employers who violated the still-intact affirmative action regulations, and appointed federal judges known for their anti-affirmative action positions. Under presidents Bush (1989–1993) and Clinton (1993–2001) the attack of affirmative action continued, though less firmly, with both administrations further dismantling the extensive regulatory apparatus and practices developed in the early 1970s (Kelly and Dobbin, 1998). With governors in several states (California, Louisiana, and Florida) taking decisive steps to end affirmative action, and judges placing ever more restrictions on racial preferences and the use of "suspect classifications" (such as race) (Skrentny, 2002: 340–341), in the 1990s the days of affirmative action looked numbered indeed.

The eventuality that affirmative action might soon come to an end loomed large in the minds of representative bureaucracy researchers who – at that very time – started reporting positive linkages between passive and active representation for minority groups. Finding themselves normatively in tune with affirmative action defenders they attempted to justify (and save) the policy by developing the pragmatic argument that it actually *worked*, through the logic of representative bureaucracy.

To illustrate: after finding positive linkages between passive and active representation for several minorities in the Farmers' Home Administration (an agency tasked with the allocation of housing subsidies to poor farmers), Sally Coleman Selden concluded:

> These findings confirm that increasing the number of minority employees makes a real difference in how resources are allocated [...] The elimination of affirmative action policies could ultimately reduce the percentage of racial and ethnic minorities employed by public bureaucracies. If colleges and universities abandon affirmative action programs, the percentage of minorities graduating with college degrees may fall. As a result, agencies would have a more difficult time recruiting minority candidates, and therefore minority agency employment would decline. Subsequently, declining entry-level minority employment will lead to fewer minorities in a position to advance into key agency decision-making positions. Moreover, if agencies abandon affirmative action policies, they might place a lower priority on recruiting, hiring and promoting minorities and women. In some cases, such as the FmHA, increasing minority representation has proven to be a tangible means of addressing historic program inequities and biases; unfortunately, however, reducing minority representation could hinder future progress. The results of this study suggest than an effective means of ensuring that minority interests are represented in administrative decision-making processes is to employ minority administrators. (Selden, 1997: 141–142)

In other words, passive representation leads to active representation leads to substantive benefits for represented minorities. And by implication: the elimination of affirmative action leads to less passive representation leads to less active representation leads to less benefits for minorities, and to more "program inequities and biases".

Selden and other researchers, to be sure, did not *only* find positive linkages in their studies. In fact, the strength of the observed linkages typically varied considerably across minority groups. And for some groups, in some cases, positive linkages were not established at all. Selden herself, for instance, found the linkage for African Americans to be much *stronger* than that for Hispanics and Asian Americans, and found *no* significant linkage for Native Americans (Selden, 1997). Characteristic of the post-1990 empirical passive-to-active literature, however, is that while these mixed and occasionally negative results do get reported, it is typically the positive linkages that get highlighted and receive center stage in the studies' discussions and conclusion sections (Selden, for instance, titled her study *The Promise of Representative Bureaucracy*).

Also, in as far as disappointing or negative results are treated as anomalies they are typically not allowed to affect the basic premise of the normative theory, that is, that passive representation leads (or, at the least, *is likely* to lead, under *certain conditions*) to active representation (and hence warrants protection by affirmative action). Subsequent studies, in any case, do not tend to pick up upon them. Recent empirical passive-to-active studies can thus be understood as an example of what Charles Lindblom has called "partisan analysis", which focuses especially on proposals and policies that seem unlikely to succeed without additional information (h.l. affirmative action) and seeks to convert political adversaries or indifferent participants through "informed and reasoned persuasion [...] regarding particular aspects of an issue" (h.l. the compensatory distributive effects of bureaucratic representation) (Lindblom and Woodhouse, 1993 [1968]: 129; Lindblom, 1979).

This partisan streak in recent representative bureaucracy studies is further exemplified by researchers' tendency to increasingly frame their more promising findings as organizational benefits of demographic "diversity". Starting in the late 1980s, diversity policy discourse and rhetoric were developed by American human resources managers and affirmative action specialists in response to the uncertain future of affirmative action. In an effort to safeguard the affirmative action programs and practices (on which their positions, paychecks and professional identities depended), they began to replace the "shopworn", "moralistic" arguments for it with a more "practical, business-friendly rationale" (Lynch, 2005: xii). This new "dollars-and-demographic" discourse of diversity downplayed the "social justice" case for affirmative action in favor of its "business case". In short, organizations that took "diversity" seriously – by hiring minorities and women, and by creating inclusive cultures in which differences between organization members are recognized, respected, valued, embraced and celebrated – would be repaid with more efficiency and innovative capacity and, hence, better organizational *performance* (Kelly and Dobbin, 1998; Lynch, 2005; Herring, 2009; Wrench, 2005; Edelman et al., 2001).

Representative bureaucracy scholars have been heeding this discursive shift, increasingly exchanging theoretical concepts associated with the old social justice case for affirmative action ("bureaucracy", "passive representation", "active representation") for newer ones associated with the business case for diversity ("public organization", "diversity", "performance"). In a parallel development, the substantive research focus of scholars in the field is gradually but perceptibly shifting from singular groups to whole organizations (cf. e.g. Selden and Selden, 2001; Pitts, 2005; Pitts and Jarry, 2007, 2009; Pitts and Wise, 2010).

CONCLUSION

This chapter has traced the origin and capricious evolution of representative bureaucracy from a descriptive Marxist theory of bureaucracy to a normative theory of diversity for public organizations. In doing so, it has found much truth in Thomas Kuhn's observation that apparently arbitrary elements of personal and historical accident are formative ingredients in the development of scientific theories. As the case of representative bureaucracy theory suggests, explanations for the apparent arbitrariness of theoretical evolution can also be found in large measure *outside* the scientific enterprise, rather than in the elements internal to it stressed by Kuhn. The neatness with which representative bureaucracy theorizing and research has time and again been influenced, *dictated* almost, by political currents and events and by the policy discourses spawned by them is striking.

Also, it is difficult not to appreciate the irony in seeing a theory retaining its name while transforming itself into virtually its exact opposite. Harold Laski would have ridiculed the suggestion that the "governing classes" should voluntarily and willfully condone, accept, facilitate and guarantee bureaucratic representation to society's "lower" segments as childishly naïve; yet it was this very idea that – decades later

– inspired and entertained a new generation of American scholars tracing their work to his disciple J. Donald Kingsley.

NOTES

1. Kingsley referred to the establishment of a *Civil Service Commission* (1855) to hold entry examinations and the *Civil Service Order in Council* (1870), which introduced open competitive entry examinations for most departments.
2. This also went for *association* with Laski, his work, and even his memory. After his death in 1950, some of his American friends tried to buy Laski's immense book collection and present it to the London School of Economics for installation in a "Laski room". The effort remained fruitless. Fundraiser Warburg explained: "[T]he project has become socially unacceptable […] People are scared – scared to speak, write and even think – scared to be seen in certain company – scared to be seen reading *The Nation* – scared to have a book by Keynes or Laski lying on their table […] Three years ago, I am sure the job could have been done. Today, I doubt very much whether anyone could do it" (Newman, 2009: 357).
3. For reasons of brevity this description imputes more linearity and deliberateness to the second stream's reformulation of the theory than there actually was. For instance, second stream scholars long struggled to find a satisfactory conceptualization of 'representation' for their new brand of representative bureaucracy theory *before* falling back on Mosher's concepts (cf. e.g. Saltzstein, 1979). Also, many replaced "class" with the minority rights revolution categories of "race", "ethnicity", "minority", and "gender" without showing any sense of discontinuity with the original Laski–Kingsley theory, explicitly and exclusively class-based though it was. Moreover, some read Kingsley's book as a plea for making bureaucracies more representative. To them, representative bureaucracy already *was* a normative theory, and needed not be made into one.
4. To be sure, more nuanced positions also exist. Many Americans, for instance, only oppose the kind of "hard", "specific", "second-generation" affirmative action involving sanctioned numerical group quotas which emerged during the minority rights revolution; *not* the 'generic', 'soft', 'outreach' type of affirmative action originally envisaged and endorsed in the Civil Rights Act (Sowell, 2004; Morning and Sabbagh, 2005; Sabbagh, 2007).

References

Aberbach, J.D., Putnam, R.D., and Rockman, B.A. (1981). *Bureaucrats and Politicians in Western Democracies*. Cambridge, MA: Harvard University Press.

Acemoglu, D. and Robinson, J. (2012). *Why Nations Fail: The Origins of Power, Prosperity and Poverty.* New York: Random House.

Acquavita, S.P., Pittman, J., Gibbons, M., and Castellanos-Brown, K. (2009). Personal and organizational diversity factors' impact on social workers' job satisfaction: results from a national internet-based survey. *Administration in Social Work*, **33**(2), 151–166.

Alford, C.F. (1985). The 'Iron Law of Oligarchy' in the Athenian Polis and today. *Canadian Journal of Political Science/Revue canadienne de science politique*, **18**(2), 295–312.

Allen, J., Massey, D., and Cochrane, A. (1998). *Rethinking the Region.* London: Routledge.

Amin, A. (2002). Ethnicity and the multi-cultural city: living with diversity. *Environment and Planning A*, **34**, 959–980.

Amin, A. and Graham, S. (1999). Cities of connection and disconnection. In J. Allen, D. Massey, and M. Pryke (eds), *Unsettling Cities*? London: Routledge, pp. 8–38.

Ancona, D. and Caldwell, D.E. (1992). Cross functional teams: blessing or curse for new product development. In T. Kochan and M. Useem (eds), *Transforming Organizations.* Oxford: Oxford University Press, pp. 154–168.

Andrews, R. (2009). Civic engagement, ethnic heterogeneity, and social capital in urban areas. *Urban Affairs Review*, **44**(3), 428–440.

Andrews, R. (2013). Representative bureaucracy in the United Kingdom. In P. von Maravić, B. Guy Peters, and E. Schröter (eds), *Representative Bureaucracy in Action*. Cheltenham, UK, and Northampton, MA: Edward Elgar, pp. 156–168.

Andrews, R., Boyne, G.A., Meier, K.J., O'Toole, J., and Walker, R.M. (2005). Representative bureaucracy, organizational strategy, and public service performance: an empirical analysis of English local government. *Journal of Public Administration Research and Theory*, **15**(4), 489–504.

Ansell, C.K. (2011). *Pragmatist Democracy: Evolutionary Learning as Public Philosophy*. Oxford: Oxford University Press.

Armenta, A. (2009). Policing immigrants: the local dilemmas of immigration enforcement. Paper presented at the annual meeting of the Law and Society Association. Denver.

Ashworth, R. and Andrews, R. (2010). Representative bureaucracy and fire service performance: evidence from England. Unpublished paper. Cardiff School of Business, Cardiff, Wales.

Bache, I. and Flinders, M. (2004). Multi-level governance and the study of the British state. *Public Policy and Administration*, **19**(1), 31–51.

Back, L. (1996). *New Ethnicities and Urban Culture*. London: UCL Press.

Badash, L. (2000). Science and McCarthyism. *Minerva*, **38**(1), 53–80.

Baker, P. and Eversley, J. (eds) (2000). *Multilingual Capital: The Languages of London's Schoolchildren and their Relevance to Economic, Social and Educational Policies.* London: Battlebridge.

Barnard, C. (1938). *The Functions of the Executive.* Cambridge, MA: Harvard University Press.

Bauböck, R. (2005). Expansive citizenship: voting beyond territory and membership. *Political Science and Politics*, **38**, 683–7.

Bauer, O. (1923 [1965]). *Die österreichische Revolution*. Wien: Wiener Volksbuchhandlung.

Becker, G.S. (1974). A theory of social interactions. *The Journal of Political Economy*, **82**, 1063–1093.

Begg, I. (2002). *Urban Competitiveness : Policies for Dynamic Cities*. Bristol: Policy Press

Bellah, R. N. (2005). McCarthyism at Harvard. *The New York Review of Books*, February 10.

Benavides, A.D. and Hernandez, J.C.T. (2007). Serving diverse communities: cultural competency. *Public Management*, **89**(6), 14–18.

Bendix, R. (1946). Representative bureaucracy: an interpretation of the British civil service. *American Journal of Sociology*, **51**, 75–76.

Bendix, R. (1980). *Kings Or People: Power and the Mandate to Rule*. Oakland, CA: University of California Press.

Benhabib, S. (2002). *The Claims of Culture. Quality and Diversity in the Global Era*. Princeton, NJ: Princeton University Press.

Ben-Tovim, G., Gabriel, J., Law, I., and Stredder, K. (1986). *The Local Politics of Race.* Basingstoke and New York: Palgrave.

Béteille, A. (1991). Distributive justice and institutional well-being. *Economic and Political Weekly*, **26**(11), 591–600.

Bigley, G.A. and Roberts, K.H. (2001). The incident command system: high reliability organizing for complex and volatile task environment. *Academy of Management Journal*, **44**(6), 1281–1300.

Birnbaum, P. (1977). *The Heights of Power.* Chicago, IL: Chicago University Press.

Blake, G., Diamond, J., Foot, J., Gidley, B., Mayo, M., Shukra, M., and Yarnit, M. (2008). Community engagement and community cohesion. Joseph Rowntree Foundation report, York, UK.

Blanc, M. and Beaumont, J. (2005). Local democracy within european urban development programmes. *Tijdschrift voor Economische en Sociale Geografie*, **96**(4), 409–420.

Blomgren Bingham, L. (2006). The new urban governance: processes for engaging citizens and stakeholders. *Review of Policy Research*, **23**(4), 816–826.

Bollens, S.A. (2003). Managing urban ethnic conflict. In R. Hambleton, H.V. Savitch and M. Stewart (eds), *Globalism and Local Democracy*. Basingstoke and New York: Palgrave, pp. 108–124.

Bolotin, F.N. and Cingranelli, D.L. (1983). Equity and urban policy: the underclass hypothesis revisited. *The Journal of Politics*, **45**(1), 209–219.

Bradbury, M.D. and Kellough, J.E. (2008). Representative bureaucracy: exploring the potential for active representation in local government. *Journal of Public Administration Research and Theory*,**18**, 697–714.

Brink, van der, H. (2004). Ethnisch-kulturelle Konflikte: Ursachen, Folgen und Handlungsempfehlungen am Beispiel der Stadt Duisburg. University of Duisburg, Institute of Geography, Discussion Paper, 1/2004.

Brubaker, R. (1992). *Citizenship and Nationhood in France and Germany*. Cambridge, MA: Harvard University Press.

Brudney, J.L., Hebert, F.T., and Wright, D.S. (2000). *From organizational values to organizational roles: examining representative bureaucracy in state administration. Journal of Public Administration Research and Theory*, **10**(3), 491–512.

Burger, M. and Buskens, V. (2009). Social context and network formation: an experimental study. *Social Networks*, **31**(1), 63–75.

Burns, D., Hambleton, R., and Hoggett, P. (1994) *The Politics of Decentralization. Revitalising Local Democracy*. Basingstoke and New York: Palgrave.

Calhoun, C. (1993). Civil society and the public sphere. *Public Culture*, **5**(2), 267–280.

California State Auditor (1999). Dymally-Alatorre bilingual services act: state and local governments could do more to address their clients' needs for bilingual services. Report No. 99110. Bureau of State Audits, Sacramento.

Capano, G. and Carboni, N. (2013). Representative bureaucracy in Italy. In P. von Maravić, E. Schröter, and B.G. Peters (eds), *Representative Bureaucracy in Action: Country Profiles from the Americas, Europe,*

Africa and Asia. Cheltenham, UK, and Northampton, MA: Edward Elgar, pp. 11–128.

Carpenter, D.P. (2002). *The Forging of Bureaucratic Autonomy*. Princeton, NJ: Princeton University Press.

Castles, S. and Miller, M.J. (2009). *The Age of Migration: International Population Movements in the Modern World*, 4th edn. New York: The Guilford Press.

Checkoway B. (2009). Community change for diverse democracy. *Community Development Journal*, **44**(1), 5–21.

Choi, S. (2009). Diversity in the US Federal Government: diversity management and employee turnover in federal agencies. *Journal of Public Administration Research and Theory*, **19**(3), 603 –630.

Chrisafis A. (2010). Immigration: France sees tensions rise five years on from Paris riots. *The Guardian*, 16 November.

Clark, T. and Hoffman-Martinot, V. (eds) (1998). *The New Public Culture*. Oxford, UK: Westview Press.

Clarke, S. (2006). Regimes of immigrant incorporation in London boroughs. Urban Affairs Association Annual Meeting.

Cooke, M. (2008). "What we might become": the lives, aspirations, and education of young migrants in the London area. *Journal of Language, Identity and Education*, **7**(1), 22–40.

Cornwall, A. (2008). *Democratising Engagement. What the UK Can Learn from International Experience.* London: DEMOS.

Councillors Commission (Chaired by Dame Jane Roberts) (2007). *Representing the Future.* London: Department of Communities and Local Government.

Cox, K. (1997). *Spaces of Globalization: Reasserting the Power of the Local*. New York: Guilford Press.

Cox, T. and Blake, S. (1991). Managing cultural diversity: implications for organizational competitiveness. *The Academy of Management Executive* (AME), **5**(3), 45–56.

Cox, T. H., Lobel, S.A., and McLeod, P.L. (1991). Effects of ethnic group cultural differences on cooperative and competitive behavior on a group task. *The Academy of Management Journal*, **34**(4), 827–847.

Dahl, R.A. (1991). *Democracy and Its Critics*. New Haven, CT: Yale University Press.

Dahlstedt, M. and Hertzberg, F. (2007). Democracy the Swedish way? The exclusion of "immigrants" in Swedish politics. *Scandinavian Political Studies*, **30**(2), 175–203.

Daley, D. (1984). Political and occupational barriers to the implementation of affirmative action: administrative, executive, and legislative attitudes towards representative bureaucracy. *Review of Public Personnel Administration*, **4**, 4–15

Daley, D. (1985). Administrative responsibility and control of the bureaucracy: the dog that did not bite. *State and Local Government Review*, **17**, 195–199.

Davies J.S. (2007). Against partnership: toward a local challenge to global neoliberalism. In R. Hambleton and J.S. Gross (eds), *Governing Cities in a Global Era*. Basingstoke and New York: Palgrave, pp. 199–2010.

Davies J.S. and Imbroscio D.L. (eds) (2009). *Theories of Urban Politics*. London: Sage.

Davis M. (1992). *City of Quartz. Excavating the Future of Los Angeles*. London: Vintage.

Davis M. (2006). *Planet of Slums*. London: Verso.

Deane, H.A. (1972). *The Political Ideas of Harold J. Laski*. Hamden, CT: The Shoe String Press.

Dee, T.S. (2004). Teachers, race and student achievement in a randomized experiment. *Review of Economics and Statistics*, **86**, 195–210.

Denters, B. and Rose, L.E. (2005). *Comparing Local Governance. Trends and Developments*. Basingstoke and New York: Palgrave.

Derlien, H.-U., and Mayntz, R. (1989). Party patronage and politicization of the West German administrative elite 1970-1987 – towards hybridization? *Governance*, **2**, 384-404.

Di Gaetano, A. and Klemanski, J.S. (1999). *Power and City Governance. Comparative Perspectives on Urban Development*. Minneapolis, MN: University of Minnesota Press.

Dobbin, F. (2009). *Inventing Equal Opportunity*. Princeton, NJ: Princeton University Press.

Dolan, J. and Rosenbloom, D.H. (2003). *Representative Bureaucracy: Classic Readings and Continuing Controversies*. New York: M.E. Sharpe. Preface, pp. xi–xiii.

Downs, A. (1967). *Inside Bureaucracy*. Boston, MA: Little, Brown and Company.

Drage, J. (2008). *A Balancing Act. Decision-making and Representation in New Zealand's Local Government*. Wellington, NZ: Institute of Policy Studies, Victoria University of Wellington.

Dresang, D.L. (1974). Ethnic politics, representative bureaucracy and development administration: the Zambian case. *American Political Science Review*, **68**(4), 1605–1617.

Dryzek, J.S. and Niemeyer, S. (2008). Discursive representation. *American Political Science Review*, **102**, 481–493.

Du Bois, W.E.B. (1899). *The Philadelphia Negro: A Social Study*. Publications of the University of Pennsylvania: Series in Political Economy and Law. Philadelphia, PA: University of Pennsylania.

Dubois, V. (2010). *The Bureaucrat and the Poor: Encounters in a French Welfare Office.* Aldershot, UK: Ashgate.
Dudek, S.M. (2009). *Diversity in Uniform? Geschlecht und Migrationshintergrund in der Berliner Schutzpolizei.* Wiesbaden, Germany: VS Verlag.
Dudek, S. M. (2009). Diversity in Uniform? Geschlecht und Migrationshintergrund in der Berliner Schutzpolizei. Wiesbaden: VS Verlag.
Easton, D. (1965). *A Systems Analysis of Political Life.* New York: Wiley
Easton, D. (1975). A re-assessment of the concept of political support. *British Journal of Political Science*, **5**(4), 435–457.
Edelman, L.B., Riggs F.W. and Mara-Drita, I. (2001). Diversity rhetoric and the managerialization of law. *The American Journal of Sociology*, **106**(6), 1589–1641.
Eliaeson, S. (2000). Max Weber's methodology: an ideal-type. *Journal of the History of the Behavioral Sciences*, **36**(3), 241–263.
Elkins, D.J. and Simeon, R.E.B. (1979). A cause in search of its effects, or what does political culture explain. *Comparative Politics*, **11**, 127–154.
Ely, R. J. (2004). A field study of group diversity, participation in diversity education programs, and performance. *Journal of Organizational Behavior*, **25** (6), 755-780. doi:10.1002/job.268
Engels, F. (1968). Introduction. In K. Marx, *The Civil War in France: The Paris Commune*. New York: International Publishers, pp. 9–22.
Escobar-Lemmon, M. and Taylor-Robinson, M.M. (2005). Women ministers in Latin American government: when, where, and why? *American Journal of Political Science*, **49**(4), 829–844.
Etzioni-Halevy, E. (1983). *Bureaucracy and Democracy: A Political Dilemma.* Boston, MA: Routledge and Kegan Paul.
Eulau, H. and Wahlke, Hrsg., J.C. (1978). *Politics of Representation: Continuities Theory and Research*. London: Sage Publications, Inc.
Eurocities (2010a). Cities accommodating diversity. Findings and recommendations from the peer review project 'Diversity and equality in European cities'. Brussels: European Commission. Available at http://www.integratingcities.eu/.
Eurocities (2010b). Eurocities charter on integrating cities. Brussels: European Commission. Available at http://www.integratingcities.eu/.
European Commission (EC) (2001). White Paper on European Governance. Brussels: European Commission.
Fischer, F. (1993). Citizen participation and democratization of policy expertise: From theoretical inquiry to practical cases. *Policy Sciences*, **26**(3), 165–187.
Florida, R. (2002). *The Rise of the Creative Class.* New York: Basic Books.

Florida, R. (2008). *Who's Your City?* New York: Basic Books.

Fox, J. (1994). The difficult transition from clientelism to citizenship: lessons form Mexico, World Politics, **46**(2), 151–184.

Frederickson, H.G. (2005). Transcending the community: local leadership in a world of shared power. *Public Management*, **87**(10), 8–15.

Fukuyama, F. (2006). Identity, immigration and democracy. *Electoral Systems Today, Journal of Democracy*, **17**(2), 4–20.

Gandhi, J. (2010). *Political Institutions under Dictatorship*. Auflage reprint. New York: Cambridge University Press.

Gandhi, J. and Lust-Okar, E. (2009. Elections under authoritarianism. *Annual Review of Political Science* **12**(1), 403–422.

Garbaye, R. (2002). Ethnic minority participation in British and French cities: a historical–institutionalist perspective. *International Journal of Urban and Regional Research*, **26**(3), 555–570.

García, M. (2006). Citizenship practices and urban governance in European cities. *Urban Studies*, **43**(4) 745–765.

García, M. (2010). The breakdown of the Spanish urban growth model: social and territorial effects of the global crisis. *International Journal of Urban and Regional Research*, **34**(4), 967–980.

Gaventa, J., Dunn A., Foot, J., and Zipfel, T. (2007). *Champions of Participation. Engaging Citizens in Local Governance*. Brighton: Institute for Development Studies.

Geddes, A. (2003). *The Politics of Migration and Immigration in Europe*. London: Sage

Gerth, H.H. and Mills, C.W. (1948). *From Max Weber: Essays in Sociology*. London: Routledge.

Gilchrist, A. (2004). *The Well-connected Community*. Bristol: The Policy Press.

Gleeson, S. (2011). To protect one, we must protect all: bureaucratic scripts for protecting undocumented workers. Paper presented at the annual meeting of the American Sociological Association, Las Vegas, NV.

Golden, M. (2003) Electoral connections: the effects of the personal vote on political patronage, bureaucracy and legislation in post-war Italy. *British Journal of Political Science*, **23**, 189–212.

Gonzales, R.G. (2007). Wasted talent and broken dreams: the lost potential of undocumented students. *Immigration Policy in Focus*, **5**(13), 1–11.

Goodman, S.W. (2012) Fortifying citizenship: political strategies for civic integration in Europe. *World Politics*, **64**, 659–98.

Goodsell, C.T. (2010). *The Case for Bureaucracy*, 5th edn. Washington DC: CQ Press.

Gormley, Jr., W.T. and Balla, S.J. (2004). *Bureaucracy and Democracy: Accountability and Performance.* Washington DC: CQ Press.

Gornick, J.C., Myers, M. K., and Ross, K.E. (1997) Supporting the employment of mothers: policy variation across fourteen welfare states. *Journal of European Social Policy*, **7**, 45–70.

Gouldner, A.W. (1954). *Patterns of Industrial Bureaucracy: A Case Study of Modern Factory Administration.* New York: The Free Press.

Green, K.W., Whitten, D., and Medlin, B. (2005). Impact of relational differences on supervisor/subordinate dyad. *Industrial Management and Data Systems*, **105**(3), 369–383.

Greene, V., Coleman, S., and Brewer, G. (2000). Measuring power and presence: bureaucratic representation in the American states. *Journal of Public Administration Research and Theory*, **11**(3), 379–402.

Grindle, M.S. (2012). *Jobs for the Boys.* Cambridge, MA: Harvard University Press.

Groeneveld, S. and Walle, S.V.D. (2010). A contingency approach to representative bureaucracy: power, equal opportunities and diversity. *International Review of Administrative Science*, **76**(2), 239–258.

Gross J.S. (2007). Diversity and the democratic challenge: governing world cities. In R. Hambleton and J.S. Gross (eds), *Governing Cities in a Global Era. Urban Innovation, Competition and Democratic Reform.* Basingstoke and New York: Palgrave.

Gruber, J. E. (1987). *Controlling Bureaucracies: Dilemmas in Democratic Governance.* Berkeley, CA: University of California Press.

Guajardo, S.A. (1996). Representative bureaucracy: an estimation of the reliability and validity of the Nachmias-Rosenbloom MV Index. *Public Administration Review*, **56**(5), 467–476.

Guy, M.E., Newman, M.A., and Mastracci, S.H. (2008). *Emotional Labor: Putting the Service in Public Service.* Armonk, NY: M.E. Sharpe.

Guyot, J.F. (1993). Argument and evidence in ethnic analysis. *Public Administration Review*, **53**(6), 567–569.

Guyot, J.F. (1998). Representative bureaucracy recast. *Public Administration Review*, **58**(4), 376–377.

Habyarimana, J., Humphreys, M., Posner, D., and Weinstein, J.M. (2009). *Coethnicity: Diversity and the Dilemmas of Collective Action.* New York: Russell Sage Foundation.

Hajer, M. and Wagenaar, H. (2003). *Deliberative Policy Analysis: Understanding Governance in the Network Society.* Cambridge, UK: Cambridge University Press

Halfmann, J. (1998). Citizenship universalism, migration and the risks of exclusion. *The British Journal of Sociology*, **49**(4), 513–533.

Hall, P. (1988). *Cities of Tomorrow.* Oxford, UK: Blackwell.

Hambleton, R. (2007). New leadership for democratic urban space. In R. Hambleton and J.S. Gross, *Governing Cities in a Global Era. Urban Innovation, Competition and Democratic Reform*. Basingstoke and New York: Palgrave, pp. 163–176.

Hambleton, R. (2009). Civic Leadership for Auckland. An International Perspective, Report of the Royal Commission on Auckland Governance. Auckland: Royal Commission on Auckland Governance.

Hambleton, R. and Gross, J. S. (2007). *Governing Cities in a Global Era. Urban Innovation, Competition and Democratic Reform*. Basingstoke,UK, and New York: Palgrave.

Hambleton, R. and Howard, J. (2012). *Public Sector Innovation and Local Leadership in the UK and The Netherlands*. York, UK: Joseph Rowntree Foundation.

Hambleton, R. and Sweeting, D. (2004) US-style leadership for English local government? *Public Administration Review*, **64**(4), 474–488.

Hambleton R., Howard J., Buser M., and Taylor M. (2009) International insights on civic leadership and public service innovation. Report for the Local Authority Research Council Initiative (LARCI). Swindon: LARCI.

Hamilton, B. H., Nickerson, J.A., and Owan, H. (2004). Diversity and productivity in production teams. SSRN eLibrary. Available at: http://papers.ssrn.com/sol3/papers.cfm?abstract_id=547963.

Harriss, J. (2005). Political participation, representation and the urban poor findings from research in Delhi. *Economic and Political Weekly*, March (12), 1041–1054.

Harvey, D. (1989). *From Managerialism to Entrepreneurialism: The Transformation in Urban Governance in Late Capitalism*. Stockholm: Stockholm University

Heclo, H. (1977). *A Government of Strangers*. Washington DC: Brookings Institution

Heeg, S., Klagge, B., and Ossenbrügge, J. (2003). Metropolitan cooperation in Europe: theoretical issues and perspectives for urban networking. *European Planning Studies*, **11**(2), 139–153.

Heinelt, H., Sweeting D., and Getimis P. (2006). *Legitimacy and Urban Governance*. London: Routledge.

Heisler, M.O. (1974). The European polity model. In M.O. Heisler (ed.), *Politics in Western Europe*. New York: David McKay, pp. 26–56.

Hellström, M. (2010). The impact of labour market administration on immigrant agency in Canada and Sweden. Paper presented at the Canadian Political Science Association Annual Conference, Concordia University, Montreal, 1–3 June, 2010.

Helmke, G. and Levitsky, S. (2004). Informal institutions and comparative politics: a research agenda. *Perspectives on Politics*, **2**(4), 725–740.

Henderson, L.J. (1979). *Administrative Advocacy: Black Administrators in Urban Bureaucracy.* Palo Alto, CA: R & E Research Associates.

Henjak, A. (2010). Political cleavages and socio-economic context: how welfare regimes and historical divisions shape political cleavages. *West European Politics*, **33**, 474–504.

Herbert, A.W. (1974). The minority administrator: problems, prospects, and challenges. *Public Administration Review*, **34**(6), 556–563.

Herbert, I. (2007). Leicester to be first city where white people are minority. *The Independent*, September 11, 2007.

Hero, R. (1986). The urban service delivery literature: some questions and considerations. *Polity*, **18**(4), 659–677.

Herring, C. (2009). Does diversity pay? Race, gender, and the business case for diversity. *American Sociological Review*, **74**(2), (208–224.

Herrschel, T. (2000). Population shifts and local government: challenges to policy-making autonomy in eastern Germany. *GeoJournal*, **50**(2), 213–223.

Herrschel, T. (2009). Regionalisation, 'virtual' spaces and 'real' territories: a view from Europe and North America. *International Journal of Public Sector Management*, **22**(3), 261–272.

Herrschel, T. and Newman, P. (2002). *Governance of Europe's City Regions*. London: Routledge.

Hickman, M., Crowley, H., and Mai, N. (2008). *Immigration and Social Cohesion in the UK.* York, UK: Joseph Rowntree Trust

Hill, M. and Hupe, P. (2002). *Implementing Public Policy.* Thousand Oaks, CA: Sage Publications.

Hindera, J.J. (1993). Representative bureaucracy: further evidence of active representation in the EEOC district offices. *Journal of Public Administration Research and Theory*, **3**(4), 415–429.

Hjern, B. and Porter, D.O. (1981). Implementation structures: a new unit of administrative analysis. *Organization Studies*, **3**(2), 211–227.

HM Government (2010a). *The Coalition: Our Programme for Government.* London: Cabinet Office.

HM Government (2010b). Decentralisation and the Localism Bill: an essential guide. December. London: Department for Communities and Local Government.

HM Government (2011). Open Public Services White Paper. Cmnd 8145. July. London: HM Government.

Hood, C. (2000). *The Art of the State: Culture, Rhetoric, and Public Management*. Oxford: Oxford University Press.

Hood, C. (2002). Control, bargains, and cheating: the politics of public-service reform. *Journal of Public Administration Research and Theory*, **12**(3), 309–332.

Hooghe, M., Trappers, A., Meuleman, B., and Reeskens, T. (2008). Migration to European countries: a structural explanation of patterns, 1980–2004. *International Migration Review*, **42**(2), 476–504.

Horowitz, D.L. (1993). Democracy in divided societies. *Journal of Democracy*, **4**(4), 18–38.

Htun, M.N. and Jones, M.P. (2001). Engendering the right to participate in decision-making: electoral quotas and women's leadership in Latin America. In J. Craske and M. Molyneux (eds), *Gender and the Politics of Rights and Democracy in Latin America*. New York: Palgrave Macmillian, pp. 32–56.

Huber, J.D. and Shipan, C.R. (2002). *Deliberate Discretion: The Institutional Foundations of Bureaucratic Autonomy*. New York: Cambridge University Press.

Hueglin, T.O. and Fenna, A. (2005). *Comparative Federalism: A Systematic Inquiry*. Peterborough, Canada: Broadview Press.

Hughes, J. and Sasse, G. (2001). *Ethnicity and Territory in the Former Soviet Union: Regions in Conflict*. Sasse, 6. London: Frank Class.

Huth, S. (2006). Bürgerschaftliches Engagement von Migrantinnen und Migranten. In H. Voesgen (ed.), *Brückenschläge – Neue Partnerschaften zwischen institutioneller Erwachsenenbildung und bürgerschaftlichem Engagement*. Bielefeld: Bertelsmann, pp. 91–204.

Imrie, K. and Raco, M. (1999). How new is the new local governance? Lessons from the United Kingdom. *Transactions: Institute of British Geographers*, **24**(1), 45–64.

Jenson, J. (2005). La citoyenneté: ses frontières et ses lisières. Communication colloque: La citoyenneté dans tous ses états. Université Libre de Bruxelles, Brussels, 23–25 March.

Jones-Correa, M. (2008). Immigrant incorporation in suburbia: the role of bureaucratic norms in education. In D. Massey (ed.), *New Faces in New Places*. New York: Russell Sage Foundation Press, pp. 308–34.

Joppke, C. (1998). *Challenge to the Nation-State: Immigration in Western Europe and the United States*. Oxford, UK: Oxford University Press.

Judd, D.R. and Smith, J.M. (2007). The new ecology of urban governance: special purpose authorities and urban development. In R. Hambleton and J.S. Gross (eds), *Governing Cities in a Global Era*. Basingstoke, UK, and New York: Palgrave, pp. 150–161.

Kahane, A. (2004). *Solving Tough Problems. An Open Way of Talking, Listening and Creating New Realities*. San Francisco, CA: Berrett–Koehler Publishers, Inc.

Kanter, R.M. (1993). *Men and Women of the Corporation*. New York: Basic Books.

Kantor, P. (2008). Varieties of city regionalism and the quest for political cooperation: a comparative perspective. *Urban Research and Practice*, **1**(2), 111–129.

Kato, J. (1998). When the party breaks up: exit and voice among Japanese legislators. *American Political Science Review*, **92**(4), 857–870.

Katzenstein, P.J. (1985). *Small States in World Markets: Industrial Policy in Europe*. Ithaca, NY: Cornell University Press.

Katzenstein, P.J. (1987a). *Policy and Politics in West Germany. The Growth of a Semisovereign State*. Philadelphia, PA: Temple University Press.

Katzenstein, P.J. (1987b). *Corporatism and Change: Austria, Switzerland and the Politics of Industry*. Ithaca, NY: Cornell University Press.

Katznelson, I. (2006). *When Affirmative Action Was White: An Untold History of Racial Inequality in Twentieth-Century America*. New York: W.W. Norton & Co.

Kearns, A. and Paddison, R. (2000). New challenges for urban governance: introduction to the review issue. *Urban Studies*, **37**(5), 845–850.

Keating, M. (1998). *The New Regionalism in Western Europe: Territorial Restructuring and Political Change*. Cheltenham, UK, and Northampton, MA: Edward Elgar.

Keiser, L.R., Wilkins, V.M., Meier, K.M. and Holland, C.A. (2002). Lipstick and logarithms: gender, institutional context, and representative bureaucracy. *American Political Science Review*, **96**(3), 553–564.

Kellough, J. E. (1998). Reliability, validity, and the MV index: toward the clarification of some fundamental issues. *Public Administration Review*, **58**(2), 167–173.

Kellough, J.E. (2006). *Understanding Affirmative Action: Politics, Discrimination, And the Search for Justice*. Washington DC: Georgetown University Press.

Kelly, E. and Dobbin, F. (1998). How affirmative action became diversity management: employer response to antidiscrimination law, 1961 to 1996. *American Behavioral Scientist*, **41**(7), 960–984.

Kelsen, H. (1920). *The Essence and Value of Democracy*. Lanham, MD: Rowman & Littlefield Publishers.

Kerner Report (1968). *Report of the National Commission on Civil Disorders*. New York: Bantam Books.

Kestila, E. and Soderlund, P. (2007). Subnational political opportunity structures and the success of the radical right. *European Journal of Political Research*, **46**(4), 773–796.

Kim, P.S. and Lewis, G. (1994). Asian Americans in the public service: success, diversity, and discrimination. *Public Administration Review*, **54**(3), 285–290.

King, D. (1995). *Separate and Unequal: Black Americans and the US Federal Government*. Oxford: New York: Oxford University Press.

Kingsley, J.D. (1944). *Representative Bureaucracy. An Interpretation of the British Civil Service*. Yellow Springs, OH: The Antioch Press.

Kingsley, J.D. (1951). Migration from Europe: a report by the director-general [J. Donald Kingsley] to the General council of the International refugee organization on experience gained in the field of migration through the processing and transportation for resettlement of more than one million refugees and other migrants. Geneva: International Refugee Organization.

Kingsley, J.D. (1956). Immigration and our foreign policy objectives. *Law and Contemporary Problems*, **21**(2), 299–310.

Kingsley, J.D. (1957). The problems of tomorrow's city. *Journal of Educational Sociology*, **31**(1), 4–7.

Kingsley, J.D. (1958). Staffing, organizational and training problems in the public service of the Western Region (unpublished report).

Kingsley, J.D. (2003). Representative bureaucracy. In J. Dolan and R.H. Rosenbloom (eds), *Representative Bureaucracy: Classic Readings and Continuing Controversies*. Armonk, NY: M.E. Sharpe, pp. 12–19.

Kitschelt, H.P. (1986). Political opportunity structures and political protest: anti-nuclear movements in four democracies. *British Journal of Political Science*, **16**, 57–86.

Knight, J. (1992). *Institutions and Social Conflict*. New York: Cambridge University Press.

Koopmans, R. (1999). Political. Opportunity. Structure. Some splitting to balance the lumping. *Sociological Forum*, **14**(1), 93–105.

Koopmans, R. (2004). Migrant mobilisation and political opportunities: variation among German cities and a comparison with the United Kingdom and the Netherlands. *Journal of Ethnic and Migration Studies*, **30**(3), 449–470.

Kramnick, I. and Sheerman, B. (1993). *Harold Laski: A Life on the Left*. London: Hamish Hamilton.

Krislov, S. (1967). *The Negro in Federal Employment: The Quest for Equal Opportunity*. Minneapolis, MN: University of Minnesota Press.

Krislov, S. (1974). *Representative Bureaucracy*. Englewood Cliffs, NJ: Prentice Hall, Inc.

Krislov, S. and Rosenbloom, D.H. (1981). *Representative Bureaucracy and the American Political System*. New York: Praeger.

Kübler, D. (2013) Representative Bureaucracy in Switzerland. In P. Von Maravić, E. Schröter, and B.G. Peters (eds), *Representative Bureaucracy in Action: Country Profiles from the Americas, Europe, Africa and Asia.* Cheltenham, UK, and Northampton, MA: Edward Elgar.

Kuhn, T.S. (1970 [1962]). *The Structure of Scientific Revolutions.* Chicago, IL, and London: The University of Chicago Press.

Kymlicka, W. (2010). The rise and fall of multiculturalism? New debates on inclusion and accommodation in diverse societies. In S. Vertovec and S. Wessendorf (eds), *The Multiculturalism Backlash. European Discourses, Policies and Practices.* London and New York: Routledge, pp. 32–49.

Lamb, P. (1999). Harold Laski (1893–1950): political theorist of a world in crisis. *Review of International Studies*, **25**(2), 329–342.

Landis, D., Bennett, J. and Bennett, M. (2004). *Handbook of Intercultural Training.* London: Sage.

LaPalombara, J. (1964). *Interest Groups in Italian Politics.* Princeton, NJ: Princeton University Press

LaPorte, T. and Consolini, P. (1998). Working in practice but not in theory: theoretical challenges of high reliability organizations. *Journal of Public Administration Research and Theory*, **1**(1), 19–48.

LaPorte, T., Rochlin, G. and Roberts, K. (1989). *High-Reliability Organizations: The Research Challenge.* Berkeley, CA: Institute of Governmental Studies, University of California.

Laski, H.J. (1921). *The Foundations of Sovereignty, and Other Essays.* New York: Harcourt, Brace and Company.

Laski, H.J. (1930). Aristocracy still the ruling class in England. *Current History*, **32**(4), 666–673.

Laski, H.J. (1931). The danger of being a gentleman: reflections on the ruling class of England. *Harper's Monthly Magazine*, August, 367–375.

Laski, H.J. (1935). *The State in Theory and Practice.* London: George Allen and Unwin Ltd.

Laski, H.J. (1938). *Parliamentary Government in England.* London: George Allen and Unwin Ltd.

Law, J. and Hassard, J. (1999). *Actor Network Theory and After.* Oxford: Blackwell

Lee, S. (2003). A review of language and other communication barriers in health care. Retrieved November 30, (2011, from http://aspe.hhs.gov/pic/fullreports/06/711B-2.pdf.

Lehmbruch, G. (1967). *Proporzdemokratie.* Tübingen, Germany: Mohr Siebeck.

Lehmbruch, G. (1977). Liberal corporatism and party government. *Comparative Political Studies*, **10**(1), 91–126.

Leung, A., Maddux, W.W., Galinsky, A.D. and Chiu, C.-yue. (2008). Multicultural experience enhances creativity: the when and how. *American Psychologist*, **63**(3), 169–181.

Levin, J. and Rabrenovic, G. (2004). *Why We Hate.* New York: Prometheus Books.

Lewis, P.G. and Ramakrishnan, S.K. (2007). Police practices in immigrant-destination cities: Political control or bureaucratic professionalism? *Urban Affairs Review*, **42**(6), 874–900.

Liebig, T. and Widmaier, S. (2009). *Children of Migrants in the Labour Market of EU and OECD Countries: An Overview.* Paris: OECD.

Light, I. (2006). *Deflecting Immigration: Networks, Markets, and Regulation in Los Angeles.* New York: Russell Sage Foundation.

Light, P.C. (1995). *Thickening Government: Federal Hierarchy and the Diffusion of Responsibility*. Washington DC: The Brookings Institution.

Lijphart, A. (1976). *The Politics of Accommodation: Pluralism and Democracy in the Netherlands*. 2. Berkeley, CA: University of California Press.

Lijphart, A. (1977). *Democracy in Plural Societies: A Comparative Exploration*. New Haven, CT: Yale University Press.

Lijphart, A. (1999). *Patterns of Democracy. Government Forms and Performance in Thirty-Six Countries*. New Haven, CT: Yale University Press.

Lim, H. (2006). Representative bureaucracy: rethinking substantive effects and active representation. *Public Administration Review*, **66**(2), 193–204.

Lindblom, C.E. (1979). Still muddling, not yet through. *Public Administration Review*, **39**(6), 517–526.

Lindblom, C.E. (2002). *The Market System: What it is, How it Works, and What to Make of it*. New Haven, CT: Yale University Press.

Lindblom, C.E. and Woodhouse, E.J. (1968 [1993]). *The Policy-Making Process*, 3rd edn. Englewood Cliffs, NJ: Prentice Hall.

Lineberry, R.L. (1977). *Equality and Public Policy: The Distribution of Municipal Public Services.* Beverly Hills, CA: Sage Publications.

Linz, J.J. and Stepan, A. (1996). *Problems of Democratic Transition and Consolidation: Southern Europe, South America, and Post-Communist Europe*. Baltimore, MD: JHU Press.

Lipset, S. and Rokkan, S. (eds) (1967). *Party Systems and Voter Alignments: Cross-National Perspectives.* New York: The Free Press.

Lipset, S. and Stein, R. (1967). Cleavage structures, party systems, and voter alignments: an introduction. In S. Lipset and S. Rokkan (eds), *Party Systems and Voter Alignments: Cross-National Perspectives*. New York: The Free Press, pp. 1–64.

Long, N.E. (1952). Bureaucracy and constitutionalism. *American Political Science Review*, **46**(3), 808–818.

Luton, L.S. (2003). Administrative State and society: a case study of the United States of America. In B. Guy Peters and J. Pierre (eds), *Handbook of Public Administration*. London: Sage, pp. 69–176.

Lynch, F.R. (2005). *The Diversity Machine: The Drive to Change the "White Male Workplace"* New Brunswick, CT, and London: Transaction Publishers.

MacLeod, G. (2002). From urban entrepreneurialism to a "revanchist city"? On the spatial injustices of Glasgow's renaissance, *Antipode*, **34**(3), 602–624.

MacMahon, A.W. (1946). *Representative Bureaucracy: An Interpretation of the British Civil Service* review. *The American Historical Review*, **52**(1), 129–132.

Manin, B. (1997). *The Principles of Representative Government*. Cambridge: Cambridge University Press.

Mann, M. (1987). Ruling class strategies and citizenship. *Sociology*, **21**(3), 339–354.

Mansbridge, J. (1999). Should blacks represent blacks and women represent women? A contingent "yes". *The Journal of Politics*, **61**(3), 628–657.

Mansbridge, J. (2003). Rethinking representation. *American Political Science Review*, **97**(04), 515–528.

Mansbridge, J. (2011). Clarifying the concept of representation. *American Political Science Review*, **105**(03), 621–630.

Marshall, J. (1997). Michel Foucault: governmentality and liberal education. *Studies in Philosophy and Education*, **14**(1), 23–34.

Martiniello, M. (2000). The residential concentration and political participation of immigrants in European cities. In M. Martiniello and S. Body-Gendrot (eds), *Minorities in European Cities. The Dynamics of Social Integration and Social Exclusion at the Neighbourhood Level*. Houndsmill, UK: Macmillan, pp. 119–128.

Martiniello, M. (2005). Political participation, mobilisation and representation of immigrants and their offspring in Europe. Willy Brandt Series of Working Papers in International Migration and Ethnic Relations, 1/05. Malmö: Malmö University. Available at: http://195.178.227.4/bitstream/handle/2043/1495/WB_1-05.pdf?sequence=1, accessed February 2011.

Marx, K. (1968). *The Civil War in France: The Paris Commune*. New York: International Publishers.

McCarney, P.L. and Stren, R.E. (2003). *Governance on the Ground. Innovations and Discontinuities in Cities of the Developing World.* Baltimore, MD: Johns Hopkins University Press.

McLeod, P.L., Lobel, S.A., and Cox, T.H. (1996). Ethnic diversity and creativity in small groups. *Small Group Research*, **27**(2), 248–264.

Meier, K.J. (1975). Representative bureaucracy: an empirical analysis. *The American Political Science Review*, **69**(2), 526–542.

Meier, K.J. (1993a). Latinos and representative bureaucracy: testing the Thompson and Henderson hypotheses. *Journal of Public Administration Research and Theory*, **3**(4), 393–414.

Meier, K.J. (1993b). *Politics and the Bureaucracy: Policymaking in the Fourth Branch of Government,* 3rd edn. Pacific Grove, CA: Brooks/ Cole Publishing Company.

Meier, K.J. (1993c). Representative bureaucracy: a theoretical and empirical exposition. In J.L. Perry (ed), *Research in Public Administration*, Volume 2. Greenwich, CT: Jai Press Inc, pp. 1–36.

Meier, K.J. and Bohte, J. (2001). Structure and discretion: missing links in representative bureaucracy. *Journal of Public Administration Research and Theory*, **11**(4), 455–470.

Meier, K.J. and Hawes D.P. (2009). Ethnic conflict in France. A case for representative bureaucracy? *American Review of Public Administration*, **39**(3), 269–285.

Meier, K.J. and Nicholson-Crotty, J. (2006). Gender, representative bureaucracy, and law enforcement: the case of sexual assault. *Public Administration Review*, **66**(6), 850–860.

Meier, K.J. and Nigro, L. (1976), Representative bureaucracy and policy preferences: a study in the attitudes of federal executives. *Public Administration Review*, **36**(4), 458–469.

Meier, K.J. and O'Toole, L.J. (2006). Political control versus bureaucratic values: reframing the debate. *Public Administration Review*, **66**(2), 177–192.

Meier, K.J. and Smith, K.B. (1994). Representative democracy and representative bureaucracy: examining the top down and the bottom up linkages. *Social Science Quarterly*, **75**(4), 790–803.

Meier, K.J., and Stewart Jr., J. (1992). The impact of representative bureaucracies: educational systems and public policies. *The American Review of Public Administration*, **22**(3), 157–171.

Meier, K.J., Eller, W., Wrinkle R., and Polinard, J.L.(2001). Zen and the art of policy analysis. *Journal of Politics*, **63**(2), 616–629.

Meier, K.J., Pennington, M.S. and Eller, W.S. (2005). Race, sex, and Clarence Thomas: representation change in the EEOC. *Public Administration Review*, **65**(2), 171–179.

Meier, K.J., Wrinkle, J.R., and Polinard, J.L. (1999). Representative bureaucracy and distributional equity: addressing the hard question. *Journal of Politics*, **61**(4), 1025–1039.

Merton, R.K. (1957). *Social Theory and Social Structure*. New York: Simon and Schuster.

Meyer, M.K. and Nielsen, V.L. (2012). Street level bureaucracy. In Peters, B.G. and Pierre, J. (eds), *The Handbook of Public Administration*, 2nd edn. London: Sage, pp. 305–318.

Miles, R and Thränhardt, D (1995). Introduction: European integration, migration and processes of inclusion and exclusion. In R Miles and D Thränhardt (eds), *Migration and European Integration: The Dynamics of Inclusion and Exclusion*. London: Pinter, pp. 1–12.

Minton, A. (2009). *Ground Control. Fear and Happiness in the 21st Century City*. London: Penguin.

Mokre, M. and Puntscher Riekmann, S. (2007). From good governance to democratic governance? A policy review of the first wave of European governance research. Series EU Research in Social Sciences and Humanities Policy Synthesis of Research Results, No. 2. Brussels: European Communities

Morning, A. and Sabbagh, D. (2005). From sword to plowshare: using race for discrimination and antidiscrimination in the United States. *International Social Science Journal*, **57**(183), 57–73.

Mosher, F.C. (1968). *Democracy and the Public Service*. New York: Oxford University Press.

Moulin, L. (1971). La Politisation de l'Administration en Belgique et en France. *Res Publica*, **13**(2), 161–242.

Nachmias, D. and Rosenbloom, D.H. (1973). Measuring bureaucratic representation and integration. *Public Administration Review*, **6**(6), 590–597.

Nalbandian, J. (1991). *Professionalism in Local Government: Transformations in the Roles, Responsibilities and Values of City Managers*. San Francisco, CA: Jossey-Bass.

Nalbandian, J. (2007). Professionals and the conflicting forces of administrative modernization and civic engagement. In R. Hambleton and J.S. Gross (eds), *Governing Cities in a Global Era*. Basingstoke and New York: Palgrave, pp. 189–198.

Newman, M. (1991 [2009]). *Harold Laski: A Political Biography*. Pontypool, Wales: The Merlin Press.

Niskanen, W.A. (1971). *Bureaucracy and Representative Government*. Piscataway, NJ: Transaction Publishers.

Norman, J. (2010). *The Big Society: The Anatomy of the New Politics*. Buckingham, UK: University of Buckingham Press.

Obama, B. (2008). A more perfect union. Speech at the National Constitution Centre, Philadelphia.

Oberti, M. (2000). Diversity and complexity in local forms of urban anti-poverty strategies in Europe. *International Journal of Urban and Regional Research*, **24**(3), 536–553.

Odalm, P. (2004). Civil Society, Migrant organisations and political parties: theoretical linkages and applications to the Swedish context. *Journal of Ethnic and Migration Studies*, **30**(3), 471–489.

Olsen, J.P. (2010. *Governing through Institution Building: Institutional Theory and Recent European Experiments in Democratic Organization*. Oxford: Oxford University Press.

OSI (Open Society Institute) (2010a). *Muslims in Leicester. At Home in Europe Project.* London: Open Society Institute.

OSI (Open Society Institute) (2010b). *Muslims in Europe. A Report on 11 EU Cities. At Home in Europe Project.* London: Open Society Institute

Ouseley Report (2001). Community Pride not Prejudice. Bradford City Council: Bradford.

Özmal, L. (2008). Kommunikation und zivilgesellschaftliches Engagement am Beispiel des Projekts „Begegnungsstätte in der Moschee" in Duisburg-Marxloh. In A. Häusler (ed.), *Rechtspopulismus als Bürgerbewegung*. Wiesbaden, Germany: Verlag für Sozialwissenschaften.

Painter, M. and Peters, B.G. (2010). *Tradition and Public Administration*. London: Palgrave Macmillan.

Pardo, M. (2013). Representative bureaucracy in Mexico. In P. von Maravić, B.G. Peters, and E. Schröter (eds), *Representative Bureaucracy in Action*. Cheltenham: Elgar Publishing, pp. 48–66.

Parekh, B. (2006). *Rethinking Multiculturalism*, 2nd edn. London and New York: Palgrave Macmillan.

Parkinson, M (1991). The rise of the entrepreneurial European city: strategic responses to economic changes in the 1980s. *Ekistics*, **350**(1), 299–307.

Pelled, L.H., Eisenhardt, K.M., and Xin, K.R. (1999). Exploring the black box: an analysis of work group diversity, conflict, and performance. *Administrative Science Quarterly*, **44**(1), 1–28.

Perrow, C. (1984). *Normal Accidents: Living with High Reliability Technologies.* New York: Basic Books.

Peters, B.G. (1987). Politicians and bureaucrats in the politics of policy-making. In J.E. Lane (ed.), *Bureaucracy and Public Choice*. New York: Sage, pp. 256–282.

Peters, B.G. (1989). *The Politics of Bureaucracy*. New York and London: Longman.

Peters, B.G. (2011). Steering, rowing, drifting or sinking? Changing patterns of governance. *Urban Research and Practice*, **4**(1), 5–12.

Peters, B.G. (2013). Representative bureaucracy in the United States. In P. von Maravić, E. Schröter, and B.G. Peters (eds), *Representative Bureaucracy in Action: Country Profiles from the Americas, Europe, Africa and Asia*. Cheltenham, UK, and Northampton, MA: Edward Elgar, pp. 21–34.

Peters, B.G. and Pierre, J. (2004). Politicization of the civil service. Concepts, causes, consequences. In B.G. Peters and J. Pierre (eds), *The Politicization of the Civil Service in Comparative Perspective: A Quest for Control*. London: Routledge Chapman & Hall, pp. 1–13.

Peterson, P.E. (1981). *City Limits*. Chicago, IL: University of Chicago Press.

Pierre, J (1999). Models of urban governance: the institutional dimension of urban politics. *Urban Affairs Review*, **34**(3), 372–396.

Pitkin, H.F. (1967). *The Concept of Representation*. Berkeley, CA: University of California Press.

Pitts, D.W. (2005). Diversity, representation, and performance: evidence about race and ethnicity in public organizations. *Journal of Public Administration Research and Theory*, **15**(4), 615–631.

Pitts, D.W. (2006). Modeling the impact of diversity management. *Review of Public Personnel Administration*, **26**(3), 245–268.

Pitts, D.W. (2009). Diversity management, job satisfaction, and performance: evidence from US federal agencies. *Public Administration Review*, **69**(2), 328–338.

Pitts, D.W. and Jarry, E.M. (2007). Ethnic diversity and organizational performance: assessing diversity effects at the managerial and street levels. *International Public Management Journal*, **10**(2), 233–254.

Pitts, D.W. and Jarry, E.M. (2009). Getting to know you: ethnic diversity, time, and performance in public organizations. *Public Administration*, **87**(3), 503–518.

Pitts, D.W. and Wise, L.R. (2010). Workforce diversity in the new millennium: prospects for research. *Review of Public Personnel Administration*, **30**(1), 44–69.

Pitts, D.W., Hicklin, A.K., Hawes, D.P., and Melton, E. (2010). What drives the implementation of diversity management programs? Evidence from public organizations. *Journal of Public Administration Research Theory*, **20**(4), 867–886.

Pollitt, C. and Bouckaert, G. (2004). *Public Management Reform: A Comparative Analysis*, 2nd edn. Oxford: Oxford University Press.

Porter, M. (2000). Location, competition, and economic development: local clusters in a global economy. *Economic Development Quarterly*, **14**(1), 15–34.

Posner, D.N. (2006). *Institutions and Ethnic Politics in Africa*. New York: Cambridge University Press.

Price, D.H. (2004). *Threatening Anthropology: McCarthyism and the FBI's Surveillance of Activist Anthropologists*. Durham, NC, and London: Duke University Press.

Provan, K.G. and Kenis, P. (2008). Modes of network governance: structure, management, and effectiveness. *Journal of Public Administration Research and Theory*, **18**(2), 229–252.

Putnam R.D. (2000). *Bowling Alone: The Collapse and Revival of American Community*. New York: Simon and Schuster.

Putnam R.D. (2007) E pluribus unum: diversity and community in the 21st century. *Scandinavian Political Studies*, **30**(2), 137–174.

Quinnipiac University (2000). Little support for giving kids more time in bad schools, New Yorkers tell Quinnipiac University poll; Increase in immigration is good for the city. Available at: http://www.quinnipiac.edu/x1302.xml?ReleaseID=635, accessed November 30, 2011.

Quinnipiac University (2006). New Yorkers tell NJ government to stay out of ground zero, Quinnipiac University poll finds; Most approve memorial and oppose admission charge. Available at: http://www.quinnipiac.edu/x1302.xml?ReleaseID=901, accessed November 30, 2011.

Quirk, P.J. (1980). Food and Drug Administration. In J.Q. Wilson (ed.), *The Politics of Regulation*. New York: Basic Books, pp. 217–218.

Raco, M. (1999). Competition, collaboration and the new industrial districts: examining the institutional turn in local economic development. *Urban Studies*, **36**(5), 951–968.

Ramakrishnan, K.S. and Wong, T. (2010). Partisanship, not Spanish: explaining municipal ordinances affecting undocumented immigrants. In M.W. Varsanyi (ed.), *Taking Local Control: Immigration Policy Activism in US Cities and States*. Stanford, CA: Stanford University Press, pp. 73–93.

Ramirez, F.O., Soysal, Y. and Shanahan, S. (1997). The changing logic of political citizenship: cross-national acquisition of women's suffrage rights, 1890 to 1990. *American Sociological Review*, **62**(5): 735–745.

Ranney D. (2003). *Global Decisions, Local Collisions*. Philadelphia, PA: Temple University Press.

Rehfuss, J.A. (1986). A representative bureaucracy? Women and minority executives in the California Career Service. *Public Administration Review*, **46**(5), 454–460.

Rhys, A., Boyne, G.A., Meier, K.J., O'Toole Jr., L., and Walker, R.M. (2005). Representative bureaucracy, organizational strategy and public service performance: an empirical analysis of english local government. *Journal of Public Administration Research and Theory*, **15**(4), 489–504.

Riccucci, N.M. (1987). Black employment in municipal work forces. *Public Administration Quarterly*, **11**(1), 76–89.
Riggs, F.W. (2002). Globalization, ethnic diversity, and nationalism: the challenge for democracies. *Annals of the American Academy of Political & Social Science*, Special Issue, 35–47.
Roberts, N. (2004) Public deliberation in an age of direct citizen participation. *American Review of Public Administration*, **34**(4), 315–353.
Roch, C.H., Pitts, D.W., and Navarro, I. (2010). Representative bureaucracy and policy tools: Ethnicity, student discipline, and representation in public schools. *Administration & Society*, **42**(1), 38–65.
Roe, E. and Schulman, P. R. (2008). *High Reliability Management: Operating on the Edge.* Palo Alto, CA: Stanford University Press
Roeder, P.G. (1999). Peoples and States after 1989: The Political Costs of Incomplete National Revolutions. *Slavic Review*, **58** (Winter): 854–882.
Rogers, A. and Tillie, J. (2001). *Multicultural Policies and Modes of Citizenship in European Cities*. Aldershot, UK: Ashgate
Rohr, J.A. (1995). *Founding republics in France and America.* Lawrence, KS: University of Kansas Press.
Romzek, B.S. and Hendricks, J.S. (1982). Organizational involvement and representative bureaucracy: can we have it both ways? *The American Political Science Review*, **76**(1), 75–82.
Rose, R. (1984). *Understanding Big Government: The Programme Approach*. London: Sage.
Rose, R. (1985). *Public Employment in Western Nations*. Cambridge: Cambridge University Press.
Rose, W.H. and Chia T.P. (1978). The impact of the Equal Employment Opportunity Act of 1972 on black employment in the federal service: a preliminary analysis. *Public Administration Review*, **38**(3), 245–251.
Rossi, P. (1987). *Vom Historismus zur historischen Sozialwissenschaft. Heidelberger Max Weber- Vorlesungen 1985.* 1. Aufl. Suhrkamp.
Roth, G. (1968). Personal rulership, patrimonialism, and empire-building in the new states. *World Politics*, **20**(2), 194–206.
Rourke, F.E. (1984). *Bureaucracy, Politics, and Public Policy*. Boston, MA: Little Brown.
Rucker, A. and Kingsley, J.D. (1961). Staffing and development of the public service of Nigeria. Unpublished report. Kaduna, Nigeria.
Sabatini, J. (2006). City vows to fix translations. *San Francisco Examiner*, September 8.
Sabbagh, D. (2003). Judicial uses of subterfuge: affirmative action reconsidered. *Political Science Quarterly*, **118**(3), 411–436.

Sabbagh, D. (2007). *Equality and Transparency: A Strategic Perspective on Affirmative Action in American Law*. New York: Palgrave MacMillan.

Saidel, J.R. and Loscocco, K. (2005). Agency leaders, gendered institutions, and representative bureaucracy. *Public Administration Review*, **65**(2), 158–170.

Saltzstein, G.H. (1979). Representative bureaucracy and bureaucratic responsibility. *Administration and Society*, **10**(4), 465.

Saltzstein, G.H. (1986). Female mayors and women in municipal jobs. *American Journal of Political Science*, **30**(1), 140–164.

San Francisco (2006a). Report concerning the status of San Francisco's equal access to services ordinance. Immigrant Rights Commission, City and County of San Francisco.

San Francisco (2006b). Cultural competency task force report. Office of the Mayor, City and County of San Francisco.

Sapat, A. (2004). Devolution and innovation: the adoption of state environmental policy innovations by administrative agencies. *Public Administration Review*, **64**(2), 141–151.

Sartori, G. (1973). *Democratic Theory*. Santa Barbara, CA: Praeger.

Saunders, D. (2010). *Arrival City*. London: William Heinneman.

Savitch, H.V. and Kantor, P. (2002). *Cities in the International Marketplace*. Princeton, NJ: Princeton University Press.

Scarman Report (1981). The Brixton Disorders, 10–12 April (1981: Report of an Inquiry by Lord Scarman. London: HMSO.

Schattschneider, E. E. (1960). *The Semi-sovereign People: A Realist's View of Democracy in America*. New York: Holt, Rinehart, and Winston.

Schmidt, V.A. (2010). Taking ideas and discourse seriously: explaining change through discursive institutionalism and the fourth 'New Institutionalism'. *European Political Science Review*, **2**, 1–25.

Schmitt, C. (1928). *Constitutional Theory*. Durham, NC: Duke University Press.

Schmitter, P.C. (1974). Still the century of corporatism? *The Review of Politics*, **36**(1), 85–131.

Schmitter, P.C. (2009). The nature and future of comparative politics. *European Political Science Review*, **1**(1), 33–61.

Schrecker, E.W. (1986). *No Ivory Tower: McCarthyism and the Universities*. New York and Oxford: Oxford University Press.

Schultze, C. (2003). Cities and EU governance: policy-takers or policymakers? *Regional and Federal Studies*, **13**(1), 121–147.

Schwartz, S. (2001). Immigrant access to food stamps: overcoming barriers to participation. *Journal of Poverty Law and Policy*, **5**, 260–275.

Selden, S.C. (1997). Representative bureaucracy. examining the linkage between passive and active representation in the Farmers Home Administration. *American Review of Public Administration*, **27**(1), 22–42.

Selden, S.C. (1998). *The Promise of Representative Bureaucracy: Diversity and Responsiveness in a Government Agency*. Armonk, NY: M. E. Sharpe.

Selden, S.C. and Selden, F. (2001). Rethinking diversity in public organizations for the 21st century. *Administration and Society*, **33**(2), 303–329.

Selden, S.C., Brudney J.L., and Kellough, J.E. (1998). Bureaucracy as a representative institution: toward reconciliation of bureaucratic government and democratic theory. *American Journal of Political Science*, **42**(3), 719–744.

Self, P. (1993). *Government by the Market? The Politics of Public Choice*. Boulder, CO: Westview Press.

Self, P. (2000). *Rolling Back the Market: Economic Dogma and Political Choice.* London: Palgrave Macmillan.

Shah, S., Rahman, I., and Khashu, A. (2007). *Overcoming Language Barriers: Solutions for Law Enforcement*. New York: Vera Institute of Justice.

Shepsle, K. (1979). Institutional arrangements and equilibrium in multidimensional voting models. *American Journal of Political Science*, **23**(1), 27–59.

Silberman, B.S. (1993. *Cages of Reason: The Rise of the Rational State in France, Japan, the United States, and Great Britain*. 1. Aufl. Chicago, IL: University Of Chicago Press.

Simon, H.A. (1947). *The Administrative State.* New York: The Free Press.

Simons, T., Pelled, L.H., and Smith, K.A. (1999). Making use of difference: diversity, debate, and decision comprehensiveness in top management teams. *The Academy of Management Journal*, *42*(6), 662–673.

Singer, A. (2004). *The rise of new immigrant gateways*. Washington DC: The Brookings Institution.

Sisneros, A. (1993). Hispanics in the public service in the late twentieth century. *Public Administration Review*, **53**(1), 1–7.

Skocpol, T. (1976). France, Russia, China: a structural analysis of social revolutions. *Comparative Studies in Society and History*, **18**(2), 175–210.

Skrentny, J.D. (1996). *The Ironies of Affirmative Action: Politics, Culture, and Justice in America*. Chicago, IL: University of Chicago Press.

Skrentny, J.D. (2002). *The Minority Rights Revolution*. Cambridge, MA: Belknap Press of Harvard University Press.

Smith, C.R. and Fernandez, S. (2010). Equity in federal contracting: examining the link between minority representation and federal procurement decisions. *Public Administration Review*, **70**(1), 87–96.

Smith, R.L. (1980). Representative bureaucracy: a research note on demographic representation in state bureaucracies. *Review of Public Personnel Administration*, **1**(1), 1–14.

Sowa, J.E. and Selden, S.C. (2003). Administrative discretion and active representation: an expansion of the theory of representative bureaucracy. *Public Administration Review*, **63**(6), 700–710.

Sowell, T. (2004). *Affirmative Action Around the World: An Empirical Study*. New Haven, CT: Yale University Press.

Stiglitz, J. (2006). *Making Globalization Work*. London: Allen Lane.

Stillman, R.J. (1991). *A Preface to Public Administration*. New York: St. Martin's.

Stillman, R.J. (2003). Twenty-first century United States governance: statecraft as reform craft and the peculiar governing paradox it perpetuates. *Public Administration*, **81**(1), 19–40.

Stoker, G. (2000). Urban political science and the challenge of urban governance. In J. Pierre (ed.), *Debating Governance: Authority, Steering, and Democracy*. Oxford: Oxford University Press, pp. 91–109.

Stone, C. (1989). *Regime Politics. Governing Atlanta, 1946–1988*. Lawrence, KS: University of Kansas.

Stubager, R. (2010) The development of the education cleavage: Denmark as a critical case. *West European Politics*, **33**, 505–33.

Subramaniam, V. (1967). Representative bureaucracy: a reassessment. *The American Political Science Review*, **61**(4), 1010–1019.

Suleiman, E.N. (1974). *Politics, Power, and Bureaucracy in France: The Administrative Elite*. Princeton, NJ: Princeton University Press.

Suleiman, E.N. (1984). From right to left: bureaucracy and politics in France. In E.N. Suleiman (ed.), *Bureaucrats and Policy-Making*. New York: Holmes & Meier, pp. 107–135.

Swyngedouw, E. (2004). Globalisation or "glocalisation"? Networks, territories and rescaling. *Cambridge Review of International Affairs*, **17**(1), 25–48.

Tarrow, S. (1988). National politics and collective action: recent theory and research in Western Europe and the United States. *Annual Review of Sociology*, **14**, 421–440.

Taylor, C. and Gutman, A. (eds). (1994). *Multiculturalism: Examining the Politics of Recognition*. Princeton, NJ: Princeton University Press.

Taylor, M. (2003). *Public Policy in the Community*. Basingstoke, UK, and New York: Palgrave.

Taylor, M. (2007) Community participation in the real world: opportunities and pitfalls in new governance spaces. *Urban Studies*, **44**(2), 297–317.

Teodoro, M.P. (2010). Contingent professionalism: bureaucratic mobility and the adoption of water conservation rates. *Journal of Public Administration Research and Theory*, **20**(2), 437–459.

Theobald, N.A. (2007). Muestreme el dinero: assessing the linkage between Latino school superintendents and English language learner program resources. In R. Espino, D.L. Leal and K.J. Meier (eds), Latino Politics: Identity, Mobilization and Representation. Charlottesville, VA: University of Virginia Press, pp. 249–264.

Thielemann, G.S. and Stewart Jr., J. (1996). A demand-side perspective on the importance of representative bureaucracy: AIDS, ethnicity, gender, and sexual orientation. *Public Administration Review*, **56**(2), 168–173.

Thomas, D.A. and Ely, R.J. (1996). Making differences matter: a new paradigm for diversity management. *Harvard Business Review*, **74**(5), 79–90.

Thompson, F.J. (1976). Minority groups in public bureaucracies: are passive and active representation linked? *Administration and Society*, **8**(2), 201–226.

Tidd, J., Bessant J., and Pavitt K. (2005). *Managing Innovation.* Chichester, UK: John Wiley and Son.

Trogen, P.C. (2001). Devolution or dissolution? Decentralization in the Former Soviet Union, Czechoslovakia, and the Russian Federation. In A. Farazmand (ed.), *Handbook of Comparative and Development Public Administration*. Boca Raton, FL: CRC Press, pp. 366–391.

Tuddenham, R. (ed.) (2010). *The "Big Society": Next Practice and Public Service Futures.* SOLACE Foundation Imprint. London: Society of Local Authority Chief Executives.

Turgeon, L. and Gagnon, A.G. (2013). Representative bureaucracy in Canada. In P. von Maravić, E. Schröter, and B.G. Peters (eds), *Representative Bureaucracy in Action: Country Profiles from the Americas, Europe, Africa and Asia*. Cheltenham, UK, and Northampton, MA: Edward Elgar, pp. 35–47.

Turney, K. and Kao, G. (2009). Barriers to school involvement: are immigrant parents disadvantaged? *Journal of Educational Research*, **102**(4), 257–271.

Uitermark, J., Rossi, U., and Van Houtum, H. (2005). Reinventing multiculturalism: urban citizenship and the negotiation of ethnic diversity in Amsterdam. *International Journal of Urban and Regional Research*, **29**(3), 622–640.

Urbinati, N. (2002). *Mill on Democracy: From the Athenian polis to Representative Democracy*. Chicago, IL: University of Chicago Press.

US Census Bureau (2005). 2005 American Community Survey, 1-year estimates; table S0501 (selected characteristics of the native and foreign-born populations) for New York City and San Francisco. Available at: http://factfinder2.census.gov.

US Census Bureau (2009). 2009 American Community Survey, 1-year estimates and 2005-2009 American Community Survey, 5-year estimates; table S0501 (selected characteristics of the native and foreign-born populations) for the United States, New York City, and San Francisco. Available at: http://factfinder2.census.gov.

van de Walle, S., Groeneveld, S. and Vandenbussche, L. (2013). Representative bureaucracy in Belgium: power sharing or diversity. In P. von Maravić, E. Schröter, and B.G. Peters (eds), *Representative Bureaucracy in Action: Country Profiles from the Americas, Europe, Africa and Asia*. Cheltenham, UK, and Northampton, MA: Edward Elgar, pp. 69–86.

van der Meer, F.M. and Roborgh, R.L.J. (1996). Civil Servants and Representativeness. In H.A.G. Beeke (ed.), *Civil Service Systems in Comparative Perspective*. Bloomington, IN: Indiana University Press, pp. 119–136.

Van Derbeken, J. (2001). Death in a cell: how sick man spent final hours in S.F. jail. *San Francisco Chronicle*, September 26.

van Gool, B. and de Zwart, F. (2013). Politics of representative bureaucracy in India. In P. von Maravić, E. Schröter, and B.G. Peters (eds), *Representative Bureaucracy in Action: Country Profiles from the Americas, Europe, Africa and Asia*, pp. 188–203.

Van Riper, P.P. (1958). *History of the United States Civil Service*. Evanston, IL, and White Plains, New York: Row, Peterson and Company.

Vega, C.M. (2008). City making clear illegals can obtain services here. *San Francisco Chronicle*, B-1, April 3.

Vertovec, S. (1996). Multiculturalism, culturalism and public incorporation. *Ethnic and Racial Studies*, **19**(1), 49–69.

Vertovec, S. (2006). Emergence of Superdiversity in Britain. WP 25, University of Oxford, COMPAS.

Vertovec, S. and Wessendorf, S. (2010). Introduction: assessing the backlash against multiculturalism in Europe. In S. Vertovec and S. Wessendorf (eds), *The Multiculturalism Backlash. European Discourses, Policies and Practices*. London and New York: Routledge, p. 1–31.

Viitanen, T.K. (2005). *Informal Elderly Care and Women's Labour Force Participation Across Europe*. Bonn: Institute for the Study of Labour.

von Bergen, C.W., Soper, B., and Foster, T. (2002). Unintended negative effects of diversity management. *Public Personnel Management*, **31**(2), 239–251.

von Maravić, P., Schröter, E., and Peters, B.G., eds. (2013). *Representative Bureaucracy in Action: Country Profiles from the Americas, Europe, Africa and Asia*. Cheltenham, UK, and Northampton, MA: Edward Elgar,.

Wainwright H. (2003). *Reclaim the State. Experiments in Popular Democracy*. London and New York: Verso.

Warner, C. M. (1997). Political parties and the opportunity costs of patronage. *Party Politics*, **3**(4), 533–548.

Warner, C.M. (2001). Mass parties and clientelism in France and Italy. In S. Piatonni (ed.), *Clientelism, Interests and Democratic Representation: The European Experience in Historical and Comparative Perspective*. Cambridge, UK: Cambridge University Press.

Warren, M.E. (2009). Governance driven democratization. *Critical Policy Studies*, **3**, 3–13.

Webber, M.M. (1968). The urban place and the non-place urban realm. In M. Webber, J.W. Dyckman, D. Foley, A.Z. Guttenberg, W.L.C. Wheaton, and C.B. Wurster (eds), *Explorations in Urban Structure*. Philadelphia: University of Pennsylvania Press, pp. 79–153.

Weber, M. (1922). *Wirtschaft und Gesellschaft. Die Wirtschaft und die gesellschaftlichen Ordnungen und Nachlässe. Nachlaß*. Bd. Teilband 4: Herrschaft. Tübingen: Mohr.

Weber, Max. (2002). *Economy and Society*. [Nachdr.]. Berkeley, CA: University of California Press.

Wilkins, V.M. and Keiser, L.R. (2004). Linking passive and active representation by gender: the case of child support agencies. *Journal of Public Administration Research and Theory*, **16**(1), 87–102.

Williams, A.M. (2009). International migration, uneven regional development and polarisation: an introduction. *European Urban and Regional Studies*, **16**(3), 309–322.

Wilson, W. (1887). The study of administration. *Political Science Quarterly*, **2**(2), 197–222.

Wimmer, A. (1997). Who owns the State? Understanding ethnic conflict in post-colonial societies. *Nations and Nationalism*, **3**(4), 631–665.

Wolffe, R. (2009). *Renegade. The Making of Barack Obama*. London: Random Books.

Wood, P. and Landry, C. (2008). *The Intercultural City*. London: Earthscan.

Wrench, J. (2005). Diversity management can be bad for you. *Race and Class*, **46**(3), 73–84.

Yates, D. (1982). *Bureaucratic Democracy: The Search for Democracy and Efficiency in American Government*. Cambridge, UK: Harvard University Press.

Yeoh, B.S.A. and Huang, S. (1999). Spaces at the margins: migrant domestic workers and the development of civil society in Singapore. *Environment and Planning A*, **31**(7), 1149–1167.

Young, C. (1976). *The Politics of Cultural Pluralism*. Madison, WI: University of Wisconsin Press.

Zachary, G.P. (2000). *The Global Me. New Cosmopolitans and the Competitive Edge*. New York: Perseus Books.

Index